MEDIA/THEORY

A grasp of an enormous body of work is displayed adroitly … overall the book is a genuine contribution to the literature. It should help to shape the future of critical reflections on media institutions and practices.

David Chaney, Emeritus Professor of Sociology, University of Durham.

This is an accomplished and elegant set of discussions, where an unusually broad range of theory from the humanities and social sciences, much of it to do with media but much of it not, is examined and organized.

Graeme Turner, Professor of Cultural Studies, University of Queensland.

Media/Theory is an accessible yet challenging guide to ways of thinking about media and communications in modern life.

Shaun Moores connects the analysis of media and communications with key themes in contemporary social theory:

- Time
- Space
- Relationships
- Meanings
- Experiences

He insists that media studies are not simply about studying media. Rather, they require an understanding of how technologically mediated communication is bound up with wider processes in the modern world, from the reproduction of social life on an everyday basis to the reorganisation of social relations on a global scale.

Drawing on ideas from a range of disciplines in the humanities and social sciences, *Media/Theory* makes a distinctive contribution towards rethinking the shape and direction of media studies today.

Shaun Moores is Associate Professor of Media and Communications at the University of Melbourne. His previous books include *Interpreting Audiences* (1993) and *Media and Everyday Life in Modern Society* (2000).

COMEDIA
Series Editor: David Morley

Comedia titles available from Routledge:

ADVERTISING INTERNATIONAL
The Privatisation of Public Space
Armand Mattelart translated by Michael Chanan

BLACK BRITISH CULTURE AND SOCIETY
A Text Reader
Edited by Kwesi Owusu

THE CONSUMERIST MANIFESTO
Advertising in Postmodern Times
Martin Davidson

CULTURAL SNIPING
The Art of Transgression
Jo Spence

CULTURE AFTER HUMANISM
History, Culture, Subjectivity
Iain Chambers

CULTURE IN THE COMMUNICATION AGE
Edited by James Lull

CULTURES OF CONSUMPTION
Masculinities and Social Space in Late Twentieth-century Britain
Frank Mort

CUT 'N' MIX
Culture, Identity and Caribbean Music
Dick Hebdige

THE DYNASTY YEARS
Hollywood Television and Critical Media Studies
Jostein Gripsrud

FAMILY TELEVISION
Cultural Power and Domestic Leisure
David Morley

A GAME OF TWO HALVES
Football, Television and Globalisation
Cornel Sandvoss

HIDING IN THE LIGHT
On Images and Things
Dick Hebdige

HOME TERRITORIES
Media, Mobility and Identity
David Morley

IMPOSSIBLE BODIES
Femininity and Masculinity at the Movies
Chris Holmlund

THE KNOWN WORLD OF BROADCAST NEWS
Stanley Baran and Roger Wallis

MEDIASPACE
Place, Scale and Culture in a Media Age
Edited by Nick Couldry and Anna McCarthy

MEDIA/THEORY
Thinking About Media and
Communications
Shaun Moores

MIGRANCY, CULTURE,
IDENTITY
Iain Chambers

THE PHOTOGRAPHIC IMAGE
IN DIGITAL CULTURE
Edited by Martin Lister

THE PLACE OF MEDIA POWER
Pilgrims and Witnesses of the Media
Age
Nick Couldry

SPECTACULAR BODIES
Gender, Genre and the Action
Cinema
Yvonne Tasker

STUART HALL
Critical Dialogues in Cultural Studies
*Edited by Kuan-Hsing Chen and
David Morley*

TEACHING THE MEDIA
Len Masterman

TELEVISION AND COMMON
KNOWLEDGE
Edited by Jostein Gripsrud

TELEVISION, AUDIENCES AND
CULTURAL STUDIES
David Morley

TELEVISION, ETHNICITY AND
CULTURAL CHANGE
Marie Gillespie

TIMES OF THE
TECHNOCULTURE
From the Information Society to the
Virtual Life
Kevin Robins and Frank Webster

TO BE CONTINUED....
Soap Opera Around the World
Edited by Robert C. Allen

TRANSNATIONAL
CONNECTIONS
Culture, People, Places
Ulf Hannerz

VIDEO PLAYTIME
The Gendering of a Leisure
Technology
Ann Gray

MEDIA/THEORY

Thinking about media and communications

Shaun Moores

Routledge
Taylor & Francis Group

LONDON AND NEW YORK

First published 2005
by Routledge
2 Park Square, Milton Park, Abingdon, Oxon OX14 4RN

Simultaneously published in the USA and Canada
by Routledge
270 Madison Ave, New York, NY 10016

Routledge is an imprint of the Taylor & Francis Group

© 2005 Shaun Moores

Typeset in Galliard by Taylor & Francis Books
Printed and bound in Great Britain by TJ International Ltd, Padstow, Cornwall

British Library Cataloguing in Publication Data
A catalogue record for this book is available from the British Library

Library of Congress Cataloging in Publication Data
A catalog record for this book has been requested

ISBN 0–415–24383–1 (hbk)
ISBN 0–415–24384–X (pbk)

TO KAREN, EVE AND RUBY

CONTENTS

Acknowledgements   xi

Introduction   1

Part I
Time and space   7

1   **Cyclicity**   9
    Structuration 9
    Routines 10
    Traditions 14
    Dailiness 16
    Seriality 19
    Scheduling 20
    Ordinariness 22
    Hourliness 25
    Lifetime 27
    Eventfulness 29

2   **Extensionality**   35
    Globalisation 35
    Stretching 38
    Medium 42
    Shrinking 46
    Unevenness 50
    Network 51
    Flow 53
    Empires 56
    Permeability 58
    Virtuality 64

Part II
Relationships, meanings and experiences   67

3   Interaction   69
Typology 69
Mix 73
Intimacy 74
Grief 78
Pathologisation 81
Sociability 83
Conversationalisation 91
Face 93
Friendliness 98
Doubling 99

4   Signification   103
Connotation 103
Multiaccentuality 106
Decoding 109
Export 112
Acts 118
Context 120
Technologies 122
Tastes 126
Fallacy 133
Authentication 135

5   Identity   139
Trust 139
Inattention 141
Reflexivity 143
Risk 146
Labour 153
Performativity 158
MUDding 160
Community 163
Diasporas 169
Dwellings 173

Afterword   177

Bibliography   179
Index   199

ACKNOWLEDGEMENTS

This book took shape in the North-East of England and was completed in South-Eastern Australia. I am grateful to colleagues in the media and cultural studies subject group at the University of Sunderland for supporting a semester's sabbatical leave that gave me room to get much of the writing done. John Storey and Sue Thornham assisted with overall organisation of the sabbatical. Myra Macdonald coordinated the MA scheme in my absence. Helen Davis, Tony Purvis and Amir Saeed covered lectures I would otherwise have given. Andrew Crisell and Angela Werndly, the two other members of the group during that period, were supportive in less direct but equally appreciated ways. In the final stages of preparing the typescript, my colleagues in the media and communications programme at the University of Melbourne (Peter Collingwood, Simon Cottle, Ramaswami Harindranath, Umi Khattab, Carolyne Lee, Scott McQuire, David Nolan and Sally Young) helped to provide a stimulating environment in which to work.

As the material in this book is intended primarily for use by students, and relates indirectly to various courses that I have taught over the years since 1986 (at the Polytechnic of Wales and Queen Margaret College, Edinburgh, as well as in Sunderland and Melbourne), I would like to acknowledge the input of those who attended my classes. Conversations with Karen Qureshi, in particular, helped me to clarify my thinking on a range of matters while she was an undergraduate and then a successful research student in Edinburgh. In addition, I am grateful to my series editor, David Morley, for his patience in waiting for the typescript to be completed and his constructive feedback on a first draft. Mario Morcellini and his colleagues in sociology and communications at University of Rome *La Sapienza* also deserve a mention here. They kindly invited me to be their Visiting Professor of Communications back in 2002–3, enabling a discussion of many ideas about media in social life that have found their way into the book. Thanks especially to Kety Momamji-Kebati for assisting with arrangements for the trip, and to Raffaella Bagnara for her two-way translations in the sessions I led in Rome and Naples. Chiara Giaccardi and her colleagues at University of Milan *Cattolica*, too, generously extended an invitation to visit Italy in 2003, facilitating a productive dialogue with their postgraduates in social communications.

ACKNOWLEDGEMENTS

Most importantly, though, I dedicate the book with love to Karen Atkinson,
Eve Moores Atkinson and Ruby Moores Atkinson.

Parkville, 2005

INTRODUCTION

I intend this book to be used by students who are taking media courses at advanced undergraduate and taught postgraduate levels, either in the field of media studies or else in other areas of the humanities and social sciences. My main aim in writing it has been to provide an accessible yet challenging guide to some ways of thinking about media and communications in modern life. From the start, though, I ought to declare that this is not straightforwardly a book about 'media theory', at least not in the conventional sense in which that term has come to be understood today. Rather, my title, *Media/Theory*, should be taken to indicate a commitment to connecting the analysis of media and communications with selected themes in contemporary social (and, to an extent, cultural) theory. These are themes of time and space, relationships, meanings and experiences.

While this is primarily a book for students, I also hope, of course, that it will be read by lecturers and researchers who, like me, are teaching media courses in higher education. For a number of those people, my choice of themes and associated headings on the contents pages may appear at first sight to be unusual. As I will explain, my approach does not involve replicating the existing structures that are employed within this genre of academic writing (although see Thompson 1995; and Silverstone 1999, for perhaps the closest relatives to the present book). A secondary aim, then, has been to make a distinctive contribution towards our rethinking of the shape and direction of media studies, by suggesting a revised conceptual vocabulary and framework for inquiry. There is a cumulative narrative in what follows, so that we begin with core issues of time and space, of 'cyclicity' and 'extensionality', enabling us to move on to intimately related matters of social interaction, signification and identity. Allowing for the regular incorporation of fresh material along the way, the book's story builds from chapter to chapter.

By deciding to organise things thematically in this manner, I am departing from previous, often highly productive, ways of telling. For example, in an introductory guide to cultural theory and popular culture, John Storey (2001) offers a clear and helpful tour of the 'isms' ('culturalism', 'structuralism and post-structuralism', 'Marxisms', 'feminisms' and 'postmodernism'). Some of

1

these traditions of thought get a mention in my own discussion, alongside less obvious schools like phenomenology, ethnomethodology and conversation analysis, yet they are not absolutely pivotal to the plot. Another approach for teaching in the humanities and social sciences is to focus on 'key thinkers' (for instance, Stones 1998; Hubbard *et al.* 2004). Again, I believe that line of inquiry has considerable merit. It will soon become evident that several such theorists are identified in my commentary. The writings of sociologist Anthony Giddens, for example, are cited at various points throughout, as is Paddy Scannell's work on communications via broadcasting. However, on this occasion I have resisted the temptation to let individual academic authors, as opposed to key ideas and themes, give an overall order to the book.

In media and cultural studies, probably the most common categories now used in writing and teaching about media are those of 'production', 'representation' and 'consumption'. Indeed, my impression is that this has become the standard framework for introducing media theory to students in higher education. That conceptual division, or a version of it, is found in recent publications by Jostein Gripsrud (2002) and Kevin Williams (2003) amongst others. They deal with the three categories in different sequences, with Gripsrud electing to start with audiences or consumers, before ending with industries and producers, but their perspectives are broadly similar. A few years ago, I contributed to a university distance-learning course that adopted a 'circuit of culture' model of roughly the same sort (Moores 1997), and so my sympathy for the 'industry/text/audience' framework is already on record. Still, I have decided not to employ it in this book as an overarching theoretical model.

To be sure, there will be numerous occasions when practices of media production, representation and consumption get referred to in the pages ahead. My current view, though, is that there are certain limitations to the use of these categories (see also Moores 2004). While they are suitable for the study of what has been termed 'mass communications' (radio, television, newspapers and so on), they cannot always be applied so successfully to particular forms of electronically mediated communication conducted via telephone, including mobile phones, and the internet. These are media that we must surely now bring within the scope of 'media studies', forcing us to bridge what I would see as the unhelpful divide between work on mass and 'interpersonal communications' or, for that matter, between discussions of so-called 'new media' (Harries 2002; Flew 2005) and older, more established modes of technologically mediated communication. In live telephone and computer-mediated dialogue, there will be performers and audiences of a kind, but rather than the institutionalised gap between production and consumption found in broadcasting or print journalism, the positions of the participants are constantly shifting as they typically do in physically co-present, face-to-face communication. It might even be appropriate for us to conceptualise radio and television as involving a sort of social interaction with listeners and viewers, as explored in the latter part of this book.

2

Just two further, general points ought to be made at this preliminary stage, before I proceed to open up the particular themes that will give a distinctive structure to the book. The first has to do with the definition of our field of interest. In my experience, a common misconception, certainly among students setting out on their degrees, is the belief that media studies are simply about 'studying media' in isolation. They are not, or, at least, I want to argue very strongly that they should not be. Instead, it is necessary to appreciate the complex ways in which media of communication are bound up with wider institutional, technological and political processes in the modern world, from the reproduction of social life on an everyday basis to the reorganisation of social relations on a global scale. For that reason, many topics apparently unconnected with media are discussed in the book, from home decoration practices to the interpersonal rituals of strangers in a city street to patterns of transnational migration and resettlement. Above all, then, my conviction is that media have to be understood in their broad social and cultural contexts. Partly as a consequence of that need for contextualisation, doing media studies can mean coming to terms with ideas drawn from a formidable range of disciplines in the humanities and social sciences (for instance, from history, geography, philosophy, linguistics, anthropology, psychology and sociology). Far from being the 'easy option' at university, as some ill-informed critics have suggested, the analysis of media and communications is, in actual fact, often a highly demanding activity for students, precisely because of its interdisciplinary character.

The other general point I wish to make here is concerned with the link between theory and research. Anybody who knows my own previous work (see, for example, Moores 1993; 1996; 2000) may be surprised to discover that this is a 'theory' book, since in the past I have always insisted on the importance of empirical investigation. However, if the present book represents something of a change of emphasis for me, it is not the result of any fundamental change of heart. I remain firmly committed to the empirical, as well as the theoretical, dimension of media inquiry. Indeed, there are many references in the coming chapters to the findings of research projects, either because they serve to illustrate conceptual issues or else because they give rise to specific ideas and concepts. Theory requires a level of abstraction, of course, yet it is best regarded as intertwined with ongoing empirical research on contemporary social existence.

Having spent a while explaining what this book is not, let me now start to discuss, in a more positive vein, the key themes I have chosen, so as to prepare the reader a little for the story that unfolds in the chapters to follow. I begin with time and space. Writing back in the 1970s, Giddens (1979: 202) notes that 'neither time nor space have been incorporated into the centre of social theory'. The principal reason, he suggests, was a problematic tendency to treat the temporal and the spatial as external 'environments' within which social life is conducted, as the special concerns of historians, geographers or philosophers. Attempting to counter this earlier tendency, he argues that 'time–space relations' should be seen as an in-built and fundamental feature of social interaction. They are, in his view, integral to the organisation of human societies rather than backgrounds to them, and therefore deserve to be at the 'very core' of our thinking about the conduct of social life (see also Giddens 1981).

Today, by the 2000s, time and space have become absolutely central themes for social theorists, while divisions between academic disciplines in the humanities and social sciences are increasingly 'blurred', and I believe that these themes should be at the core of our efforts to theorise the role of media in modern societies. Of course, it is not my intention to imply here that Giddens is somehow single-handedly responsible for such a major shift in thinking, but his own writings do contain valuable insights into time–space relations, which will be considered over the coming pages. Other social theorists cited in the first part of the book include Barbara Adam, Manuel Castells, David Harvey, Doreen Massey and John Urry. Although the focus of their attention is not on media, all of them have interesting things to say about communication technologies and practices. In addition, I will refer to several authors whose work does concentrate more fully on media, time and space, like Scannell, whose name I have already mentioned in this introduction, Marshall McLuhan (an influence on Giddens), Joshua Meyrowitz, Kay Richardson and Ulrike Meinhof, and Roger Silverstone.

Drawing on a range of material, then, I am proposing that we need to understand media as operating in the wider temporal and spatial arrangements of society, but also as contributing, reciprocally, to the creation, maintenance or transformation of social time and space. Chapters 1 and 2, on cyclicity and extensionality respectively, both deal with this two-way connection, yet each has a specific emphasis. Expressing it as simply as possible, one is mainly about 'round-and-round' movements in time-space, while the other has to do with what might be called a 'reaching out', and a 'collapsing in', of social life in the contemporary period. As well as explaining such movements and metaphors, these two opening chapters raise a number of issues to be pursued in the second part of the book, which is concerned with human relationships, meanings and experiences in circumstances of technologically mediated communication.

If, as Giddens (1979: 3) puts it, 'we must grasp the time–space relations inherent in the constitution of all social interaction', then logically the next step, after asking about matters of media, time and space, is to consider questions of media and interaction. Chapter 3 does this, exploring at length, without completely exhausting, the theme of changing social relationships with others in the modern era. An important element of this change is the social deployment of communications technology, which helps to establish interactions and interaction 'mixes' of a novel sort, involving mediated intimacies and sociabilities. Some of the writings I review there do start to address practices of meaning construction in people's relationships (both face-to-face and mediated), but it is only in Chapter 4 that we turn to look in detail at theories of signification. In the field of cultural studies, in particular, the making of meanings and value distinctions has been a central theme, and so my commentary on media and signification will offer an overview of conceptual developments that are mostly associated with this academic area. What becomes clear in the course of the discussion is that I favour those approaches to signification in which meanings are seen to be socially variable, context-specific and multi-dimensional. Following that commentary, my focus shifts to issues of self and collective identity in Chapter 5, where I place an emphasis on the theme of experiences that are distinctive to contemporary living. Any attempt to comprehend patterns of social interaction and signification calls, ultimately, for our close attention to the formations of modern subjectivity and community. Once again, though, my preference for certain theoretical perspectives will be evident, and in discussing media and identity I favour the notion of a reflexive or performative self, remaining suspicious of the wholesale 'decentring of the subject' found in structuralist and poststructuralist thinking, which tends to dismiss the category of human experience far too easily.

Among the theorists cited in the second part of the book are Roland Barthes (known primarily as a poststructuralist, although his late work on photography marks a radical departure from this school of thought), Pierre Bourdieu, Erving Goffman, Arlie Hochschild and Valentin Volosinov. The three chapters in that part will also include references to authors like Stuart Hall, Donald Horton and Richard Wohl, John Thompson and Sherry Turkle, whose publications include useful reflections on the dynamics of electronically mediated communication. Whilst I am not, in every case, wholly sympathetic to their ideas, all of the academics listed here provide highly relevant concepts for students of media and communications.

Part I
TIME AND SPACE

1

CYCLICITY

In this opening chapter, I want us to consider some ideas about the 'cyclical' or 'recursive' character of social life and, in particular, arguments about the significance of routines and traditions. We will be focusing on the role of radio and television in basic processes of social reproduction (looking, for instance, at their constructions of 'dailiness' and 'eventfulness', see Scannell 1996), but to begin with, it is necessary to lay a foundation for that discussion of communications via broadcasting by thinking more generally about the temporal and spatial arrangements of day-to-day lives and social institutions. My starting point is the theory of 'structuration' outlined by Anthony Giddens (1981; 1984), since an important aspect of this theory is its concern with 'recursiveness'.

Structuration

The theory of structuration is Giddens' ambitious attempt to transcend the division between 'structure' and 'action', or 'agency', in sociological thinking. For Giddens (1984: 25), social structures and actors are not to be thought of as 'two independently given sets of phenomena, a dualism', but rather as interdependent (a 'duality') so that the 'structural properties of social systems' can be seen as 'both medium and outcome of the practices they recursively organize'. His aim is to resolve a long-running dispute between, on the one hand, those theoretical approaches that emphasise the structural determination of actions and, on the other hand, those that tend to privilege human agency or the capacity of individuals to act on (and interact in) the social world. Indeed, he employs the rather awkward concept of structuration as part of his attempt to think beyond the very terms of this separation, understanding structures and actors as mutually constitutive. Setting out his own 'new rules of sociological method', he states: 'To enquire into the structuration of social practices is to seek to explain how it comes about that structure is constituted through action, and reciprocally how action is constituted structurally' (Giddens 1993: 169).

When asked in an interview to reflect on the theory of structuration 'in fairly straightforward terms', Giddens explains that he rejects certain conceptions of structure in which it is thought to have 'some given form, even a visible form', and that he also tries 'to get away from the idea that agency is just contained within the individual' (Giddens and Pierson 1998: 76). These points are then illustrated with reference to the example of 'speaking a language':

> Language has structure, language has form, but it isn't visible and it is only 'there' in so far as it actually forms part of what people do in their day-to-day use of it. That is what I call the recursive quality of language. I didn't claim that society 'is like a language' ... but language gives us clues as to how recursiveness happens. 'Society' can be understood as a complex of recurrent practices which form institutions. ... That is, society only has form and that form only has effects on people in so far as structure is produced and reproduced in what people do.
>
> (Giddens and Pierson 1998: 76–7)

Even when it is expressed and illustrated in this way, though, it might not be easy to grasp his argument about 'the structuration of social practices' immediately. We must therefore unpack what Giddens is suggesting here when he talks about 'how recursiveness happens' in social life. Later, we will see what he has to say about 'institutional time' and tradition, but first it is necessary for us to consider his reflections on routine.

Routines

At one level, recursiveness happens in day-to-day routines. Giddens (1981: 38) writes that:

> It is the routinised, or largely taken-for-granted, character of life in society, in most contexts of time and place, which gives meaning to the phrases 'daily life' or 'day-to-day life' as a regular round of activities. In all societies the vast bulk of daily activity consists of habitual practices, in which individuals move through definite 'stations' in time-space.

His reference at the end of this passage to ' "stations" in time-space' reveals the influence of an approach known as 'time-geography'. This approach is associated especially with the work of a geographer, Torsten Hägerstrand (1975), who is concerned to map the highly routinised 'time-space paths' of individuals in their daily movements and biographical 'projects', as they pass through various stations or 'time-space locations' (for some detailed discussions of Hägerstrand's time-geography, see Gregory and Urry 1985; Pred 1996).

Although Giddens is by no means uncritical of Hägerstrand's work, pointing to a tendency there 'to treat "individuals" as constituted independently of the social settings which they confront in their day-to-day lives' (Giddens 1984: 117), he believes that time-geography is helpful in shedding light on cyclical patterns of social activity. Of course, these patterns are likely to be modified to a certain extent through what is often called 'the life-cycle':

> A person may live in the house of his or her parents, for example, until establishing a new residence on marriage. This may be associated with a change of job, such that both home and workplace, as 'stations' along the daily trajectory, become altered. Mobility within the housing market, marital separation or career progression, amid a host of other possible factors, may influence typical life paths.
>
> (Giddens 1984: 113)

However, at any particular 'stage of life', it is usual for daily physical movements through time-space to be fairly settled and ordered (for empirical evidence, see Jarvis *et al.* 2001), allowing for variations such as the difference between 'working week' and 'weekend', to which I will return below.

Giddens (1981: 37) proposes that the typically settled and ordered routine has a significant emotional dimension: 'The routinisation of day-to-day life ... is the single most important source of ontological security.' 'Ontological security' is a term that appears across a range of his writings (see Giddens 1981; 1984; 1990; 1991). He defines it as experiencing a basic sense of 'confidence' in the 'continuity' of self-identity and the 'constancy' of the surrounding, everyday social world (Giddens 1990: 92). This confidence can only blossom and grow when social life has at least a degree of predictability to it. Perhaps the best way of illustrating the concept, and its relationship to 'routinisation', is to consider exceptional cases of 'radical ontological insecurity'. These are to be found in extreme 'critical situations' where the certitudes of routine are threatened. Referring to an account that psychoanalyst Bruno Bettelheim (1960) gives of life in Nazi concentration camps during the Second World War, Giddens (1984: 62) discusses one such case in which predictability was destroyed 'by the manifestly contingent character of even the hope that the next day would arrive'. By throwing the concept of ontological security into sharp relief in this way, it might be possible for us to start to see the emotional investment that many people have in the taken-for-granted and predictable features of ordinary daily life.

According to Michael Young (1992), 'the day-to-day' is marked above all by practices of repetition. He asks:

> Why do people repeat themselves so much? Why do they do more or less the same thing ... every day as they go about their daily rounds, getting out of bed in the morning, washing, dressing, getting break-fast, reading the paper, opening the mail ... as on other days?
>
> (Young 1992: 25–6)

His answer to these questions is that routine practices are driven by 'the force of habit and its extension, custom – the tendency we all have, in greater or lesser measure, to do again what we have done before' (Young 1992: 26; and see Felski 2000 on repetition, home and habit in everyday life). That answer is plausible enough, yet Giddens warns us against understanding repetition in day-to-day routines as a matter of 'blind habit'. Drawing on the perspective of ethnomethodology (see Garfinkel 1984; Heritage 1984), he insists that predictability is an ongoing 'skilled accomplishment': 'The predictable character of the social world is "made to happen" as a condition and result of the knowl-edgeable application of rules and resources by actors in the constitution of interaction' (Giddens 1981: 64). Although such an accomplishment of predictability, or an 'achievement' of routine (Schegloff 1986), requires effort, much of it is done apparently 'effortlessly' since we possess what Giddens (1984: xxiii) calls 'practical consciousness', 'all the things which actors know tacitly about how to "go on" in the contexts of social life without being able to give them direct discursive expression'.

Furthermore, if Young's assertion that we constantly repeat ourselves indi-cates a significant degree of social 'stability', then Giddens wants the concept of 'reproduction' to allow for the possibility of social 'change' and innovation too. 'Every act which contributes to the reproduction of structure', Giddens (1993: 134) tells us, 'is also an act of production, a novel enterprise, and as such may initiate change by altering that structure ... as it reproduces it.' Returning to the example of speaking a language, it is important to recognise how the mean-ings of words are not wholly stable. They can be transformed in and through everyday talk or 'speech acts'.

Another plausible answer to Young's opening question is that, for many people, specific repetitive activities are performed because they have to be, in order for those people to earn a wage. Most workers in conditions of capitalist industrialism are subject to regimes of 'work-discipline' that involve the temporal regulation of their labour. The social historian Edward Thompson (1993: 368) notes that 'a general diffusion of clocks and watches is occurring ... at the exact moment when the industrial revolution demanded a greater synchronisation of labour'. Similarly, citing the work of Lewis Mumford (1973), Giddens (1981: 133) remarks:

> The commodification of time in the emergence of capitalism was ... closely integrated with specific technical innovations – particularly, of course, those involved in the construction of clocks. ... Mumford has suggested, in fact, that it is the clock rather than the steam engine that should be regarded as the epitome of capitalist industrialism.

The timed 'working day' gave rise, in turn, to two 'opposed modes of time-consciousness, "working time" and "one's own" or "free time"' (Giddens 1981: 137).

In addition to the commodification of time, capitalism brought a 'commodifi-cation of space' (Giddens 1984: 144). For example, there has been a spatial (and gendered) separation of the private household from the public workplace, which was bound up with the creation of a kind of unpaid labour called 'housework' (Matrix Collective 1984). Moreover, each of these settings was 'regionalised internally'. Within the domestic context, writes Giddens (1981: 40), rooms 'are usually categorised in respect of their characteristic usage in time-space, as "living rooms", "kitchens", "bedrooms", etc.', while there is a 'differentiation of the "office" from the "shop floor" in industrial organisations' (see also Foucault 1979; 1980, who makes related points about the temporal and spatial arrangements of modern institutions such as the prison, the school, the household and the factory).

Before extending this discussion of routines, I want us to reflect on one of several criticisms of the theory of structuration that is put to Giddens by a fellow sociologist, John Urry (1991). Amongst other things, he writes on issues of tourism, leisure and travel (Urry 1990; 1995), and so we should not be too surprised when he alleges that:

> Giddens' conception of human activity is too routinized, too boring, and it is difficult in his framework to conceptualize pleasure-producing activities such as travel, leisure, holiday-making, sightseeing, shopping, playing sport, visiting friends and so on.
>
> (Urry 1991: 168)

This criticism does ring true in some ways. While Giddens takes account of the importance of transportation (and media) technologies for the transformation of time-space relations in modern society, as I will explain in due course, it seems reasonable to conclude that his emphasis on the routine features of ordinary daily life is at the expense of considering hedonistic or 'escapist' cultural practices (even if he later went on to publish a book on eroticism, love, sex and intimacy, see Giddens 1992).

However, Urry's criticism seems to me to miss a crucial point that he acknowledges elsewhere, which is that the 'pleasure-producing activities' listed above only have meaning in relation to cultures of the everyday. For instance, Urry (1990: 2–3) observes how tourism is 'a leisure activity which presupposes its opposite, namely regulated and organised work', and he remarks on how it involves journeys to 'sites which are outside the normal places of residence and work'. Without an understanding of routines, then, holidays make little sense. In an historical essay on the 'social production of the vacation house', Anthony King (1980) advances a similar argument, tracing the temporal and spatial shifts that produced the vacation house as a retreat or a 'place apart' from modern urban life. He charts the 'emergence of the weekend', which has become 'one of the most important leisure institutions' (King 1980: 204), but he recognises that this leisure time depends on the 'industrial time' of the working week. The weekend returns, routinely and predictably, at the end of each working week.

Let us now look more closely at the features of 'clock time', which, as we have seen, is so vital for the organisation of modern industrial societies. Barbara

Adam (1995: 25) refers to the mechanical clock as 'a material embodiment of classical mechanics, designed to the principles of idealized invariance ... motion without change and reversibility'. Its invariance results in the fact that it 'measures the "same" twenty-four hours in Iceland during the winter as in Britain during the summer' (Adam 1995: 24), providing an opportunity for the global standardisation of time-measurement, which will be one of the topics covered in the next chapter. For the moment, we can concentrate on the principles of 'motion without change' and 'reversibility'.

Giddens (1984: 35) contrasts the 'reversible time' of day-to-day life, symbolised by the mechanical clock, with the finite and 'irreversible' time of the life of a human being, which, alluding to Martin Heidegger's phenomenological philosophy (Heidegger 1962), he characterises as 'being towards death'. While the term 'life-cycle' is often used to describe the passage through socially constructed stages in human lifetime, this is actually a little misleading when applied to a particular person, since our lives are usually experienced as 'passing away' without the option of 'turning back time' and beginning again from birth (unless, that is, we believe in reincarnation). Each day, though, and twice a day if its face is divided into twelve hour-long units, the clock turns 'full circle' to start again. The daily movement of its hands or electronic digits is repetitive and cyclical.

Writing an essay devoted to the analysis of time and social organisation, Giddens (1987a: 143) pushes this point about the reversibility of clock time by asking us to imagine 'a clock that goes backwards':

> Such clocks are in fact on sale as amusing gadgets. A clock that goes backwards is actually very easy to adjust to, although at the beginning it seems specifically unnatural. The example drives home the fact that clocks have little to do with the 'linear' notion of time which we might imagine dominates in modern culture. The hands on a clock need not move in any particular direction; the important thing is that the clock conforms to the repetition of the day-to-day cycle.

On the basis of these comments, perhaps it is inappropriate to speak about the hands on a clock moving either 'forwards' or 'backwards'. As he makes clear, the linear notion of time as progression, expressed in a phrase like 'the arrow of time', does not fit the case of the clock. Put simply, clocks go round and round in circles, whether that is in a 'clockwise' or an 'anti-clockwise' direction.

Traditions

The cyclical or reversible time of day-to-day life is linked to a further, overlapping level of recursiveness in social life, 'the "supra-individual" *durée* of the long-term existence of institutions' (Giddens 1984: 35). Borrowing a phrase coined by the historian Fernand Braudel (1973), Giddens refers to this as the '*longue durée*' of institutional time that exceeds individual lifetimes. Earlier in this chapter, I quoted an extract from an interview with Giddens in which he asserts that what gets called 'society' is 'a complex of recurrent practices which form institutions' (Giddens and Pierson 1998: 77). His statement there hints at the integral connection between 'the *durée* of daily life' and the slower movement of institutional time, which he explains more fully in the following way:

> The reversible time of institutions is both the condition and the outcome of the practices organized in the continuity of daily life. ... It would not be true, however ... to say that the routines of daily life are the 'foundation' upon which institutional forms of societal organization are built in time-space. Rather, each enters into the constitution of the other, as they both do into the constitution of the acting self.
>
> (Giddens 1984: 36)

To understand that connection between the day-to-day and the *longue durée*, we might consider the link between routines and traditions.

Tradition is an enduring concept in Giddens' work, from his first writings on time and space through to his more recent reflections on modernity and globalisation. He says of its relationship to routine that:

> Routine is strongest when it is sanctioned, or sanctified, by tradition: when 'reversible time' is invoked in connecting past and present in social reproduction. ... Routine is closely linked to tradition in the sense that tradition 'underwrites' the continuity of practices in the elapsing of time.
>
> (Giddens 1979: 219–20)

Although he contends that contemporary society is, in certain respects, 'post-traditional' (Giddens 1994), characterised by greater 'institutional reflexivity' (Giddens 1991) so that routine actions in daily life are increasingly being 'opened up from the hold of tradition' (Giddens 1999: 43), his analysis also acknowledges the persistence of many traditions today. We could perhaps say that there is an intermingling of tradition and modernity, rather than simply a replacement of one by the other. 'Traditions are needed, and will always persist', insists Giddens (1999: 44–5), 'because they give continuity and form to life.' It is argued by some, indeed, that the necessity of tradition in modern cultures has led to its 'invention' (see Hobsbawm and Ranger 1983). Giddens (1999: 37) picks up on this point, noting that 'much of what we think of as traditional, and steeped in the mists of time, is actually a product at most of the last couple of centuries and is often much more recent than that'. He adds that there was no 'generic notion' of tradition in pre-modern cultures, 'precisely because tradition and custom were everywhere' (Giddens 1999: 39).

Providing us with an interesting and salient example of one of these invented traditions, Giddens discusses the case of the annual Christmas Day speech delivered by the British monarch, originally on radio and later on television too. This is an established institutional tradition yet 'it started only in 1932' (Giddens 1999: 41). A ritual occasion, it is a repetitive and predictable part of 'the broadcast calendar' (Scannell 1988) in the UK, even if not all the listeners and viewers to whom it is addressed choose to incorporate it into their Christmas holidays each year.

Dailiness

I am now ready to focus our attention on broadcasting and cyclicity, building on the foundation laid so far. Among those academics specialising in the study of media and communications, Paddy Scannell has probably done most to apply and expand on this aspect of the theory of structuration. He engages directly with Giddens' work in an essay on the 'temporal arrangements of broadcasting' (Scannell 1988), and a concern with the recursive character of social life (of cultural production and consumption in particular) is evident throughout his writings. The rest of this chapter will therefore include, but is by no means restricted to, several references to these reflections on radio, television and their audiences. My first concern here is with the concept of dailiness (Scannell 1996), which serves to crystallise many of his earlier attempts at theorising the role of broadcasting in processes of social reproduction (although he is not the only one to have used it, see Silverstone 1993; 1994).

Scannell (1996: 149), in defining this key concept, poses himself the question 'what is dailiness?' and responds at length as follows:

> We might begin with what it is to provide a daily service – of say bread or milk, newspapers, trains or whatever. In order to bring it about that an everyday service is produced every day … a routinization of the production of the service is required in such a way that that, precisely, is the outcome. Now it is one thing – complex enough – to produce a single good (a newspaper, a pint of milk) in such a way that it is there for anyone on their doorstep each morning. It is another thing to produce a daily service that fills each day, that runs right through the day, that appears as a continuous, uninterrupted, never-ending flow – through all the hours of the day, today, tomorrow and tomorrow and tomorrow. What does that mean? What is it to have such a service in such a way that it appears as no more than what I or anyone am entitled to expect as an aspect of my days?

Clearly, it is the provision of a 'daily service' by radio and television that he has in mind, yet running a train service (one of his examples above) no doubt entails many similar problems for its operators. Their aim, if not always their achievement, is to ensure a continuously flowing service for users, who feel 'entitled' to expect it, at a price, as a routine and reliable aspect of their days.

This feeling of entitlement best 'shows up', as Scannell might say, on occasions when a daily service is not delivered for some reason. While they are not the critical situations that Giddens (1984) writes about when he discusses feelings of ontological insecurity, commuters may still get upset when trains do not arrive to take them to work in a morning, and householders can be 'put out' if milk deliveries fail to turn up on their doorsteps as requested. Such disturbances have to do with the consequent inconvenience, of course, as when there is nothing to pour over the breakfast cereal, but they are also felt as a disruption of stable routines and everyday rituals.

Hermann Bausinger (1984: 344), a cultural theorist and researcher, argues that newspaper readers experience a disruption when 'it happens from time to time that newspapers ... are not delivered in the morning':

> Is this a question of the missing content of the newspaper, or isn't it rather that one misses the newspaper itself? Because the newspaper is part of it, reading it proves that the breakfast-time world is still in order – hence the newspaper is a mark of confirmation.

What Bausinger identifies in this passage is precisely the dailiness of the 'daily paper' for its regular readers. It has a ritual function and emotional significance in their day-to-day cultures. However, I think he is in danger of downplaying the 'missing content of the newspaper' (or, certainly, its style) a little too much, since readers tend to choose a particular publication to form part of their 'breakfast-time world'. They become familiar with the newspaper's layout and its distinctive brand of journalism, and so if the 'wrong paper' gets delivered then similar upset is likely to occur.

Let us consider the related case of breakfast-time broadcasting. Telling a story about his own mornings in Britain, Scannell (1996: 149–50) writes:

> I usually get up with *Today* (BBC Radio 4), whose very name defines its function of orienting me-or-anyone to the day today. So *Today*, with its formatted time-structure, has regular time-checks, updates and reports on the weather and traffic conditions. All such matter chimes in with my concerns, the tasks that face me now, of gearing up for another day today. *Today* brings me 'news': what's happened since I went to bed, what's happening 'now', what's coming up later in the day.

Today seems to provide, for Scannell at least, what Bausinger terms a 'mark of confirmation', helping to order his everyday social world. The programme also offers him a sense of 'liveness' and 'immediacy', like many other programmes on radio and television, marking the now of the time of day and distinguishing it from 'past time-in-the-day or time that is yet-to-come' (Scannell 1996: 149). Whether he is right to assert that the programme is for 'me-or-anyone' is highly debatable, though. In principle, anyone with the technology to pick up Radio 4 transmissions can tune in to *Today*, but its style is pitched at the 'serious' news listener, and listeners are assumed to have specific cultural competences. Indeed, Scannell (1996: 150) appears to recognise this when he notes that 'different significances are picked out in different morning media services': 'Today may be a fun-day on *The Big Breakfast* (TV, Channel 4) or in the *Sun* newspaper.' Nevertheless, he suggests that any of these services (and, presumably, their equivalents in other countries) will make an important contribution to the 'meaningfulness of days' for consumers. We could add that this may be so even when everyday media use itself is experienced as relatively 'meaningless' (see Hermes 1993; 1995).

Alluding to the reversible or cyclical motion of clock time in day-to-day life, and seeking to locate broadcasting's position in relation to it, Scannell (1996: 150) indicates 'the way in which any moment, in its own now-point, is caught in a double movement away from and towards':

> This movement shows up ... in the ways that time-through-the-day is zoned from breakfast time to bed time. These zones are part of the fundamental way in which broadcast services are arranged to be appropriate to the time of day – which means appropriate to who in particular is available to watch or listen at what time and in what circumstances.

The 'zoning' that Scannell points to is repeated, by and large, day after day, 'today, tomorrow and tomorrow and tomorrow', as he puts it in the lengthy extract I quoted earlier (although there are routine variations across the weeks, notably in the distinction which broadcasters have long appreciated between the industrial time of the working week and the institutionalised leisure time of the weekend). There are recursive 'time-through-the-week', as well as 'time-through-the-day', zones of radio and television output.

As an historian, and not just a theorist, of broadcasting (for a major social history of broadcasting in Britain during the 1920s and 1930s, see Scannell and Cardiff 1991), Scannell is able to look at what he calls the 'routinization of the production of the service' in the process of its historical emergence. He understands this routinisation in terms of the initial problems faced by those at the BBC whose job it was to offer 'public service broadcasting' to radio listeners in return for the payment of a licence fee. Ways of organising programme-making and broadcast output that are largely taken-for-granted and unproblematic today, for producers and audiences alike, then needed to be worked out for the first time. 'It is worth remembering', cautions Scannell (1995: 7), 'that there was a moment when "how to do broadcasting", in all respects, had to be discovered.' At the outset, the operators of radio services had no methodical and reproducible ways of 'doing broadcasting'. The solution to this fundamental problem (which was, above all, one of filling the available 'air time') was to be found chiefly in serial production and fixed schedules. I will therefore deal next with issues of 'seriality' and 'scheduling'.

Seriality

Serial production (in general, as opposed to the more specific sense of making 'continuous serials', see Geraghty 1981) involves the creation of standardised programme formats for current affairs, situation comedies, game shows and so on. These are reproducible on a regular basis and audiences can come to find them familiar. 'Program formats', observes Scannell (1995: 8), 'include the use of signature tunes, regular presenters, standardized openings and closings; set sequences for the program material; and routines for moving through the sequences and for maintaining continuity.' Within a 'fiction' format, there is usually a group of regular characters interacting in an established setting or range of settings, representing rooms in a household or workplace, streets in a neighbourhood, public bars or wherever.

John Ellis (1982: 122–3) notes that 'repetition' is one of the defining principles of broadcasting, with the production of television serials and series facilitating 'a form of continuity-with-difference'. The basic format of a programme remains unchanged while the detail of its content alters from day to day, week to week or, in the case of some contemporary news broadcasts, hour to hour (see Richardson and Meinhof 1999). For example, in a studio discussion programme, there is always the same host (Robert Kilroy-Silk in *Kilroy!*, Oprah Winfrey in *The Oprah Winfrey Show*, or whoever) in the same setting, but the studio audience and the precise topic of discussion shift from one show to the next. It should also be emphasised that, just as Giddens wants to allow for the possibility of transformation in processes of social reproduction, so we must recognise innovation as well as repetition in broadcasting, such as when, for instance, elements of previously distinct programme formats are combined in a hybrid genre like the 'docu-soap'.

Programme production is typically, though not exclusively, studio-based, and so once the main features of the set are established, there is no need to create them anew for every broadcast. Scannell (1991: 2) comments that the studio is 'the institutional discursive space of radio and television ... a public space in which and from which institutional authority is maintained and displayed'. However, he comprehends how the output of broadcasting has to be oriented to the 'conditions of reception':

> From the start it was recognized that listening and viewing took place
> in the sphere of domesticity, within the spaces of the household and
> normatively in the small, family living room. How broadcasters
> attempted to produce programmes that fitted in to the domestic
> sphere and the daily round, that were appropriate to the conditions of
> reception, has a long and uneven history in relation to different types
> of output. But as it was increasingly understood that broadcasting,
> because it could not compel its audiences to listen or to behave as the
> broadcasters ideally wished, must adapt the form and content of its
> programmes to fit in with the circumstances of viewing and listening,

attention focused on ways of achieving this. It was recognized that broadcast output, though articulated in the public domain as public discourse, was received within the sphere of privacy, as an optional leisure resource. Within this sphere ... people did not expect to be talked down to, lectured or 'got at'. They expected to be spoken to in a familiar, friendly and informal manner as if they were equals on the same footing as the speaker.

(Scannell 1991: 3)

Historically, these spatial features of communication via radio and television forced the broadcasters 'to understand that while they could, and did, control what went on in their place (typically the studio), they did not, indeed could not, control what went on in the places of listening and viewing' (Scannell 1995: 9–10). The fuller implications of that arrangement for broadcasting's serialised 'public discourse' will be explored later in the book. On a final note in this section, though, we ought to remember that daily life in the household has a serial quality of its own, a set of routines into which the schedules of radio and television are designed to fit.

Scheduling

Fixed schedules, in which the same programme is put on at the same time of the day (each day, each week or several times each day and week), mean that audiences can come to find the overall shape of output to be ordered and predictable. Within the British model of public service broadcasting, this scheduling tends to operate on the principle of providing 'mixed programming', 'a wide range of different kinds of programmes delivered on a single channel' (Scannell 1992: 320). Richard Paterson (1993: 144–5), in an account of such scheduling practices on television, contends that 'the keystone of the schedule's architecture' is a particular conception of the 'family audience'. For instance, he refers to UK policy guidelines for schedulers on family viewing, which prescribe what types of material are suitable (and 'unsuitable') to be screened in specific 'time-bands'. More generally, schedulers make programming decisions that are based on cultural assumptions about which household members are available to watch television at what times of the day and week. These decisions are taken in an effort to 'target' certain groups of viewers and maximise viewing figures, especially in the commercial broadcasting sector where 'the ratings' help to determine the price at which advertising slots can be sold (for a critical analysis of this economic dimension of the television industry, especially in the USA, see Ang 1991).

Scannell's historical perspective allows us to see the origins of fixed schedules that are planned around a notion of the family audience. He reports that, after an initial period during which any regularity of programming was 'deliberately shunned' by the BBC:

Greater care was taken to organise the daily output on more routinised, regular lines. Popular programmes were increasingly given fixed time slots. *Monday Night at Seven*, as its name implies, was an early and successful attempt to produce a fireside show that recurred at a known time and could pleasurably be anticipated as a predictable enjoyment in the week. By the late 1930s programme-planners were adjusting daily output to chime in with the time routines of day-to-day life through the weekend and the working week. Today the pattern of output is carefully arranged to match what is known of the daily working, domestic and leisure patterns of the population.

(Scannell 1988: 24–5)

His reference to the late 1930s as a turning point is significant, because the BBC had just set up an audience research unit at that time. Since it was founded, one of its main purposes has been to carry out investigations into the temporal rhythms of the day-to-day. Indeed, he describes two of the surveys conducted by this unit in the 1970s and 1980s as constituting a sort of time-geography. Although researchers at the BBC were not directly influenced by Hägerstrand's approach, these surveys effectively charted people's time-space paths through the day, paying special attention to when family members were routinely in or out of the house and therefore available, or unavailable, to listen and view.

The resulting 'pattern of output' in broadcasting is predominantly based around the times of paid labour, and leisure outside such labour, but during the daytime, broadcasting provides important resources for those in the household (usually women) who spend their days doing the unpaid labour of housework and childcare (see Johnson 1981; 1988, on the targeting of the 'modern house-wife' by early Australian radio). This kind of work, carried out in what Michèle Mattelart (1986) calls 'feminine time', is characterised by its 'structurelessness' in comparison with the temporal organisation of industrial production. 'It is ... difficult', write Sue Hemmings *et al.* (2002: 280), 'to trace the boundaries between work and leisure in the everyday lives of women.' However, as Dorothy Hobson (1980: 105) reports in her ethnography of British working-class housewives in Birmingham, 'the time boundaries provided by radio are important in the women's own division of their time'. According to Hobson, the regular daily features of programming and the frequent time-checks function as temporal markers, enabling women in that social context to punctuate their days and sequence their housework practices while listening to the radio, which is often a 'secondary activity'.

Gender, as might be expected, is one of the 'key variables' identified in the time-use research done by the BBC's audience research unit. The other main variable is age or, more accurately, life-stage. 'Thus what emerges from the study', writes Scannell (1988: 26), 'is the interlocking of lifetime with the time-structures of the day ... what is mapped here synchronically are the different

disposals of time-in-the-day by individuals at different stages in their life-cycles.'
Near the start of this chapter, in my discussion of Giddens on routinisation, I
touched on his argument that recursive patterns of social activity are subject to
change as individuals make the transition into a new stage of life. Such shifts in
daily time-space paths can involve modified relationships with media, as David
Gauntlett and Annette Hill (1999) illustrate in their report of findings from an
innovative 'audience tracking study' of television and everyday life. That
research involved a 'longitudinal' analysis of television viewing habits over
several years (see also Petrie and Willis 1995). For instance, the extract reproduced below is taken from the solicited diary entry of a woman in her early
twenties:

> When the study began I lived with my parents and although we did
> watch some TV together I spent a lot more time in my room listening
> to music. TV is more important to me now, in that I need to relax
> when I come home from work. As I live in a horrible bedsit on my
> own, I switch on the TV the minute I get in the door.
>
> (in Gauntlett and Hill 1999: 95)

This young woman, having acquired her first job and moved away from family
and friends, found that the continuous flow of television, accessed as soon as
she returned to her flat, played a 'more important' role in day-to-day routine
than it had done previously (see Williams 1990, who argues that we should
focus not only on the 'separable items' of television but also on the experience
of its flow of scheduled programming).

Ordinariness

If we add to those production and scheduling methods outlined above the
discovery of 'continuity techniques' in broadcasting (the use of 'links' and
'trailers' announcing what is coming up next or later) then it is possible to
recognise that, as Scannell (1995: 8) puts it:

> The net effect of all these techniques is cumulative. In and through
> time, program output, in all its parts and as a whole, takes on a settled,
> familiar, known and taken-for-granted character as the recursive condi-
> tion of its daily occurrence. That it is so is by virtue of techniques
> discovered and applied to make it so.

This contributes to making radio and television profoundly 'ordinary' media.
According to Scannell (1995: 4), when it is said sometimes that there is
'nothing on telly', this does not mean that there is 'literally nothing to watch',
rather, there is 'nothing out of the ordinary, merely the usual programs on the
usual channels at the usual times' (his conception of 'ordinariness' here is drawn

from Sacks 1984; 1995, who speaks of television viewing as one of the many ways of 'doing "being an ordinary person"' in daily life). As Frances Bonner (2003: 32) writes, the routine fare of contemporary television itself 'calls on ordinary, everyday concerns and patterns of behaviour', in 'lifestyle programming' and so-called 'reality TV', as well as in advice, chat and talk shows.

To borrow Giddens' words, we could say that broadcasting's ordinariness, familiarity and predictability are the skilled accomplishments of various groups of people (technicians, presenters and schedulers, for instance) who are collectively responsible for putting programmes on our radio sets and television screens, or for 'doing' broadcasting. Of course, these things are also the seemingly effortless practical accomplishments of listeners and viewers, who know how to 'go on' in their habitual use of broadcasting, typically in private household settings (my choice of the term 'habitual' is not necessarily intended to convey a sense of 'addiction' to radio and television). Possession of such basic 'know how', an element of practical consciousness, appears unremarkable, and yet, as ever, there is an historical dimension to this. Tim O'Sullivan (1991) in the UK and Lynn Spigel (1992a; 1992b) in the USA have each shown how the performance of television viewing had to be 'learnt' back in the 1950s, when there was uncertainty about the ways in which the technology ought to be incorporated into day-to-day, domestic life. Some consumers were still unsure as to which spatial 'region' of the household television was to be placed in, and precisely how it was to be watched.

Alongside Scannell, another theorist who emphasises the ordinariness of broadcasting, focusing on the medium of television, is Roger Silverstone. Before Scannell employed the term, Silverstone (1993: 574–5) had already asked about what he calls 'television's veritable dailiness':

> How is it that such a technology and medium has found its way so profoundly and intimately into the fabric of our daily lives? How is it that it stays there? ... Television accompanies us as we wake up, as we breakfast, as we have our tea and as we drink in bars. It comforts us when we are alone. It helps us sleep. It gives us pleasure, it bores us and sometimes it challenges us. It provides us with opportunities to be both sociable and solitary. ... Although ... it was not always so ... we now take television entirely for granted, in a way similar to how we take everyday life for granted.

Not all readers of this passage will identify with the 'our', 'we' or 'us' of his specific examples. Nevertheless, I believe Silverstone is absolutely right to suggest that television has the capacity to be a constantly available cultural resource (one that is 'ready-to-hand', in phenomenological terms) and may get stitched into day-to-day routines. Like Scannell, he sees broadcasting as 'very much part of the seriality and spatiality of everyday life', so that its ordered schedules help to 'reproduce (or define) the structure of the household day (itself significantly determined by the temporality of work in industrial society)' (Silverstone 1993: 592).

Silverstone's distinctive contribution to our understanding of broadcasting and cyclicity is to be found in his reflections on television and ontological security (see Silverstone 1993; 1994). He draws on Giddens' concept to provide answers to his questions about how television has become, and continues to be, part of the 'fabric' of ordinary daily life, developing an account of the ongoing emotional significance that the medium can have for its viewers. If it is generally the case that 'ontological security is sustained through the familiar and predictable' (Silverstone 1993: 591), then familiarity and predictability are, as we have seen, the intended features of most broadcast output. In modern society, television therefore offers at least some of those elements of continuity and constancy that are required by social actors in order to feel a basic sense of confidence in the quotidian world. The ways in which this offer is taken up by viewers in particular settings will be uneven, but it is the overall stability of output that has the potential to contribute to ontological security.

Unlike cinema, which tends to be consumed as a 'special event' in public contexts (Ellis 1982; Jancovich et al. 2003), television is, Silverstone (1994: 24) confirms, predominantly a 'domestic medium': 'It is watched at home. Ignored at home. Discussed at home. Watched in private and with members of family or friends.' There are exceptions to this general rule (for an illuminating account of the social uses of television in public places, see McCarthy 2001), say when a crowd of strangers gathers in a bar to watch live coverage of a big sports match, yet viewing remains, by and large, a routine and ordinary domestic experience. Whereas film constructs the spectacular, television is typically mundane and 'underwhelming'. Broadcasting is a cultural 'utility', 'always on tap like water, gas or electricity' (Scannell 1988: 24). 'Switching it off', adds Silverstone (1993: 587), 'does not destroy it ... switch it on again and it demonstrates its invulnerability and its dependability.' Still, as with Bausinger's story of the disruption caused by an undelivered newspaper, there are moments when the dependability of broadcast output can be briefly threatened. I am thinking of instances such as the 'moving' of *The BBC Nine O'Clock News*, which for many years was a 'fixture' on British television, to a different slot an hour later in the evening schedule, changing its name to *The BBC Ten O'Clock News*. This provoked a heated response from a number of viewers who were upset by the alteration. As Scannell (1996: 155) comments, 'if ... temporal regularity ... is disturbed it gives rise to ... remarkings'.

Today, with the widespread use of domestic video technology since the 1980s, it is possible for viewers themselves to disrupt the schedules 'from below' if they wish, 'time-shifting' television programmes to suit their personal circumstances rather than having to fit in completely with the pre-determined slots. For example, it is now quite common for people to record selected programmes whilst having a 'night out', before returning to watch the tape later (a few hours after the point of transmission or else in the following days). When playing the tape, too, they might 'zip' through any advertisements and 'boring bits'. Adopting a perspective on everyday life that is associated with the cultural theorist Michel de Certeau (1984), Ien Ang (1992: 138–9) has referred to such practices as 'tactical manoeuvres viewers engage in, in order to construct their own television experience'. She is justified, I think, in seeing video time-shifting and zipping as specific 'tactics' of television consumption that are making it more difficult for broadcasters to 'know' their audiences, but we must be careful not to get carried away because these activities do not necessarily mean that viewers are 'resisting' routinisation and ordinariness. On the contrary, it could be that they are occasionally recording programmes they usually watch at the scheduled time, so as not to miss out on what Scannell terms 'a predictable enjoyment'.

Hourliness

Following the arrival of video, other new technologies (cable, satellite and now digital television) provide programme services that are beginning to rework the temporal arrangements of broadcasting, as well as its spatial arrangements, in more fundamental ways. In their critique and development of Scannell's ideas on broadcasting and cyclicity, Kay Richardson and Ulrike Meinhof (1999) contend that, whilst he is correct in highlighting the recursiveness of radio and television output, his writings take insufficient account of programming strategies in 'non-terrestrial' broadcasting within Western Europe. I would want to argue that this is one shortcoming of his generally valuable historical perspective. Indeed, Richardson and Meinhof (1999: 23) imply that Scannell is less comfortable with 'the age of multi-channel television' than he is with the formations of public service broadcasting. His focus is on the established production and scheduling methods of mixed programming, yet non-terrestrial television is characterised by a strong 'branding' of channels devoted entirely to news, sport, music and so on. The 'internal pluralism' of terrestrial output is being replaced by 'external pluralism' in the new multi-channel viewing environment (see Collins 1990; 1992).

Considering the emergence of 'rolling' news channels such as CNN, Sky News and the BBC's own News 24 digital station, Richardson and Meinhof (1999: 8–9) observe how:

> 24-hour news channels address the 'need' for TV news-on-demand, and thus break with the tradition which ties news programming to specific times of the day. This is one aspect of changes in scheduling ... which arguably give a different kind of basis for the temporal relations between TV and its audiences. Television becomes less important than heretofore in constructing 'dailiness' on the basis of predictably different 'mornings', 'afternoons' and 'evenings'. ... In place of the rhythms of the (working) day, 24-hour news foregrounds its hourly cycles of repetition.

Rather than dailiness, then, we might say that the main characteristic of these channels is their 'hourliness' (in fact, within the hourly cycle, the headlines on some news channels are summarised every fifteen minutes). This temporal organisation of news is closely related to 'the recency principle': 'the principle that reportage should be as close as possible in time to the moment of occurrence' (Richardson and Meinhof 1999: 33).

The cyclical movements of the clock remain crucial in 24-hour news. However, there is 'a significantly different relation to cyclicity':

> Cyclicity is the principle that particular programmes or segments recur on a regular, timed basis. This has always been an important part of schedule design. ... On some of the new channels, notably those which seek to combine liveness with 24-hour scheduling, cyclicity has become hourly – as well as daily and weekly. 24-hour news channels have adopted this format because it allows them, in principle, to refresh their agenda and renew their stories much more regularly than channels with fixed-point news programmes. The result in practice is considerable repetition, but on the understanding that the stories reported, the facts provided, are as immediate/recent as the best efforts of the broadcasters can manage.
>
> (Richardson and Meinhof 1999: 24)

According to Richardson and Meinhof (1999: 8), this departure from 'fixed point news programmes' also signals an important shift in which it is now possible for viewers 'to reject the temporalities of the normative lived day'. These authors see the fast-paced cycles of 24-hour news as potentially liberating for television audiences.

Indeed, Richardson and Meinhof take serious issue with both Scannell and Silverstone when judging the significance that scheduling has at the point of consumption. While the latter see the predictability of terrestrial programming as 'a benign contribution to the character of twentieth-century life', sometimes equating that predictability with 'the psychic comfort of "ontological security"', the former believe 'the routines of (traditional) television broadcasting can be seen as coercive, and we should welcome any signs that the future of television may involve less complicity with the time frames of the (national; normal and normative) working day/week/year' (Richardson and Meinhof 1999: 29). This is an interesting critique, but we need to think very carefully before adopting Richardson and Meinhof's optimistic perspective on change. Following a different line of argument developed by the social theorist Richard Sennett (1998), it would equally be possible for us to understand these alterations in schedule design as related to the emergence of 'flexitime' work patterns in the 'new capitalism' (see also Urry 2000: 128–9, on 'time–space desynchronisation'). Reflecting on these emergent modes of temporal organisation in the workplace, Sennett (1998: 59) concludes: 'The time of flexibility is the time of a new power ... not freedom from restraint.' Although flexitime is often presented as a 'reward' for employees, he contends that it does not liberate them from the employer's 'intimate grip'.

If we accept that the predictability of established routines and schedules is to some extent disrupted by non-terrestrial television (even if the 'hourly cycles of repetition' in 24-hour news have a predictability of their own), then it is also necessary to recognise that senses of familiarity are called into question as a consequence of the relative 'novelty' that cable, satellite and digital channels have for their audiences:

> Television's cultural/symbolic order has been unsettled by recent changes. ... Despite the large amounts of recycled material on the new channels, there has been a wave of televisual novelty effects rippling through our societies. People have stories to tell about the first time they saw CNN; or MTV; or the shopping channel.
>
> (Richardson and Meinhof 1999: 7)

Yet this unsettling presupposes a 'prior stability', and Richardson and Meinhof acknowledge that the new output available via fibre-optic cables, satellite dishes and digital 'set-top boxes' is in a process of 'building familiarity' with viewers. For instance, their analysis of the QVC shopping channel's 'verbal' and 'visual' discourses (Richardson and Meinhof 1999: 107–11; and see also Bucholtz 2000) details the kind of strategies being employed to construct the familiar and the intimate.

Lifetime

Earlier in the present chapter, I touched briefly on what Giddens (1984), after Heidegger (1962), refers to as the irreversible passing away of lifetime or being towards death. 'All human agents are beings who are born and die, and ... live out their lives', writes Giddens (1987a: 145), 'in consciousness of their fini-tude.' One of Scannell's concerns in looking at the temporal arrangements of broadcasting is to ask how radio and television are enmeshed not only with the reversible time of the day-to-day but also with the 'intersecting plane' of life-time (Scannell 1988). In his later work, he calls this by various other names ('phenomenological time', 'human time' or simply 'my-time'), yet a continuing interest there is the ways in which broadcasting 'articulates its time-structures to ... lifetime' (Scannell 1996: 152).

Scannell (1996: 156) invites us to think about the structure of the 'never-ending' serial or soap opera, 'that fictional narrative form which is particular to broadcasting'. Unlike the literary novel and the fiction film, where, as Christine Geraghty (1981: 13) puts it, there is an 'emphasis on resolution and closure', soap operas are distinguished by their 'endlessness' (see also Geraghty 1991). For example, *Coronation Street* is the longest running British television soap, broadcast for well over forty years and showing little sign of losing momentum. In time, this remarkable programme will no doubt 'outlive' many of its regular viewers. However, what Scannell (1988: 20) notices about such stories is that 'the time of the tale' moves in parallel with 'lifetime and its passing away'. He elaborates on that point below, spelling out the potential consequences for audience members:

> The key is the correspondence between the movement of time in the fictional world and the actual world: for, since these move together and at the same pace, it follows that the lifetime of viewers and listeners unfolds at the same rate as the lives of the characters in the stories. Thus we stand in the same relation to them as we do to our own family, relatives, friends and everyday acquaintances. Moreover access to this fictional world corresponds quite closely to the forms of access we have to people in the real world, and just as in our own lives we acquire, through the years, our own incremental biography as well as an accumulating familiar knowledge of the biographies of those around us, so too, in the same way, we come to know the people in the serials. We can recall past incidents in their lives with the same facility as we can remember events in our own lives and in the lives of those we know and have known for years. And we can drop out of the narratives for a while and later return and pick up the threads in the same way as we resume real-life situations and relationships.
>
> (Scannell 1988: 21–2)

Of course, as with the passage from Silverstone (1993: 574–5) extracted earlier, the 'inclusive "we"' here has to be qualified. Not everybody will necessarily 'come to know the people' in a soap opera, although this is undoubtedly an intended 'effect' which is worked for by the programme-makers. Anyway, Scannell is not suggesting that listeners and viewers are somehow duped into believing the fictional characters are exactly the same as what he terms 'people in the real world'. Rather, his proposal is that, among the routine pleasures to be had from watching soap opera, there is the possibility of identification with characters whose fictional lives are 'lived out' at the same 'pace' or 'rate' as our own. These are lives to which we may, if we wish to do so, gain regular 'access'.

The 'familiar knowledge' of characters accumulated by many long-term followers of a soap opera like *Coronation Street* means that, while the endlessness of the narrative makes it 'future-oriented', 'the audience's engagement is also with what has happened in the past' (Geraghty 1981: 16). For Scannell (1988: 22), this engagement with a serial's history raises issues of memory:

> Such programmes resonate in memory in a double sense: they are both a cultural resource shared by millions and ... particular to the lives of individuals. Talk about them is part of the staple currency of the

tabloid press and the small change of everyday conversation. ... The repetitiveness of day-to-day life, cross-cut by the irreversibility of life-time, is continually reproduced by these stories without beginning or ending.

Remembering past goings-on in the 'fictional world' helps listeners and viewers to speculate on and 'gossip' about what might happen next in forthcoming episodes (speculation that, as he notes, can be fuelled by popular journalism). Evidence of this type of 'soap talk' is well documented in geographically diverse studies of television and everyday life (see, for instance, Penacchioni 1984 on Brazil; Hobson 1989 on the UK; Brown 1994 on the USA and Australia).

Eventfulness

We have seen how, in the relationship between soap operas and their audi-ences, the plane of the day-to-day is 'cross-cut' by lifetime. Now it is necessary for us to focus on the ways in which broadcasting serves to articulate its daili-ness with the *longue durée* of institutional time, or with what Scannell (1988) calls 'calendrical time'. One straightforward way of understanding this articula-tion, already hinted at in the previous section, is to recognise that a long-running programme such as *Coronation Street* has become 'an institution' in British popular culture, but there is a more general sense in which radio and television could be said to operate at the intersection of routines and tradi-tions. Just as the 'humdrum' of routine helps to give holidays their special significance, so the ordinariness of much broadcast output is intimately connected to its occasional eventfulness (Scannell 1995; 1996; and see Dayan and Katz 1992, who define 'media events' as 'high holidays of mass communi-cation' that function as 'interruptions of routine'). So although 'broadcast output, like daily life, is largely uneventful ... both are occasionally punctuated (predictably and unpredictably) by eventful occasions' (Scannell 1995: 4). Many of the 'eventful occasions' in British broadcasting, such as the annual tradition of the monarch's Christmas Day speech discussed by Giddens (1999), have formed what Scannell terms a national broadcast calendar (hence his consideration of this further, intersecting plane of temporality as calendrical time). As a time-measurement device, the calendar, like the clock, is charac-terised by its repetitiveness. On a yearly rather than a daily or half-daily basis, it turns round full circle to start again.

Scannell's argument, then, is that listeners and viewers in the private sphere are granted access to what, for the vast majority of people prior to broadcasting, were once remote and inaccessible public events. For instance, ever since the early days of radio, the BBC has invested importance not just in its studio-based productions but also in its 'outside broadcasting' activities. 'In the course of the 1920s and 1930s', reports Scannell (1988: 17), 'BBC engineers arranged thou-sands upon thousands of outside broadcasts from a wide variety of sources.'

These included live coverage of state and sporting occasions, which were thereby transformed by radio and later by television:

> Consider the FA Cup Final, the Grand National or Wimbledon. All these existed before broadcasting, but whereas previously they existed only for their particular sporting publics they became, through radio and television, something more. Millions now heard or saw them who had little direct interest in the sports themselves. The events became, and have remained, punctual moments in a shared national life. Broadcasting created, in effect, a new national calendar of public events ... threaded through the continuing daily output was the cyclical reproduction, year in year out, of an orderly and regular progression of festivities, celebrations and remembrances that marked the unfolding of the broadcast year. The calendar not only organizes and co-ordinates social life, but gives it a renewable content, anticipatory pleasures, a horizon of expectations. The BBC calendar became the expressive register of a common, corporate public life that persists to this day.
>
> (Scannell 1992: 322–3)

The extent to which public service broadcasting in Britain succeeds in creating a 'common' national culture, as he suggests it does, is a matter of debate to which I will return shortly. Still, the fundamental point here concerns broadcasting's efforts to produce and reproduce eventfulness, which it attempts to achieve through the development of appropriate styles of eventful commentary and imagery (see Scannell 1996, for a detailed analysis of the coverage of royal and parliamentary occasions), as well as through the cyclicity of the broadcast calendar. Of course, ultimately, it is for listeners and viewers to experience media events as eventful in the context of their own daily lives and lifetimes.

According to Scannell (1996), who contests the view that modern media only offer 'inauthentic' cultural experiences, the liveness of radio and television can serve to enhance, rather than detract from, the special 'aura' of events. Broadcast coverage of an event helps to give it a 'halo of expectation and anticipation that includes the build-up to an occasion and that runs right through to its conclusion' (Scannell 1996: 90–1). This sense of eventfulness may be linked, in turn, to the role of radio and television in 'the invention of tradition' (Hobsbawm and Ranger 1983) and 'the reinvention of publicness' (Thompson 1995).

There are strong similarities, in my view, between this aspect of Scannell's work and elements of the social theory of media and modernity advanced by sociologist John Thompson (1994; 1995). However, whereas Scannell has a tendency to foreground modes of temporal organisation, Thompson puts greater emphasis on spatial issues. He contends that 'the mass media' in modern societies have constituted a new and distinctive kind of publicness, a 'mediated publicness'. Amongst its defining features, he argues, is the fact that it is a 'non-local' space (I would prefer to say 'trans-local'), because 'the development of communication media ... detaches the phenomenon of publicness from the sharing of a common locale: the sphere of mediated publicness is extended in time and space, and is potentially global in scope' (Thompson 1995: 246). As Daniel Dayan and Elihu Katz (1992), McKenzie Wark (1994) and Maurice Roche (2000) propose in their different case studies of media events and 'mega-events', the publics for some of those occasions (for instance, the Olympic Games, the first Gulf War or the fall of the Berlin Wall) have been 'global in scope', at least in the sense that they have been 'witnessed' by large international audiences. The same could be said of the soccer World Cup Finals, which come around every four years, or for occasions such as the death of Diana, Princess of Wales, and the 'September 11' attack on the World Trade Centre in New York. Although the last two 'happenings' listed here were unanticipated news stories rather than elements of a cyclical tradition, they did 'pierce' the ordinariness of uneventful daily life for audiences around the world. It is a mark of these particular sorts of dramatic occasion that coverage of them breaks into and disrupts the usual flow of scheduled programming. People also tend to recall, even years after, where they were and what they were doing when news of the happening broke.

Correspondingly, traditions in modern society are now largely trans-localised. This enables tradition, which in pre-modern cultures was confined to the performance of ritual in a local place, 'to be re-embedded in a multiplicity of locales and reconnected to territorial units that exceed the limits of face-to-face interaction' (Thompson 1995: 197). Given Scannell's main interest is in the history of British broadcasting, it is understandable that the primary geographical or territorial unit in his writings on institution and tradition is the space of 'the nation'. Indeed, he believes that broadcasting has made a significant contribution to the formation of this unit. While Britain clearly had a contested existence as an 'imagined community' (Anderson 1991) prior to the arrival of radio and television, the BBC's commitment to the 'principle of universal availability' in the provision of its service (Scannell 1992: 319) was intended to create a new order of 'general public' on a national scale. Even in the USA, where broadcasting has been organised along more commercial lines from the start, 'the "national networks" of CBS, NBC and ABC served as the focus for national life' (Robins 1995: 249).

Today, the basic public service idea of 'access for all to entertainment, informational and cultural resources in a common public domain' is being 'threatened', as Scannell (1992: 321) sees it, by non-terrestrial broadcasters who are providing specialised subscription channels and 'pay-per-view' transmissions to increasingly fragmented and dispersed audiences. In this regard, I think his work can be seen as a spirited defence of the 'democratic principles' of public service broadcasting against the 'enemy' of the free market, on much the same grounds that some people in Britain have fought to protect the state's

National Health Service from 'privatisation'. On the face of it, this is a laudable project, yet broadcasting and health care are not quite the same sorts of service, and Scannell refuses to accept that the BBC might have an 'ideological' function as well as a democratic one. He is, in any case, fighting against apparently irresistible forces of commercialisation and 'transnationalisation' in the contemporary media environment. There is no going back to an age of broadcasting that pre-dates cable, satellite and digital television.

As David Morley and Kevin Robins (1995: 11) point out, policies of so-called 'deregulation' ('re-regulation' would be a more accurate description, see Corner *et al.* 1994) have accompanied a decrease in the influence of national broadcasting systems within Western European countries since the 1980s:

> The political and social concerns of the public service era – with democracy and public life, with national culture and identity – have come to be regarded as factors inhibiting the development of new media markets. ... Driven now by the logic of profit and competition, the overriding objective of the new media corporations is to get their product to the largest number of consumers. There is, then, an expansionist tendency at work, pushing ceaselessly towards the construction of enlarged audiovisual spaces and markets. ... Audiovisual geographies are thus becoming detached from the symbolic spaces of national culture and realigned on the basis of the more 'universal' principles of international consumer culture. ... The new media order is set to become a global order.

What these authors are witnessing, in effect, is the declining power (though certainly not the disappearance) of the nation-state in Western Europe, and the rise of international 'audiovisual spaces', 'satellite footprints' or 'territories of transmission' (Rath 1985) that are bound up with wider processes of 'globalisation' (see also Robins 1995; Morley 1996). There continue to be barriers, of language, for example, to the 'television without frontiers' ideal espoused by 'new media corporations' (and also by the European Commission, see Schlesinger 1991; 1993), but the territorial units to which Thompson refers are now 'realigning' partly as result of economic imperatives.

At the end of his essay on the temporal arrangements of broadcasting, Scannell (1988: 29) writes in conclusion:

> In class-divided nation states, radio first and later television unobtrusively restored (or perhaps created for the first time) the possibilities of a knowable world, a world-in-common, for whole populations. ... Broadcasting brought together for a radically new kind of general public the elements of a culture-in-common for all. In doing so, it redeemed, and continues to redeem, the intelligibility of the world and the communicability of experience in the widest social sense.

Broadcasting constructed such feelings of 'commonality', he believes, by helping to sustain the cyclical or recursive character of social life 'for whole populations', both at the level of clock time (day-to-day routines) and calendrical time (annual traditions). In assessing this bold assertion, we must be careful to separate out two rather different strands of argument in his writings.

On the one hand, Scannell presents us with several highly illuminating reflections on radio, television and the movements of time (the repetitive ordering of dailiness and eventfulness, and the cross-cutting linearity of human lifetime), usefully applying and expanding on Giddens' theory of structuration. However, on the other hand, he leaves himself open to criticism with his insistence that British broadcasting is a positive force in creating a 'culture-in-common' for its listeners and viewers, a national 'public sphere' with a shared 'universe of discourse' (Scannell 1992). If this was ever the case historically, then it appears to be less and less evident in the current period, because of an increasing fragmentation and dispersal of audiences. New commonalities might well be emerging from these shifts, but they do not usually conform to the old shape of bounded national community envisaged by public service broadcasters in Western Europe.

While Morley (2000: 110) claims to be 'in sympathy with much of Scannell's approach', acknowledging that radio and television can have certain 'ritual functions', he questions the assumption made by Scannell, who was employing a concept borrowed from the social theorist Jürgen Habermas (1989), 'that there indeed is a public sphere, in the singular, and that it is a Good Thing' (Morley 2000: 113). He thinks it would be far better for us to talk about there being multiple public spheres (related to divisions of gender, generation, ethnicity and so on), some of which may be transnational or 'diasporic' (for a roughly similar critique, see Couldry 2000a: 10–11). Attending to issues of 'race', Morley (2000: 119–20) also seeks to expose what he perceives to be the predominant 'whiteness' of public service broadcasting in Britain:

> Scannell's celebration of broadcasting as a public good, 'a culture-in-common' … which needs to be defended against the fragmenting forces of deregulation, simply fails to recognise that this public culture itself is already an ethnic culture and has a colour which is only in common to some of the citizens of the nation which it supposedly reflects, and which it attempts to address.

Coming from a 'critical' perspective in media and cultural studies, Morley is alert to the significance of conflicting social interests. In comparison, rather than focusing on difference and power, Scannell is concerned with how 'intelligibility' and 'order' are co-operatively achieved in modern communications, and his own stance therefore seems to be more closely associated with a 'consensus view of society' (see Cuff et al. 1998).

To recap, Chapter 1 has focused on what I called, in the general introduction to this book, round-and-round movements in time-space. With reference to Giddens' theory of structuration, two overlapping levels of recursiveness in social life, namely the day-to-day and the *longue durée* of institutions, were identified (it was noted, too, how each of these contrasts yet intersects with life-time's irreversibility). I then considered in detail the ways in which Scannell, building on those ideas, regards broadcasting as being organised according to the cyclical rhythms of clock time and calendrical time. In his historical analysis of radio and television, he emphasises the seriality and scheduling of broadcast output, as well as the occasional interruption of its ordinariness by predictable and unpredictable events. It was also suggested, in my discussion of the work of Richardson and Meinhof, that the hourliness of some new programme services can be related to the increasing flexibility or desynchronisation of work and leisure practices.

2

EXTENSIONALITY

The emphasis in the last chapter was on routines, traditions and processes of social reproduction. Although it was acknowledged there that reproduction does involve elements of change, the focus here will be much more on patterns of social transformation. So far, in discussing day-to-day and institutional life, I have concentrated mainly on their stability and continuity (underpinned by the repetitions of the clock and calendar), but this is only part of the story. Modern institutions are also characterised by their 'dynamism', the ways in which they can 'undercut traditional habits and customs' and, crucially, their 'extensional transformations' on a potentially global scale (Giddens 1991: 1). In other words, whereas our primary concern up to now has been with cyclicity or the recursive ordering of practices in time–space, I want us to think next about some of the features of extensionality in social life. This means engaging with the arguments about globalisation touched on towards the end of the previous chapter, where we began to look at issues to do with what John Thompson (1995) calls the 'extended availability' of media messages in time and space. Whilst it is certainly not my intention to suggest that media are the principal 'motors' of change, I will be exploring the significant role they play, alongside other institutions and technologies, in globalising processes.

Globalisation

Globalisation is a term that has enjoyed 'sudden popularity' over recent years, having seemingly 'come from nowhere to be almost everywhere' (Giddens 1999: 7), yet it is important to recognise at the outset that the social changes to which it refers have not 'come from nowhere'. As Stuart Hall (1991: 19–20), a leading figure in so-called 'British cultural studies', reminds anyone who might be suffering from 'historical amnesia', globalisation 'is far from ... new'. From his critical perspective, it has its origins specifically in the 'European expansion' that started in the 'early modern age' with Europe's 'discovery of new worlds' and with the formation of a discourse in which 'the West' constructed itself in opposition to (and in a position of power and dominance over) 'the Rest' (see Hall 1992a; and also Said 1978 on the discursive practices of 'Orientalism').

More generally, for the purposes of the present chapter, let us say that today's intensified phase of globalisation is the outcome of a long-term, and ongoing, 'reorganisation' of time–space relations. Sociologist Malcolm Waters (1995: 3) defines globalisation as a set of processes 'in which the constraints of geography on social and cultural arrangements recede' (that is, the constraints of physical distance) and, in doing so, he highlights temporal and spatial shifts which will mean that 'we can expect relationships between people in disparate locations to be formed as easily as relationships between people in proximate ones'. Indeed, we could add that one of the reasons why time and space have become such central issues for social theorists is that many academics in the humanities and social sciences are attempting to account for the globalising tendencies evident in what Anthony Giddens (1991) labels the 'late modern age' (others, like Harvey 1989a, use 'postmodernity' as a label for the contemporary era).

A number of helpful concepts and metaphors have emerged from the intellectual endeavours of social theorists seeking to explain globalisation (Moores 2003a). For example, when writing on modernity, which he views as 'inherently globalising', Giddens (1990; 1991) discusses the 'separation of time and space' and the 'disembedding' of social systems. Geographer David Harvey (1989a: 240), meanwhile, reflects on experiences of 'time–space compression', which include feelings of a 'speed-up in the pace of life'. The first of these theorists focuses his discussion on how social relationships may get increasingly 'stretched' across vast distances, while the second is more interested in how the globe might appear to 'shrink' or 'collapse inwards', although those metaphors are not necessarily incompatible. As I will go on to argue, 'stretching' and 'shrinking', or 'implosion' (McLuhan 1964), could be seen as different sides of the same coin. In addition, sociologists such as Manuel Castells (1996) and John Urry (2000) employ notions of 'network' and 'flow' in an effort to come to terms with the global spread of certain institutions and relationships. Castells plots the rise of 'the network society' and Urry proposes a new sociology of 'fluids' or 'mobilities' for the twenty-first century. These notions can be connected, in turn, to arguments about the increasing 'permeability' of boundaries in the contemporary period.

We must now examine each of those approaches in greater detail, considering the voices of other key thinkers, where relevant, along the way. This involves beginning once again with the work of Giddens, but concentrating on his later writings on modernity and globalisation rather than the theory of structuration (for a useful overview, see Bryant and Jary 2001). There are clear continuities across that whole body of work. For instance, he demonstrates an unwavering commitment to theorising the temporal and spatial arrangements of social life. However, some subtle modifications are also detectable. I have already noted his growing interest in the dynamic character of modern institutions, and this is related to a further shift in his thinking, for whereas the theory of structuration makes much of the predictability of daily human conduct, he subsequently accepts that we are 'riding the juggernaut' of a 'runaway world' (see Giddens 1990; 1999) in which social processes are marked by an unprecedented degree of 'unpredictability'.

What Giddens (1999: 2–3) has in mind when he refers to unpredictability are the 'new risks and uncertainties' of late modernity:

> The world in which we find ourselves today ... seems out of our control – a runaway world. Moreover, some of the influences that were supposed to make life more certain and predictable for us, including the progress of science and technology, often have quite the opposite effect. Global climate change and its accompanying risks, for example, probably result from our intervention into the environment. They aren't natural phenomena. Science and technology are inevitably involved in our attempts to counter such risks, but they have also contributed to creating them in the first place. We face risk situations that no one in previous history has had to confront – of which global warming is only one. Many of the new risks and uncertainties affect us no matter where we live, and regardless of how privileged or deprived we are. They are bound up with globalisation.

In this passage, the collective pronouns he uses are entirely appropriate, because an environmental risk such as global warming does touch all of us in some way (although it is important to remember that several other aspects of globalisation are 'unevenly' spread). His argument is similar to that advanced by the social theorist Ulrich Beck (1992a; 1992b; 1999), who, playing with words, has suggested that the unequal 'distribution of goods' which is an established feature of modern societies is currently accompanied by an often indiscriminate distribution of 'bads' in the emerging global 'risk society'. Of course, the natural and social worlds have always contained hazards of various sorts, yet never before have we faced 'global dangers' of the type 'that arise for all of humanity from nuclear fission or the storage of radioactive waste' (Beck 1992b: 21).

At a later stage in the book, when dealing more fully with issues of self and experience, or with the 'intentionality' of personal lives (Giddens 1990; 1991), I will explain how Giddens tries to strike a balance between his existing ideas about ontological security, which is 'sustained through the familiar and the predictable' (Silverstone 1993: 591), and his newer concerns with the unpredictability of our 'global futures' (see Adam 1995). He understands senses of security and anxiety, of 'trust' and 'risk', as co-existing in 'various historically unique conjunctions in conditions of modernity' (Giddens 1991: 19). Building on his notes on trust and risk, in which little specific attention is given to electronically mediated communication, my aim will be to outline the role of media in helping to shape those distinctive 'conjunctions'.

Stretching

For the present, I intend to focus on Giddens' account of 'the intimate connections between modernity and the transformation of time and space' (Giddens 1990: 17), since it deals with issues that are pivotal to broader debates about extensionality in social life. He illustrates these connections by contrasting modern time–space relations with those of 'pre-modern cultures', where 'for the bulk of the population, and for most of the ordinary activities of day-to-day life, time and space remained essentially linked through place' (Giddens 1991: 16). 'Place' refers here to a spatial 'locale' or a 'physical setting' that is 'situated geographically', and so if time and space are 'linked through place', as he puts it above, then the 'when' of social activity remains closely tied to its localised 'where'. However, with the advent of modernity, there is a radical 'separation' of time and space as each is 'pulled away' from physical place (that is, the social organisation of time and space is abstracted from locales). As will become clear later in the chapter, this has not led to the disappearance of places. Rather, place tends to be more 'open' (and is, I will argue, instantaneously 'pluralised') as a result of modern time–space transformations.

These ideas about time, space and place may seem difficult initially, but in the course of defining his concept of time–space separation or 'distanciation', Giddens offers some basic examples of the historical transformation that he is identifying. One of them has to do with the standardisation and globalisation of time-measurement, and it requires us to return to two of the devices, the clock and the calendar, which we have encountered previously. Writing at the start of the last decade of the twentieth century, Giddens (1990: 17–18) observes:

> The invention of the mechanical clock and its diffusion to virtually all members of the population (a phenomenon which dates at its earliest from the late eighteenth century) were of key significance in the separation of time from space. The clock expressed a uniform dimension of 'empty' time, quantified in such a way as to permit the precise designation of 'zones' of the day. Time was still connected with space (and place) until the uniformity of time-measurement by the mechanical clock was matched by uniformity in the social organisation of time. This shift coincided with the expansion of modernity and was not completed until the current century. One of its main aspects is the worldwide standardisation of calendars. Everyone now follows the same dating system: the approach of the 'year 2000', for example, is a global event. Different 'New Years' continue to co-exist but are subsumed within a mode of dating which has become to all intents and purposes universal. A second aspect is the standardising of time across regions. Even in the latter part of the nineteenth century, different areas within a single state usually had different 'times', while between the borders of states the situation was even more chaotic.

This move towards globally synchronised 'unified time', with an international system of 'time zones' to complement the zoning of the day, was concretised, according to Barbara Adam (1995: 114), when the first electronic 'time-signal' was transmitted across the globe from Paris in the early twentieth century: 'Wireless signals travelling at the speed of light displaced local times and established one time for all people on this earth ... world time.' She points out that this universalisation helped to create the necessary conditions for a whole 'global network of communication', involving the coordinated flow of transportation and information.

Another example offered by Giddens in his discussion of time–space distanciation is the emergence of techniques of spatial representation associated with modern map drawing. Just as mechanical clocks are an expression of 'empty time', by which he implies time abstracted from distinct locales, so 'universal maps' have been significant in the 'emptying of space':

> The development of 'empty space' is linked above all to two sets of factors: those allowing for the representation of space without reference to a privileged locale which forms a distinct vantage-point; and those making possible the substitutability of different spatial units. ... The progressive charting of the globe that led to the creation of universal maps, in which perspective played little part in the representation of geographical position and form, established space as 'independent' of any particular place or region.
>
> (Giddens 1990: 19)

The basis of that charting was 'the "discovery" of "remote" regions' of the world by Western travellers (his inverted commas around those terms remind us that, for the 'native' peoples who inhabited them, such regions were neither 'discovered' nor 'remote') and this observation can be related back to Hall's remarks on the origins of globalisation in Europe's expansion. Giddens understands that modernity is, at least at root, a 'Western project' (even if he refuses to equate globalisation today simply with 'Westernisation', see Giddens 1999).

Having explained the role of clocks, calendars and maps in the 'process of the emptying of time and space', Giddens (1991: 17–18) asserts that this process is crucial for disembedding, 'the "lifting out" of social relations from local contexts and their rearticulation across indefinite tracts of time–space'. He identifies several 'disembedding mechanisms' that facilitate such a 'lifting out' and extending, or stretching, of relationships. I will look at just two of these mechanisms here, namely money and media of communication (and see Murdock 1993: 529–30, who lists a number of links between them).

Strictly speaking, money itself may be seen as a 'medium of exchange'. According to Giddens, it is best conceptualised as a sort of 'symbolic token'. It has a 'standardised value' that allows for the possibility of 'transactions between a multiplicity of individuals who never physically meet one another'

(Giddens 1991: 18). Of course, coins and notes are exchanged between 'co-present' participants in local contexts, say when they are passed between members of a household or over the counter in a shop, but he emphasises that many financial transactions today are between physically 'absent' others. For instance, the 'plastic money' of credit cards means that purchases might now be made over the telephone or else 'online' via the internet. These exchanges at a distance are only possible when money takes the form of 'pure information lodged as figures in a computer printout' (Giddens 1990: 25). When considering evidence of an intensification of globalising tendencies in the late modern age, he cites a dramatic increase in the level of transnational 'finance and capital flows':

> Geared as it is to electronic money – money that exists only as digits in computers – the current world economy has no parallels in earlier times. In the new global electronic economy, fund managers, banks, corporations, as well as millions of individual investors, can transfer vast amounts of capital from one side of the world to another at the click of a mouse.
>
> (Giddens 1999: 9)

His description of capital changing hands 'at the click of a mouse' helps to illustrate the interdependence of money and electronic media. There is clearly a close connection between the workings of the 'current world economy' and the technology of computer networks.

Although Giddens has never written extensively on media (something for which we can forgive him, since he is a general social theorist rather than a media specialist) his model of disembedding does take account of the enormous capacity that information technologies have to extend relationships in time and space. Talking about his social theory of modernity in an interview, he remarks: 'I do see communication, and changes in systems of communication, as particularly important to the constitution and development of societies' (Giddens and Pierson 1998: 100). In fact, he was already interested in communication media before his work on modernity, noting the historical importance of the telegraph, the first mode of electronic signalling, for temporal and spatial arrangements. Previously, information tended to move only as fast as it could be transported physically. Media 'of communication' were bound up with those 'of transportation' (Giddens 1984: 123), yet electronic media (from the telegraph to satellite transmission and the internet) have brought virtually instantaneous communications at a distance.

Thompson (1995) has similar things to say about the 'instantaneity' of modern telecommunications, observing how 'temporal delays' in the mediation of symbolic forms are 'virtually eliminated'. Moreover, he stresses a new dimension of 'simultaneity' that is thereby introduced into social life:

> In earlier historical periods the experience of simultaneity – that is, of events occurring 'at the same time' – presupposed a specific locale in

which the simultaneous events could be experienced by the individual. Simultaneity presupposed locality; 'the same time' presupposed 'the same place'. But with the uncoupling of space and time brought about by telecommunication, the experience of simultaneity was detached from the spatial condition of common locality. It became possible to experience events as simultaneous despite the fact that they occurred in locales that were spatially remote. In contrast to the concreteness of the here and now, there emerged a sense of 'now' which was no longer bound to a particular locale.

(Thompson 1995: 32)

This passage echoes his comments on the space of mediated publicness, which I quoted in the last chapter, or, to be precise, these remarks on changing senses of simultaneity serve to ground his assertion that 'the phenomenon of publicness' has become detached from 'the sharing of a common locale' (Thompson 1995: 246).

Modern mechanical transportation (including trains, cars and aeroplanes) has certainly increased travel speeds dramatically, but with electronic media the old link between communications and the 'mobility of the human body' is no longer a necessary one (see Giddens 1984). In his book on globalisation, Giddens (1999: 10–11) returns to exactly that point:

In the mid-nineteenth century, a Massachusetts portrait painter, Samuel Morse, transmitted the first message, 'What hath God wrought?', by electric telegraph. In doing so, he initiated a new phase in world history. Never before could a message be sent without someone going somewhere to carry it. Yet the advent of satellite communications marks every bit as dramatic a break with the past ... there are more than 200 such satellites above the earth, each carrying a vast range of information.

It is not quite true that, before the telegraph, no message could 'be sent without someone going somewhere to carry it', for there were basic signalling systems such as semaphore, yet these did not have the same instantaneous 'reach'. A remarkable consequence of contemporary 'satellite communications', he argues elsewhere (Giddens 1990: 141), is that people are often 'familiar with events, with actions and with the visible appearance of physical settings thousands of miles away', even when they have not actually travelled there 'in person'.

Geographer Andrew Leyshon (1995), from whom we will hear more in the coming pages, draws an historical comparison in order to illuminate the argument that familiarity with distant places is now possible via electronically mediated communication. Having described the actions of European migrants who travelled to America by ship in the nineteenth century as 'something of a leap in the dark' (since their 'knowledge of what was awaiting them when

41

they got there was necessarily partial'), he asserts that nowadays 'even the first time visitor to the US feels immediately familiar' with much of what she or he finds there, because that country 'serves as both the subject and the backdrop to countless numbers of movies and television drama series as well as news and documentary programmes' (Leyshon 1995: 13–14). Of course, there are quite complex issues to do with how popular film and television 'represent' places in the USA, constructing images that may not always 'match up' with how visitors, or the local inhabitants, find those physical settings to be. Indeed, Giddens (1991: 27) goes so far as to suggest that 'familiarity generated by mediated experience might perhaps ... produce feelings of "reality inversion" '. In these circumstances, when the place is physically encountered, it appears to have a 'less concrete existence' than its media representation (see also Baudrillard 1988, whose concept of 'hyperreality' takes this suggestion a stage further by breaking with any notion that media images can represent some prior reality).

Medium

Giddens' concern with media is not, in any case, centrally with signification (although see Giddens 1987b). Rather, he is interested in the communicative features and transformative potential of media technologies themselves. His interest in these matters arises partly out of his engagement with a body of literature that constitutes what Joshua Meyrowitz (1994) retrospectively terms 'medium theory'. Meyrowitz prefers to use the singular, 'medium', in order to distinguish this perspective from other theories of media. Considering himself to be a 'second-generation medium theorist' (his own thoughts on electronic media and place will be discussed later in this chapter), he acknowledges a debt to the two leading figures of the 'first generation', Harold Innis and Marshall McLuhan. The focus of their writings is on 'the particular characteristics of each individual medium or of each particular type of media', and their principal aim is 'to call attention to the potential influences of communication technologies ... apart from the content they convey' (Meyrowitz 1994: 50). To quote one of McLuhan's slogans, ' "the medium is the message" because it is the medium that shapes and controls the scale and form of human association and action' (McLuhan 1964: 9).

A political economist by training (see Mosco 1996: 173), Innis (1950; 1951) writes on the history of communication, culture and power. The historical scope of his work is exceptionally broad, with much of it relating to pre-modern civilisations. One of the key distinctions that he makes is between 'time-biased' and 'space-biased' media. 'A medium of communication has an important influence on the dissemination of knowledge over space and over time', remarks Innis (1951: 33), 'and it becomes necessary to study its characteristics in order to appraise its influence in its cultural setting.' As Meyrowitz (1994: 52) explains in the extract below:

42

Innis ... argues that most media of communication have a 'bias' either towards lasting a long time or towards being moved easily across great distances. He claims that the bias of a culture's dominant medium affects the degree of the culture's stability and conservatism as well as the culture's ability to take over and govern a large territory. 'Time-biased' media such as stone hieroglyphics, he argues, lead to relatively small, stable societies because stone carvings last a long time and are rarely revised, and their limited mobility makes them poor means of keeping in touch with distant places. In contrast, messages on light, 'space-biased' papyrus allowed the Romans to maintain a large empire with a centralized government that delegated authority to distant provinces.

When reading this commentary on his theory, it becomes evident that Innis identifies certain elements of extensionality in a pre-modern culture such as the Roman Empire, in which he believes 'bureaucratic development ... and success in solving problems of administration over vast areas were dependent on supplies of papyrus' (Innis 1951: 47), although Giddens reminds us that 'in the case of modernity, these traits are more inclusive and far-reaching than in any previous civilization' (Giddens and Pierson 1998: 99). Crucially, in contrast to the movement of even a 'light' medium such as papyrus, electronic signals are not at all constrained by the speed of physical transportation, as I noted earlier.

McLuhan (1964) adopts the same general approach to understanding media, but his work concentrates far more than Innis' on communications in the modern period. He pays close attention to the 'impact' of electronic media (see also McLuhan and Fiore 1967), and this difference in emphasis leads him to conclude the history of communication technologies in a distinctive way. Whilst he agrees that this story is one of 'explosion outward' by degree, for example, as 'the alteration of social groupings, and the formation of new communities, occur with the increased speed of information movement by paper messages and road transport' (McLuhan 1964: 90), he proposes that the speed-up brought about by electronic media leads to an 'instant implosion' of space. In his view, these technologies 'abolish the spatial dimension, rather than enlarge it' (McLuhan 1964: 255), and his perception that the world has 'imploded' gives rise to the famous statement that: 'We now live in a global village ... a simultaneous happening' (McLuhan and Fiore 1967: 63).

Although McLuhan (1964: 3) understands media technologies as 'exten-sions' of the human body (suggesting, in my view rather oddly, that 'we have extended our central nervous system itself in a global embrace'), his writings evoke the image of a shrunken planet. When he declares that electronic media have 'abolished' space (very similar to a recent thesis on 'the death of distance', advanced by Cairncross 1997), and when he announces that 'our world has become compressional ... electrically contracted' (McLuhan 1964: 5), this fits neatly with Harvey's ideas on time–space compression, which I will review in the next section. However, his concept of implosion need not be seen in opposition to that of extensionality. It can serve instead to complement it. In Giddens' work, for example, traces of McLuhan are to be found in the observation that media of communication have brought a growing 'intrusion of distant events into everyday consciousness' (Giddens 1991: 27), or else that: 'In conditions of modernity, place becomes increasingly phantasmagoric … locales are thoroughly penetrated by … social influences quite distant from them' (Giddens 1990: 18–19). This notion of 'phantasmagoric' places, of distant happenings and forces having a 'ghostly' presence in the physical settings of daily life, is evidently related to the assertion that an electronic medium such as television 'pours upon us instantly and continuously the concerns of all other men [*sic*]' (McLuhan and Fiore 1967: 16). As social relationships are stretched further and further beyond the confines of 'common locality', so it may sometimes feel like the globe is collapsing in on locales.

The medium theory developed by Innis and McLuhan has several strengths. Giddens (1991: 24) is quite right to praise them for their attempts at theorising 'the connections between dominant kinds of media and time–space transformations', since few theorists of media have sought, as they do, to explain the links between communications and long-term social change. In the period when they were writing, both were undoubtedly 'ahead of their time' in addressing the temporal and spatial dimensions of culture, and Thompson (1994: 29) believes their line of thought is of 'enduring significance'. An enthusiasm for McLuhan's work in some quarters today, especially among those who are concerned to study communication via the internet (Levinson 1999, for instance, insists on the continued relevance of that work for understanding media in 'the digital age'), leads his son, Eric McLuhan, and Frank Zingrone (1997a: 3) to claim that: 'Since his death in 1980, Marshall McLuhan's reputation has been in a sort of hiatus waiting for electronic reality to catch up … a surge of interest in his work emphasizes its usefulness.' There has, in Meyrowitz's words, been a 'revival' or 'resurrection' of McLuhan's ideas since the early 1990s (see Meyrowitz 2003: 205–8).

First-generation medium theory also has its weaknesses, though. The main problem is what critics of this approach call its 'technological determinism'. For example, whilst he does not explicitly cite McLuhan as the target of his attack, Raymond Williams (1990: 13) clearly has him in mind when outlining such a determinist 'view of the nature of social change':

> New technologies are discovered, by an essentially internal process of research and development, which then sets the conditions for social change and progress. Progress, in particular, is the history of these inventions, which 'created the modern world'. The effects of the technologies, whether direct or indirect, foreseen or unforeseen, are as it were the rest of history. The steam engine, the automobile, television, the atomic bomb, have made modern man [*sic*] and the modern

condition. ... The new technologies are invented as it were in an independent sphere, and then create new societies or new human
conditions.

A key difficulty with technological determinism, then, is its separation of 'technology' from 'society' and its reduction of history to a tale of isolated
innovations that have subsequently reshaped social life. In his critique of this
approach, Williams (1990: 14) is keen to point out that technologies are typically 'looked for and developed with certain purposes and practices already in
mind'. They are, to borrow a phrase from Donald MacKenzie and Judy
Wajcman (1985), 'socially shaped'. Indeed, that social shaping continues well
after 'invention', carrying over into their actual 'take up' and use (occasionally
in unexpected ways) in specific cultural circumstances (see Mackay 1995).

Accepting this critique does not mean that we have to deny the potential of
any given medium to contribute to a transformation of time and space (or that
we have to deny the 'communicative affordances' of a technology, see Hutchby
2001), but it should lead us to be cautious or 'modest' when theorising the role
of media technologies in processes of globalisation. When Giddens (1999:
10–11), in a passage reproduced earlier in the chapter, argues that 'Samuel
Morse ... initiated a new phase in world history' by inventing the telegraph, he
slips momentarily into the discourse of technological determinism that Williams
is so critical of. The danger is in thinking that a new technology could have
effects which are unaccompanied and unmediated, in the general sense of 'mediation', by other, socially shaped institutional and technological developments.

I say above that Giddens 'slips momentarily' because it is evident in his writings on extensionality in the late modern age, and from the following interview
response, that he is far from being a crude determinist. Here, he replies to a
question about whether 'the rise of electronic communication' prescribes a
specific kind of society:

> No. I think it is just one aspect of disembedding really. But it was
> certainly driven in some part by the perceived demands of the new
> society. There was an active search for quicker and more effective forms
> of communication across time and space. ... Information technology is
> bound up with the workings of a global economy, but many other
> forces are involved, including the driving power of capitalism and
> industrialism.
>
> (Giddens and Pierson 1998: 100)

His answer suggests that globalisation is 'best understood as a multifaceted or
differentiated social phenomenon' (Held *et al.* 1999: 27). He talks in this
extract about the forces of 'capitalism and industrialism', which, as he contends
elsewhere (Giddens 1990), are two of the four main 'institutional dimensions of
modernity' along with 'surveillance' and 'military power'. Rather than

proposing a 'medium-centred' account of human history in the style of Innis and McLuhan, his preference is to see media of communication as significant contributors to, not the principal motors of, social change.

Innovations in communications technology during the modern period have been closely intertwined with the broader imperatives of capitalism, industrialism, surveillance and military power. One well-documented instance of that intertwining is the beginnings of the internet in a 1960s defence research programme in the USA (for example, see Rheingold 1995; Kitchin 1998; Slevin 2000). This general programme was set up during the Cold War in a concerted effort to surpass technological advances that were being made in the Soviet Union, and, amongst other things, it gave rise to a computer networking system with military applications. Of course, what happens to this computer technology when it is adapted, marketed and appropriated for non-military use is a different matter altogether. 'The Internet', comments Urry (2000: 40), 'is one of the clearest examples of how a technology invented for one purpose, military communication within the US in the event of a nuclear attack, chaotically evolves into purposes wholly unintended by those inventing and developing it.'

A further problem with first-generation medium theory, associated with its technological determinism, has to do precisely with its proponents' focus on 'medium concerns' at the expense of what Meyrowitz (1994) names 'content concerns'. Perhaps the intensity of their focus is best summed up by McLuhan's statement that 'the content ... of any particular medium has about as much importance as the stencilling on the casing of an atomic bomb' (in McLuhan and Zingrone 1997b: 238). Still, Meyrowitz (1994: 73) concedes that:

> Ultimately, medium theory is most helpful when it is used not to supplant content concerns but to add another dimension to our understanding of the media environment. What is needed is a better integration of medium theory with other perspectives.

So if we can agree with Giddens (following Innis and McLuhan) that it is important to ask about the communicative features and transformative potential of a medium, then this must not blind us to issues of signification. These are issues relating to the cultural construction of meanings in mediated symbolic exchanges, to which I will pay attention in the second part of the book.

Shrinking

Harvey (1989a), more strongly influenced by Marxist theory than Giddens is, concentrates on the economics of capitalism in his attempt to account for experiences of time–space compression and what he terms 'the condition of postmodernity'. Indeed, his insistence on looking for the origins of contemporary cultural change in the appearance of 'more flexible modes of capital accumulation' (Harvey 1989a: vii) leaves him open to the charge of 'economic determinism'. Briefly summarised, his argument is that a capitalist economic crisis, which came to a head in the early 1970s, led to the decline of a previously dominant 'Fordist' economy, characterised by the assembly line of 'mass production' and by the 'mass consumption' of standardised goods. There followed the emergence of 'post-Fordism' (Murray 1989), or an economic system of 'flexible accumulation':

> Flexible accumulation, as I shall tentatively call it, is marked by a direct confrontation with the rigidities of Fordism. It rests on flexibility with respect to labour processes, labour markets, products and patterns of consumption. ... It has also entailed a new round of what I shall call 'time–space compression' in the capitalist world – the time horizons of both private and public decision-making have shrunk, while satellite communication and declining transport costs have made it increasingly possible to spread those decisions immediately over an ever wider and variegated space.
>
> (Harvey 1989a: 147)

For our purposes in this book, the crucial point to grasp here is the one he makes about a speeding up and spreading out of economic activity.

As Leyshon (1995: 20) elaborates, business organisations are in a competitive 'race to seek out new markets' globally and to reduce the 'turnover time of capital': 'the amount of time it takes for money advanced to fund the cost of new production to be returned with a profit through the sale of goods and services'. Taken together, these factors have certainly helped to 'shrink the world'. However, it is also necessary to recognise that, as we will explore shortly, 'the relative level of shrinkage ... and acceleration that people experience varies markedly from place to place and from person to person' (Leyshon 1995: 44).

In my account of McLuhan's ideas on electronic media and the implosion or 'abolition' of space, I suggested that there are parallels to be drawn with Harvey's thoughts on time–space compression. Interestingly, at the point where he offers us a definition of this concept, Harvey (1989a: 240–1) writes in a strikingly similar fashion about the way in which the take up of technological innovations has served to 'annihilate space through time' (Marx himself observed this at a much earlier stage), referring directly to the notion of 'a "global village" of telecommunications':

> I mean to signal by that term processes that so revolutionize the objective qualities of space and time that we are forced to alter, sometimes in quite radical ways, how we represent the world to ourselves. I use the word 'compression' because a strong case can be made that the history of capitalism has been characterized by a speed-up in the pace

of life, while so overcoming spatial barriers that the world sometimes seems to collapse inwards upon us. ... As space appears to shrink to a 'global village' of telecommunications and a 'spaceship earth' of economic and ecological interdependencies – to use just two familiar ... images – and as time horizons shorten to the point where the present is all there is ... so we have to learn how to cope with an over-whelming sense of compression of our spatial and temporal worlds.

Like Giddens, Harvey (1989a: 293) sees the significance of satellite communi-cations, which have, at least in principle, 'rendered the unit cost and time of communication invariant with respect to distance', and which now make it possible 'to experience a rush of images from different spaces almost simultane-ously, collapsing the world's spaces into a series of images on a television screen'. For instance, television news presents its viewers with a 'collage', juxta-posing happenings from around the globe, yet we must not forget that many news programmes still have a predominantly national perspective, even when they are reporting on 'international affairs' (see Baran and Wallis 1990).

If there are some similarities between Giddens and Harvey in this respect, with Giddens (1991: 26) pointing to the 'collage effect' of modern newspapers in which the individual items 'share nothing in common other than that they are "timely" ', then there are differences between them in other ways. Perhaps the most noticeable difference is in their use or non-use of the 'post' prefix to modernity. This merits closer inspection, since it is indicative of a wider debate in the humanities and social sciences about whether we continue to live in the modern period or have moved into a distinctively postmodern era.

Giddens (1990: 45) believes that 'the postmodern' is a term 'best kept to refer to styles or movements within literature, painting, the plastic arts and architecture', marking a break with the aesthetics of 'modernism'. In the early chapters of his book on the condition of postmodernity, Harvey (1989a) reviews these cultural shifts before going on to explain the economic factors that he views as giving rise to them. As a geographer with a long-standing interest in the urban environment (see Harvey 1989b), it is no surprise that he concentrates there on the growth of postmodern architectural forms. Harvey (1989a: 66) notes:

In the field of architecture and urban design, I take postmodernism broadly to signify a break with the modernist idea that planning and development should focus on large-scale, metropolitan-wide, techno-logically rational and efficient urban plans, backed by absolutely no-frills architecture (the austere 'functionalist' surfaces of ... modernism).

Instead, the postmodern aesthetic is more 'fragmented' and eclectic, involving a 'bits and pieces' mixing of past styles. Yet Giddens is unwilling to accept that such shifts signal the arrival of a new historical epoch of postmodernity, just as Harvey is unwilling to accept that today's society is 'postcapitalist'. 'Rather than entering a period of postmodernity', Giddens (1990: 3) contends, 'we are moving into one in which the consequences of modernity are becoming more radicalised and universalised than before.' Hence his choice of the label of 'late' modernity (and Beck's use of the term 'second modernity', see Beck and Willms 2004), although, like the concept of 'late capitalism' employed by Fredric Jameson (1991), I would suggest that even this has an unfortunate 'end is nigh' ring to it.

Looking beyond Harvey, another version of the global shrinkage thesis is to be found in the work of a fellow human geographer, Donald Janelle (1991). He carries out research that is concerned with 'the rates at which places move closer together ... in travel or communication time' or, in other words, with rates of 'time–space convergence' (Janelle 1991: 49). Mapping out historical patterns of convergence, he is interested in particular cases where 'space-adjusting technologies' have helped to reduce the 'friction' of distance. In the passage reproduced below, he takes the example of 'global air travel':

> Travel from Paris illustrates this shrinkage of distances. The fastest aircraft in 1950, the DC7, travelled roughly 350 miles per hour. Thus, most cities in southern and northern Europe could be reached from Paris in two hours, while flights to eastern North America took seven hours. ... The Boeing 747 jumbo jets, introduced in the late 1960s, reduced these times considerably. Flying at 640 miles per hour, northern South America, central Africa, southern Asia and central North America could be reached within six hours from Paris. The supersonic Concorde ... reduced such long-distance flights almost by half. Travelling at roughly 1,350 miles per hour, the Paris–Dakar–Rio de Janeiro flight takes only seven hours, compared to thirteen hours at subsonic speed. At Concorde speeds, New York, Moscow, Caracas, Lagos and New Delhi are reachable from Paris within four hours, and Sydney and Buenos Aires within seven hours.
>
> (Janelle 1991: 51)

His conception of places moving 'closer together' (of course, it should be noted here that Concorde is no longer in commercial use) also relates to the phenomenon of 'telephonic convergence'. Janelle (1991: 51) observes that, via the telephone, 'businesses or friends thousands of miles away can be reached in less time than someone across the street or in an office in the same building'. Near the beginning of this chapter, I quoted Waters' remark that 'relationships between people in disparate locations' may be 'formed as easily as relationships between people in proximate ones' (Waters 1995: 3). The implication of Janelle's comments on the telephone is that social relationships at a distance could even be formed more easily than physically co-present ones, at least in terms of the time taken to make contact. A word of caution is needed, though, because he does not see time–space convergence as a uniform process. There are places that, far from converging, are moving further apart in time–space, and people in rural parts of the 'developing world' who live in 'nonshrinking societies', which leads us to consider issues of global 'unevenness' and inequality.

Unevenness

Leyshon (1995: 36), who shares Harvey's emphasis on the economic aspects of globalisation, builds on the argument made by Janelle that time–space convergence is not a uniform process:

> On the one hand, some places have moved closer together in relative space. The trajectories of several national, regional and local economies have become ever more closely interconnected, held together by a dense network of financial flows and transactions. These flows have also served to bring about a greater degree of economic homogenization than hitherto, as traditional economic practices have been overwhelmed by a more powerful calculative rationale associated with the imperatives of global financial capital. But on the other hand, some places have moved further apart in relative space, as they have been subject to a process of financial exclusion, and this has led to a widening of economic and social space between such 'places of exclusion' and those localities which remain within the global financial system.

We could expand on his point about 'financial exclusion' by thinking about places (often the same ones) that are excluded from global information systems too, because of a lack of access to relevant media of communication. Jim McGuigan (1996: 184) writes of 'a yawning gulf between the information-haves and the information-have-nots', observing that, whilst a rapidly rising number of people in 'rich countries' are now participating in computer-mediated communication, 'the poor in such countries and, to a much greater extent, in the most deprived parts of the world are, nevertheless, excluded from … cyberspace'. Referring to the work of Ray Thomas (1995) on information access and inequality, he notes that most of the planet's population does not yet have private use of an 'old' technology like the telephone, let alone new digital media such as personal computers.

Doreen Massey (1992), meanwhile, has more sobering thoughts on the unevenness of globalisation and its time–space transformations. She is a geographer who is particularly suspicious of the language used by theorists of postmodernity, accusing them of employing what she calls a special type of 'hype'. 'Much of life for many people, even in the heart of the first world, still consists of waiting in a bus-shelter with your shopping for a bus that never comes', asserts Massey (1992: 8), which is 'hardly a graphic illustration of time–space compression.' Elsewhere, she invites us to reflect on 'the power geometry of time–space compression' (Massey 1994: 149–50), highlighting social divisions between those groups 'in charge' of contemporary time–space transformations, 'the jet-setters, the ones sending and receiving the faxes and the e-mail, holding the international conference calls, the ones distributing the films, controlling the news, organizing the investments and the international currency transactions', and those, in contrast, 'on the receiving end of time–space compression': 'The pensioner in a bed-sit ... eating British working-class-style fish and chips from a Chinese take-away, watching a US film on a Japanese television; and not daring to go out after dark.' The British inner-city pensioner in her example is not wholly deprived of access to communication technologies, and certainly not untouched by globalising tendencies, but that elderly person is clearly a less powerful agent in processes of social change than a member of one of the elite groups listed above.

Massey's important discussion of difference is taken up by John Tomlinson (1999: 131), who claims that globalisation is: 'uneven, not just in that it involves "winners and losers" or that it reproduces many familiar configurations of domi-nation and subordination, but also in the sense that the cultural experience it distributes is highly complex and varied'. Although there is increasing economic homogenisation, given the forces of 'global financial capital' (Leyshon 1995: 36), this does not necessarily signal a shift towards cultural homogenisation. It is true that there is evidence of greater uniformity in the sphere of culture (for instance, if we look at the remarkably standardised design of airport buildings around the world) and yet, as Tomlinson (1999: 6) reminds us:

> To decide whether the homogenization thesis really obtains you have to venture outside the security of the terminal and get progressively deeper into the dangerous cultural hinterland. ... The assertion of global homogenization of culture is a little like arriving by plane but never leaving the terminal, spending all one's time browsing amongst the global brands of the duty-free shops.

Outside airport lounges, which anthropologist Marc Augé (1995) curiously brands 'non-places', or sites such as international hotels and retail outlets, cultures continue to be largely 'heterogeneous'. That heterogeneity is not to be understood simply as a 'global mosaic' of neatly bounded regional and national entities, but is produced in part by 'transnational connections', which foster new cultural 'mixes' or 'confluences' in numerous local places (see Hannerz 1996; 2001).

Network

So far, we have considered metaphors of stretching (Giddens) and shrinking (Harvey and others). In the current section and the one following it, I will be exploring related ideas about network and flow that have been discussed by Castells (1996) and Urry (2000). A number of the social theorists whose writings I have already cited in this chapter refer to 'networks' or 'flows' in passing, but for Castells and Urry each is a pivotal term in thinking about globalisation. As Urry (2000: 33) puts it, 'the global presupposes the metaphors of network and flow'.

Let us start here with an extract from Castells' concluding definition of his concept of network:

> A network is a set of interconnected nodes. ... What a node is, concretely speaking, depends on the kind of concrete networks of which we speak. They are stock exchange markets, and their ancillary advanced services centers, in the network of global financial flows. ... They are television systems, entertainment studios, computer graphics milieux, news teams, and mobile devices generating, transmitting and receiving signals, in the global network of the new media ... in the information age. ... Networks are appropriate instruments for a capitalist economy based on innovation, globalization and decentralized concentration ... and for a social organization aiming at the supersession of space.
>
> (Castells 1996: 470–1)

Many of the strands running through that definition will be familiar by this stage. Like Giddens, Castells sees money and media of communication as two of the significant mechanisms in processes of globalisation. Meanwhile, like Harvey, he is particularly interested in capitalist economic transformations and in the overcoming of spatial barriers that is made possible by, amongst other things, the movement of information at the speed of light. The distinctive feature of his analysis is the framing of these shifts within a model of what he names the network society: 'Networks constitute the new social morphology ... processes in the information age are increasingly organized around networks' (Castells 1996: 469). There are those writers, like Tom Standage (1998) in the UK and Armand Mattelart (2000) in France, who contend that the principle of 'networking' has a long history, yet Castells (1996: 469) insists that contemporary conditions provide a unique basis 'for its pervasive expansion throughout the whole social structure'.

According to Castells, capitalism is now going through a period of 'profound restructuring'. For instance, there is the emergence of the 'network enterprise', involving a new organisational 'logic' for businesses in the global economy. As Urry (2000: 37–8) notes, ' "global" enterprises, such as American Express, McDonalds, Coca-Cola, Disney, Sony, BA and so on, are organised on the basis of a global network', as are 'some oppositional organisations such as Greenpeace'. We have also heard much from politicians in recent times about the threat, to the safety of those in the West, posed by global 'terrorist networks'. In turn, this general organisational logic is converging and inter-acting with a new 'technological paradigm' (Castells 1996: 152), which is associated with the 'information technology revolution'. Indeed, the internet is perhaps the most obvious symbol of Castells' network society (see Castells 2001; 2002), incorporating the 'World Wide Web', 'a flexible network of networks within the Internet where institutions, businesses, associations and individuals create their own "sites" ' (Castells 1996: 355). The technological design of the internet is precisely a 'set of interconnected nodes', where the 'distance' between these nodes (in operational terms) is effectively 'zero'.

Flow

Castells (1996) contends that, in the network society, the transformation of spatial arrangements entails the expansion of what he labels 'the space of flows'. This is distinguished in his work from 'the space of places', which he sees as characterised by social relations of 'physical contiguity'. His case is not that place is disappearing, since the two types of space coincide, but rather that its significance is altered by flows: 'flows of capital, flows of information, flows of technology, flows of organizational interaction, flows of images, sounds and symbols' (Castells 1996: 412). Places or locales are increasingly caught up in (or else excluded from) global networks and flows, in which there is often a virtual 'temporal immediacy'. What he terms the dominant structural logic of the space of flows therefore 'alters the meaning and dynamic of places' (Castells 1996: 428).

Pursuing much the same line of argument, Urry (2000: 38) proposes the development of 'a sociology of fluids' that would involve studying 'heteroge-neous, uneven and unpredictable mobilities' (for an earlier version of this argument about the need to understand fluidity and mobility in modern life, see Lash and Urry 1994; and for the comparable notion of 'liquid modernity', see Bauman 2000). He wants to go further than Castells, though, because a proposed emphasis on 'global fluids' and on the 'social as mobility' leads him to interrogate the whole idea of the 'social as society' (including, presumably, even the idea of a 'network society'), questioning what has been the central concept of his own academic discipline to date. For Urry (2000: 5–6), the concept of society in sociological discourse is too closely tied up with 'notions of nation-state, citizenship and national society' to be usefully redeployed in the study of flows that now criss-cross the 'porous borders' of nations. New social circum-stances, he asserts, require the setting of new rules of 'sociological method' (see Durkheim 1964; Giddens 1993), in order to get beyond the 'methodological nationalism' that has characterised sociology (Beck and Willms 2004). Whether or not we agree with him on this specific matter of terminology (quite frankly, I do wonder why he rules out any possibility of rearticulating the sign of society to suit contemporary circumstances), his general call for social theory to focus in future on various sorts of 'movement' merits further consideration.

To the kinds of flow listed by Castells above, Urry adds others. He talks, for instance, about flows of 'waste products' that bring with them 'new risks', 'the mobilities of objects' such as consumer goods and, crucially, flows consisting of people on the move. Discussing modern forms of 'corporeal travel' (see also Clifford 1992; 1997 on travelling cultures), Urry (2000: 50) observes that:

> The scale of such travelling is awesome. There are over 600 million international passenger arrivals each year. ... International travel now accounts for over one-twelfth of world trade. It constitutes by far the largest movement of people across boundaries that has occurred in the history of the world.

While these figures are indeed 'awesome', clearly supporting his case for the investigation of mobilities, an important qualification should be noted. A good deal of this international travel is for the purposes of commerce or tourism, consisting of temporary visits to other places made principally by people from Western countries (that is, by those with the economic resources to enable them to travel for business or pleasure). When these people are not 'on the move', many of them continue to live a relatively 'local life' in and around their places of work and residence. For this reason, Tomlinson (1999: 9) remains cautious of theoretical accounts that give too much weight to physical mobility (most notably, Lash and Urry 1994), suggesting that 'the paradigmatic experience of global modernity for most people ... is that of staying in one place', where they experience what globalisation 'brings to them'. Similarly, for David Morley (2000: 14), who quotes other statistics indicating that over half of the adults in Britain 'live within five miles of where they were born', it is 'in the transformation of localities, rather than in the increase of physical mobility (significant though that may be for some groups) that ... globalisation perhaps has its most important expression' (I will be returning later in the chapter to this particular issue of the 'transformation of localities').

Returning to Urry's figures for now, though, we could add that the transnational flow of people also includes more permanent migrations across the globe. A further qualification is necessary here, of course, because today there are sometimes 'strict barriers and firm counter-forces' (Papastergiadis 2000: 8) serving to resist or restrict human movement, such as the border controls set up by Western nation-states in an attempt to regulate the influx of refugee 'asylum seekers' and 'economic migrants'. In this regard, national boundaries are not so porous. If there is a 'green light for the tourists', then there is often a 'red light' for those Zygmunt Bauman (1998: 92–3) calls 'the vagabonds', who may well be 'on the move because they have been pushed from behind', and for whom staying at home just 'does not seem a feasible proposition'. Nevertheless, one of the notable consequences of global migration over recent decades, when seen in relation to 'flows of information, ... technology, ... images, sounds and symbols' (Castells 1996: 412), has been the emergence of what the anthropologist Arjun Appadurai (1996) terms 'diasporic public spheres'. These public spheres are, from his perspective, 'the crucibles of a postnational political order' (Appadurai 1996: 22).

Appadurai's reflections on global 'ethnoscapes', 'the landscape of persons who constitute the shifting world ... tourists, immigrants, refugees, exiles, guest workers, and other moving groups and individuals' (Appadurai 1996: 33), have particular relevance for those concerned to comprehend the role of media in globalising processes. This is because one of his main interests is in the connections between migration and 'mediascapes':

> As Turkish guest workers in Germany watch Turkish films in their German flats, as Koreans in Philadelphia watch the 1988 Olympics in Seoul through satellite feeds from Korea, and as Pakistani cabdrivers in Chicago listen to cassettes of sermons recorded in mosques in Pakistan or Iran, we see moving images meet deterritorialized viewers. ... Neither images nor viewers fit into circuits ... that are easily bound within local, national or regional spaces.
>
> (Appadurai 1996: 4)

He goes on to suggest that the circulation of mediated symbolic forms might provide resources to bind together 'ethnic groups' scattered well beyond the frontiers of a single 'national territory' (see also Morley 2000).

Daniel Dayan (1998; 1999) expands on this topic of 'diasporic communications'. He looks at how the use of media (not just 'conventional media' such as radio and television, but also 'small media' like audio and video cassettes) can help to maintain links across 'geographically dispersed groups' (Dayan 1999: 22). For example, referring us to selected findings from ethnographic field research carried out in London by Marie Gillespie (1995), he discusses the circulation of 'home videos' and 'video letters' exchanged by members of Punjabi families living in various parts of the world. These videos are produced in order to sustain contact with 'extended' kin, in two different senses of the word, who are in distant segments of a global diaspora.

Indeed, both Dayan and Appadurai point out that diasporic communications could force ethnographers, whose investigations have traditionally focused on the activities of social groups in specific locales, to rethink the boundaries of 'the field' when they do 'fieldwork' (see also Olwig and Hastrup 1997). 'As groups migrate, regroup in new locations ... and reconfigure their ethnic projects', notes Appadurai (1996: 48), 'the "ethno" in ethnography takes on a slippery ... quality.' Still, as I hinted at the close of this chapter's section on unevenness, there will be many distinctive local (as well as trans-local) dimensions to a reconfiguration of 'ethnic projects'. For instance, following the arrival of ' "the Rest" in "the West" ' (Hall 1992b), migrant populations have come into contact with other social groups and cultural flows in their multiple 'new locations'. So the young 'Punjabi Londoners' in Gillespie's study encounter, amongst other things, Coca-Cola advertisements and Australian soap opera on

'British television', interpreting or 'translating' these forms of media output to fit the special circumstances of place.

Empires

While Gillespie's writing, to which we will return later in the book, is mainly concerned with 'local uses' of media in 'global context' (see also Gillespie 1997), it is important for us to recognise that the study of media and globalisation throws up other, political-economic issues of ownership and control that deserve our attention. For those authors who address such issues, the term 'empires' is employed on occasion to signal the dominance of powerful organisations and business leaders in global media markets. In my earlier account of first-generation medium theory, I indicated that Innis (1950; 1951) has a general historical interest in the relationship between systems of communication and the growth of empire, but for Herbert Schiller (1992) the notion of 'American empire' serves to conceptualise what he sees as the specific influence of American communication industries on the modern world stage. His book sets out to detail the features of a 'global American electronic invasion', carried out during the second half of the twentieth century, in which large parts of the earth have been put 'under electronic siege' through the export of television programmes and films produced in the USA, and through the commercial interests of American-based companies in media production outside the USA (for further arguments about American domination of global media and 'information flows' during this period, see Tunstall 1977; Varis 1984; Schiller 1985).

Similarly, Daya Thussu (1998) describes the current growth of 'electronic empires' that are 'ruled over' by figures like Bill Gates (Microsoft Corporation) and Rupert Murdoch (News Corporation), both of whom are American citizens, although Murdoch is Australian by birth. According to Thussu (1998: 1), these heads of transnational media corporations are the 'Robert Clive and Cecil Rhodes of the twenty-first century ... constructing their electronic empires by colonising the imagination of the ... consumers of media products':

> Unlike the empires of the nineteenth century ... these new empires are not ultimately based on coercion or military might. Their aim is not to subject alien populations to imperial dictates but to persuade consumers, through ... global electronic networks, to use their media or buy the products advertised.

In the case of Murdoch's empire, his News Corporation has holdings that include a host of daily newspapers, such as *The Times* in the UK and the *New York Post* in the USA, as well as commercial television services spread right across the globe. 'The defining feature of Murdoch's global push', explains Robert McChesney (1998: 37), 'is the establishment of satellite television systems, along with the channels and programming to be displayed on them.'

Among these are numerous Sky TV channels distributed across Britain and Western Europe, the Star Television service broadcast throughout Asia, and the Latin American TV channels, *El Canal Fox* and *Fox Sport Noticias*.

McChesney's analysis of the Murdoch empire, and of other major transnational corporations such as Time Warner and Disney, certainly reveals a quite staggering concentration of media ownership and commercial power in the hands of a few (for a fuller account, see Herman and McChesney 1997). However, when Thussu (1998) refers to a 'colonising' of the imagination of consumers, there is a problematic slippage in the argument, characteristic of the broader 'political-economy perspective', in which he is in danger of conflating the control of media production and distribution systems with the ideological manipulation of media audiences or users. The difficulty, in my view, is that the latter cannot be 'read off' automatically from the former. Of course, we should be concerned with issues of ownership and control in media markets, since they tell us more about the unevenness of global economics, but it would be premature (and politically pessimistic) to assume that consumers in different cultural contexts will all be duped in the same way by the forces of 'Americanisation' or Westernisation. In advancing this position, I am indebted to a critical analysis of 'the discourse of media imperialism' offered by Tomlinson (1991). There, he presents a searching critique of the work of Schiller (1979; 1985), who is found guilty of asserting media effects without actually demonstrating that influence with reference to the domain of lived culture.

Another difficulty with arguments about American empire or Western media imperialism is that they fail to recognise the full complexity of media and information flows, which, in the words of sociologist Hugh Mackay (2000: 72), 'are not simply one-way'. Thussu (2000: 200) himself acknowledges that there are some instances of 'contraflow in global media': 'the Brazilian television giant *TV Globo* ... exports its *telenovelas* to more than 100 countries, while the Indian film industry is an example of a non-Western production centre making its presence felt in a global cultural context'. *Telenovelas* (Latin American soap operas) are broadcast in the USA and several European countries (see Giddens 1999: 16–17, who cites this as an example of 'what one could call "reverse colonisation" '), while 'Bollywood' cinema is widely consumed by South Asians living around the world. In addition, despite being a net importer of film and television, Australia has become a significant exporter of television fiction, which is perhaps best illustrated by the ratings successes of *Neighbours* and *Home and Away* in the UK:

> *Neighbours* began on BBC1 in ... 1986. ... By 1988, it had become the most popular children's and young adults' programme on British television and it has remained in the ten most-watched programmes in Britain for several years. In an effort to counter it, the ITV network ... scheduled *Home and Away* ... to immediately follow *Neighbours* in the early evening each night of the week. By ... 1989 no less than fifteen

hours a week of Australian soap opera was ... on British television, an amount far greater than the five hours of US drama.

(Cunningham and Jacka 1996: 207–8)

On a final note here, before moving on, we might also cite the considerable commercial successes of Japanese communication industries in exporting both hardware and software to the West. For instance, Sony makes most of its money from overseas sales, with America being its largest national market.

Permeability

In what remains of the chapter, I want us to concentrate on the character of places, both physical and 'virtual', in the modern world. At several points above in this discussion of extensionality, we have touched briefly on ideas about place and the ways in which it is changing (on what, following Morley 2000, could be termed the transformation of localities). For example, Giddens (1990: 19) asserts that in conditions of modernity, 'place becomes increasingly phantas-magoric' as it is 'thoroughly penetrated' by distant happenings and forces. Similarly, Castells tells us how, in the network society, the significance of places is being transformed by flows, although there is an apparent contradiction in his conceptualisation of places (see Moores 2003b), which at one point he defines, rather puzzlingly, as locales 'whose form, function and meaning are self-contained within the boundaries of physical contiguity' (Castells 1996: 423).

A further attempt to theorise these changes is to be found in Massey's account of the relative 'openness of places' in 'global times' (Massey 1995). She argues that, with 'worldwide connections' now impinging on the daily lives of millions, the boundaries of place are becoming 'far more open than they have been in the past' (Massey 1995: 58). However, in keeping with her perspective on the 'power-geometry' of contemporary time–space transformations, she is careful to qualify this remark about the permeability of boundaries, providing evidence of the complex variety of people's experiences of locality and 'inter-connectedness'.

The evidence provided by Massey (1995: 59–60) arises out of research designed to map the 'activity spaces' (the spatial locations and connections) of different social groups living in a number of small country villages in Cambridgeshire, England:

There are high-tech scientists, mainly men, whose work is based in Cambridge, though they often have computers with modem links at home as well. The companies they work for operate in a highly interna-tionalized part of the economy, and these employees spend their time in constant contact with, and physically travelling between, colleagues and customers all around the world. ... At the other extreme are people who have never been to London and only rarely ... as far as

Cambridge. When they have done so, it is usually in order to go to the shops or maybe to the hospital. ... They work locally – some on the farms, some in the village shops and services. On the whole they are older and have known one another for years. ... There are other groups, too ... people who work more or less locally ... as cleaners or caterers, but for firms which are multinational; for such firms this is just one group of workers among many scattered over the globe. There are women who are partners of the high-tech men, some of them presently at home with small children, occupied in a daily round of nurseries and child-minders. ... For shopping they are more likely to drive into Cambridge than are some of 'the locals'; for holidays they may fly off to somewhere exotic.

This study (for a comparable discussion of some other geographical settings, see Massey 1998) clearly shows, as Urry (2000: 140) puts it, how 'places can be ... understood ... as multiplex', and how the cultural boundaries of place are far more open or permeable for some (in these villages, the middle-class 'incomers' and 'out-goers') than they are for others. In addition, within that middle-class group, there are gender differences in the shaping of activity spaces. Still, even those more 'rooted', less 'routed' (Clifford 1997), working-class people referred to by the incomers as 'the locals' are linked in significant ways with wider processes. Farm workers, then, will be subject to agricultural policy decisions made in London or Brussels, and the cleaners and caterers who work for multinational firms in the area would certainly feel the force of global economics if these companies were to cut jobs.

These places featured in her description are unique, at least in the sense that they are not quite the same as any other locations in the world. Still, their 'uniqueness' is not simply the outcome of 'some long internal' history (they are far from being 'self-contained'), rather:

> The uniqueness of a place ... is constructed out of particular ... articulations of social relations, ... experiences and understandings, in a situation of co-presence, but where a large proportion of those relations, experiences and understandings are actually constructed on a far larger scale than ... the place itself.
>
> (Massey 1993: 66)

In other words, a major part of what makes a place distinctive has to do with activity spaces extending outside of it, the particular 'mix of links and interconnections' to a 'beyond': 'the global as part of what constitutes the local, the outside as part of the inside' (Massey 1994: 5). This is true for a big city as much as it is for a village in a rural area, and, for Massey (1995: 61), the openness of places is 'not a new phenomenon, just as globalization itself is not'. She shares with Hall (1991) a wish to guard against historical amnesia, pointing to the case of a port city like Liverpool, which has formed its own distinctive character out of links with other places through trade and migration over the past three centuries. What is new about globalisation in its current phase, though, is that 'the speed of it all ... and its intensity ... have increased dramatically in recent years' (Massey 1995: 46).

One of the reasons why global processes have speeded up and intensified, as we have already seen, is that the mobility of the human body through corporeal travel has been supplemented by instantaneous flows of information, images and sounds via modern telecommunications. Such electronic flows inevitably have consequences for the boundaries of a place like the domestic home, just as they do for the boundaries of villages, cities or nation-states. On the one hand, it is possible to conceptualise this change in terms of the 'imaginative' and virtual travel (see Urry 2000; 2002) done by household media users, who can sometimes feel they are 'transported elsewhere' by, say, radio and television (Larsen 1999 provides empirical evidence that suggests television viewers do sometimes feel this sense of transportation). So even when listeners and viewers are 'staying home' physically, located in a fixed 'dwelling', they might be thought of as 'going places' imaginatively (Morley 2000: 149). The reach of audience members is thereby extended, as Roger Silverstone (1994: 25) puts it, 'beyond the physical spaces of the house, or the social relations of the family, into a world of ... movement'. It is also possible, on the other hand, to conceptualise the role of media technologies as fetching 'the outside world' indoors (as part of a movement in which, to paraphrase Tomlinson 1999, 'global modernity' brings things from a distance). 'The media pitches that public world', writes Urry (2000: 68), 'into one's private world.' In doing so, a medium like television may bring news of strange and potentially disturbing happenings, but more generally it 'offers to present the world beyond the familiar and the familial ... in a familiar and familial guise' (Ellis 1982: 163), constructing a 'domesticated' view of national and international affairs.

An innovative thinker on matters of media, place and permeability is the second-generation medium theorist, Meyrowitz (1985). Making a seemingly improbable link between Erving Goffman's sociology, which is mainly concerned with situations of 'face-to-face' interaction where 'individuals are physically in one another's response presence' (Goffman 1983: 2), and the first-generation medium theory of McLuhan discussed earlier in this chapter, his proposal is that electronic media are 'changing the "situational geography" of social life' by undermining 'the traditional relationship between physical setting and social situation' (Meyrowitz 1985: 6–7). He develops a model of 'situations as information-systems' (see also Meyrowitz 1994), in which the emphasis is on how 'patterns of information flow' serve to 'define the situation'. This model does not invalidate the work done by Goffman on co-present encounters in physical settings, rather it 'extends the study of situations' to include a range of encounters in and with 'media "settings" ' (Meyrowitz 1985: 37–8). The best way of illustrating the argument is by referring to a particular instance of communication discussed by Meyrowitz (1985: 38) in the extract below:

> When two friends speak on the telephone … the situation they are 'in'
> is only marginally related to their respective physical locations. Indeed,
> the telephone tends to bring two people closer to each other, in some
> respects, than they are to other people in their physical environments.
> This explains the almost jealous response on the part of some people
> who are in the same room with someone speaking on the phone. They
> often ask 'Who is it?' 'What's she saying?' 'What's so funny?'

In his example, the telephone is a medium that enables its users to 'override' the
boundaries of 'their respective physical locations', engaging in a 'mediated
encounter' in which there is 'closeness' at a distance, although he acknowledges
that there may be interruptions from those who are physically co-present in the
rooms at either end of the line (for that reason, I think there is actually a 'plural-
ising' of setting here, as opposed to the removal of the two friends from one type
of situation, which then becomes 'marginal', and their relocation in another).

It has been suggested that the telephone has the capacity to function as an
especially 'intimate' medium, given the voice of the other participant in an
exchange is electronically proximate, 'next to the ear' (Gumpert 1990: 148). As
Ian Hutchby (2001: 31) puts it, 'intimacy … is afforded by the telephone'. Of
course, it should also be remembered that there are occasions when the caller's
immediate physical context is highly significant in shaping telephone interactions. For instance, this applies when the telephone user is a worker in a 'call
centre' (Cameron 2000), often operating with a script or 'prompt sheet' and
required to deal with a certain number of calls per hour.

Meyrowitz (1994: 67–8) points out that, although there are still separate
physical settings, many of which have walls around them (see Giddens 1981;
1984 on the commodification of space), these solid boundaries cannot stop
electronic signals from passing through:

> The telephone, radio and television make the boundaries of all social
> spheres more permeable. One can now 'witness' events without being
> physically present; one can communicate 'directly' with others without
> meeting. … The walls of the family home, for example, no longer
> wholly isolate the home from the outside community. Family members
> at home now have access to others and others have access to them. …
> Children may still be sheltered at home, but television now takes them
> across the globe before parents give them permission to cross the
> street. … And while few of us actually travel to see our leaders in the
> flesh, television now shows us our politicians close up – stammering
> and stumbling in living colour. Television blurs the line between public
> and private by bringing the public sphere into the home.

When he writes about a blurring of 'the public' and 'the private', I am put in
mind of Paddy Scannell's theory of radio, television and modern life, some

elements of which were considered in the previous chapter. Scannell (1996: 167) borrows from Martin Heidegger's philosophy the notion that broad-casting contributes to 'a de-severance of the "world" ', or 'the conquest of remoteness' (Heidegger 1962: 140), and this is evidently related to the obser-vations on permeability and 'access to others' in the passage reproduced above.

Despite clear overlaps between the theories of Meyrowitz and Scannell, though, there is also an important difference, for whereas the phrase in the title of Meyrowitz's book is 'no sense of place', Scannell (1996: 172) writes instead of 'the doubling of place' by broadcasting (for a critique of Meyrowitz, and an attempt to apply Scannell's ideas about the doubling of place in an analysis of electronically mediated communications via telephone and the internet, see Moores 2003c; 2004). Meyrowitz (1985: 308) explains that his title is intended as a 'serious pun' in which place is supposed to signify 'both social position and physical location'. Running those two meanings together, he argues that social roles and hierarchies, through which people have traditionally come to 'know their place', are being transformed as electronically mediated communication transcends the limits of physical settings. To take a dramatic (if problematic) example, he states that: 'A telephone or computer in a ghetto tenement or in a suburban teenager's bedroom is potentially as effective as a telephone or computer in a corporate suite' (Meyrowitz 1985: 169–70). His statement is questioned by Leyshon (1995: 33), who asks if the technology is 'really as effec-tive in the way that Meyrowitz suggests', because while 'the inner-city resident, the suburban teenager and the corporate executive may all be able to telephone a bank ... they would not all necessarily enjoy the privilege of being granted an audience with the bank manager'.

Whether or not we accept Meyrowitz's view on the transformation of place as 'social position' (my feeling, like Leyshon's, is that he has a tendency to be too optimistic about the prospects for challenging established social hierarchies), there is still a problem with his suggestion that place as 'physical location' is of little or no consequence today. He asserts that contemporary culture is 'relatively placeless' in comparison with the conditions of existence in previous times, and that it is therefore necessary to move 'beyond place' in theorising communica-tions. However, the permeability or openness of geographical places does not automatically lead to the loss of a sense of place. Indeed, Meyrowitz seems to concede this point, ultimately, by rejecting a perception that our existence is now completely placeless. So after remarking on how 'the social meaning of a "prison" ... has been changed as a result of electronic media of communication', because the prisoner's 'physical incarceration' no longer necessarily involves 'informational isolation' (Meyrowitz 1985: 117), he rightly acknowledges that 'regardless of media access, living in ... a prison cell and a middle class suburb are certainly not "equivalent" ' (Meyrowitz 1985: 312).

I want to propose that Scannell's conception of place (as instantaneously pluralised, not marginalised, in practices of electronic media use) is preferable to Meyrowitz's (and see Couldry 2000a: 30, who wonders why Meyrowitz does not conclude 'that media coverage massively multiplies the interconnections between places, rather than weakening our sense of place'). Scannell (1996: 76) develops his argument that radio and television ' "double" reality' in the analysis he offers of the distinctive character of public events, and of the changing experiences of 'being-in-public', in late modernity: 'Public events now occur, simultaneously, in two different places: the place of the event itself and that in which it is watched and heard. Broadcasting mediates between these two sites.' Advancing a 'phenomenological approach' to the study of radio and television, which is concerned in part with the 'ways of being in the world' (Scannell 1996: 173) that have been created for listeners and viewers, he goes on to argue that, for audience members in their dispersed, usually private settings, there are transformed 'possibilities of being: of being in two places at once' (Scannell 1996: 91). Of course, it is only ever possible for any individual to be in one place at a time physically, but broadcasting nevertheless permits a live 'witnessing' of remote happenings that can bring these happenings experientially close or 'within range', thereby removing the 'farness'. In such circumstances, listeners and viewers may come to feel they are simultaneously 'here-and-there'.

Further twists in this tale of a blurring of public and private contexts come with the arrival of a new generation of portable media, notably the 'personal stereo' and the 'mobile phone'. Writing fairly soon after their introduction on to the market, Meyrowitz (1985: 125) perceives how 'personal sound systems such as the Sony "Walkman" make public spaces private'. In their cultural analysis of the 'Walkman', Paul du Gay et al. (1997: 114) confirm Meyrowitz's initial observation, stating that the technology 'is primarily designed and marketed for mobile private listening in public ... taking private listening into the public domain'. It enables its consumers to go for an 'aural walk' with a 'portable soundtrack' (Chambers 1994). 'Tuning in' to the personal stereo helps them to 'tune out' the sounds of the city (Bull 2000; 2004). The technology lends itself to the creation of an 'impermeable' aural boundary around the listener (from the perspective of the personal stereo user), as expressed in the following interview response given to a media researcher, Michael Bull: 'Because I haven't got the external sort of noises around me I feel I'm in a bit of a world of my own ... I can't really hear ... what is going on around me' (in Bull 2000: 32).

From the perspective of people sitting near to the personal stereo user on a bus or train, things might look, or, more accurately, sound, rather different. This is because music intended for private consumption frequently 'leaks out' into public. Drawing on the work of social anthropologist Mary Douglas (1966), du Gay et al. (1997: 116–17) interpret such noise as 'matter out of place':

> The Walkman created something of a 'moral panic' when it appeared, precisely because of its transgression of established symbolic boundaries. ... In a recent case on the British railway system, a youth who had insisted on playing his Walkman at top volume had so enraged his

fellow passengers that he was forcibly evicted from the train on which he was travelling (luckily for him while it was standing at a station!) and was later taken to court and fined for breach of the peace.

A person who talks on a mobile phone while travelling on public transport may also be annoying, or at least mildly irritating, to fellow passengers, yet the practice is widespread in the UK and USA, where the technology is known as a 'cell phone'. Mobile phones are becoming common 'devices for private talk in the company of strangers' (Sussex Technology Group 2001: 205).

As sociologist Emanuel Schegloff (2002: 286–7) remarks, unwittingly echoing Scannell, when people use a mobile phone (or a personal stereo) they are 'in two places at the same time ... there are two "theres" there'. Mobile phone users are simultaneously in a physical location, typically a public one, and 'on the telephone', engaged in a private conversation. Although we are not accustomed to thinking of speaking on the telephone as an instance of what the philosopher Edward Casey (1993) calls 'being-in-place', the participants in telephone conversations share 'occasions of talk-in-interaction' (Schegloff 2002: 287) in which there is a 'real time' simulation of being 'in one another's response presence'.

Virtuality

With the rapid developments in computer-mediated communication that have occurred since Meyrowitz (1985) wrote his book on electronic media, I believe our understanding of the 'situational geography' of social life now needs to be widened to include the numerous virtual 'places in the cyberspace of the Net' (Mitchell 1995: 21). The story of two friends speaking on the telephone, in Meyrowitz's discussion of situations as information-systems, is already, in a sense, about the construction of a 'virtual co-presence' in a 'media setting'. We have also noted how broadcasting can offer us virtually immediate, 'live access' to a distant event, in such a way that 'the experience of simultaneity' is 'detached from the spatial condition of common locality' (Thompson 1995: 32). In various forms of computer-mediated communication, though, the software enables participants (who are actually positioned in front of pieces of hardware that could be thousands of miles apart) to inhabit a simulated common locality. William Mitchell (1995: 21–2) points to a few of the 'virtual realms that you can potentially enter' on the internet:

> Like architectural and urban places, these have characteristic appearances. ... A software 'there' can be a ... virtual room ... or landscape. ... Some virtual places ... are designed to serve as shared access, multiuser locations for joint activities. ... Sharing a virtual place is not quite the same thing, of course, as sharing a physical place like a room, a bed or an umbrella in the rain. Bodies need not be in close proximity

and they need not be enclosed by the same architectural or natural boundaries. The crucial thing is simultaneous electronic access to the same information. At their simplest, shared places are created by displaying the same scrolling text on multiple personal computer screens. ... Shared 'rooms' on the Net often announce themselves by descriptive or allusive names (like the signs on bars and other hang-outs) – *The Flirt's Nook, Gay and Lesbian, ... Teen Chat, Thirtysomething, Born-Again Onliners, Pet Chat* and so on. You can cruise them by scanning menus, and look in when they catch your interest, as you might bar hop down a street.

What is interesting here, from my perspective, is the regular use of the term 'rooms' to describe such virtual places. Similarly, people speak of 'visiting sites' on the World Wide Web. As the frontiers of 'cyberspace' are pushed back, some of the language associated with local physical settings and with corporeal travel is being employed there in an effort to contextualise, or to 're-embed', disembedded social relations (see also Kendall 2002, who reminds us that even when the internet user 'hangs out' in a virtual environment, then usually she or he simultaneously inhabits an 'offline' room, and so, in Scannell's terms, reality gets 'doubled').

Sherry Turkle (1996a; 1996b), a sociological and psychoanalytical theorist, reflects on questions of identity raised by presentations of self in a virtual place known as a 'multiuser domain' or MUD, in which the participants she observes are engaged in role-playing games. I will be dealing with her answers at length in the subsequent part of this book. For the moment, let us see what she writes about the basic features of this sort of 'text-based virtual reality' (or 'real virtuality', see Castells 1996): 'in many MUDs, players are invited to help build the virtual world itself ... they can make "rooms" in the game space where they are able to set the stage and define the rules' (Turkle 1996a: 156). Her work focuses on the creative possibilities of 'playing in the MUD', but its strength lies in the fact that she investigates the connections between the online fantasies of participants and their ordinary lives away from the computer screen.

While the kind of approach taken by Turkle is considered valuable by two other internet researchers, Daniel Miller and Don Slater (2000), they start out from a quite different position, and are more suspicious of ideas about cyberspace and 'virtuality' found in much of the existing literature on computer-mediated communication (for a review of this body of literature, see Kitchin 1998). The problem with these notions, according to Miller and Slater (2000: 4), is an accompanying emphasis on the constitution of 'spaces or places apart from the rest of social life' (a similar critique of the idea that cyberspace can be treated as a separate and alternative reality can be found in Robins 1996). In their own study, they argue instead that the internet ought to be treated as a 'part of everyday life' and 'as continuous with ... other social spaces' (see also Graham 2000; Wellman and Haythornthwaite 2002):

Indeed, to the extent that some people may actually treat various Internet relations as 'a world apart' from the rest of their lives, this is something that needs to be socially explained as a practical accomplishment rather than ... the assumed point of departure for investigation. How, why and when do they set 'cyberspace' apart? Where and when do they not do this? In what ways do they make use of 'virtuality' as a feature of new media?

(Miller and Slater 2000: 5)

They choose to begin by asking how the internet gets appropriated by people in a unique physical location, the Caribbean island of Trinidad, and by those in the global Trinidadian diaspora. Their research identifies a series of cultural 'alignments' or 'elective affinities' between internet use and 'being Trini', and they claim that Trinidadians, particularly those who are 'living away', 'see the Internet as a place to perform Trini-ness' (Miller and Slater 2000: 7).

Chapter 2, then, has explored the extensional transformations (the reaching out) of social life in the modern world. Various concepts or metaphors for thinking about globalisation and media were considered, such as Giddens' ideas on disembedding and time–space distanciation, and the pronouncements of McLuhan and Harvey on an experiential collapsing-in of the globe. It was argued, following Urry, that with the growth of transnational and trans-local connections greater attention now needs to be paid to the relations between corporeal, imaginative and virtual mobilities. However, I stressed that this concern with movement should not be at the expense of understanding the significance of places or localities in contemporary social existence. The boundaries of the local tend to be more permeable today, as Meyrowitz and others observe, and yet in my view (*contra* Meyrowitz) place is best thought of as instantaneously pluralised rather than marginalised by electronically mediated communication. Finally, it is important to remember the unevenness and inequalities of these different aspects of global social change, which Massey usefully theorises as their power geometry.

Part II
RELATIONSHIPS, MEANINGS AND EXPERIENCES

3

INTERACTION

In my introduction to this book, I made reference to an argument that time–space relations must be seen as 'inherent' in the constitution of social interaction (Giddens 1979). Having looked at themes of time and space in some detail, I now want to focus our attention on the study of interaction and, in particular, on issues that are raised by what John Thompson (1995) terms 'the rise of mediated interaction' in modern life. It will not be possible, nor would it be desirable, for us to leave behind entirely a discussion of temporal and spatial arrangements, since time, space and social interaction are inextricably linked. However, there is a shift of emphasis here, as we turn to examine ways of 'relating to others' (Duck 1999) in circumstances of technologically mediated communication.

Typology

Thompson's identification of 'three forms or types of interaction' (Thompson 1995: 82), in his social theory of media and modernity, provides a helpful point of departure for my discussion. The typology that he sets up involves distinguishing between 'face-to-face interaction', 'mediated interaction' (a potentially confusing category in his writing, for reasons I will explain shortly) and 'mediated quasi-interaction'. For each of these types, a number of 'interactional characteristics' is specified. As might be expected, given what we already know about his work, the list of characteristics includes the 'space–time constitution' of interactions, but this typology also specifies the 'range of symbolic cues' available to participants, the 'action orientation' of their communication and whether the form of interaction that they are engaged in is 'dialogical' or 'monological' (Thompson 1995: 85).

To begin with, though, before proceeding to deal with the characteristics of the three different forms of interaction, it is necessary for us to note that the typology is elaborated as part of a more general concern that Thompson has with processes of social change, a significant aspect of which he calls 'the transformation of interaction' (Thompson 1994). Such an historical shift is closely bound up with the development of print and electronic media technologies (see also Giddens 1991: 24, who thinks of 'the printed text and, subsequently, the electronic signal' as modernity's 'own' distinctive media). While many of these technologies have been around for a long time, Thompson (1994: 34) names them 'new media of communication' in this extract, meaning 'new' at the point of their introduction:

> In order to assess the impact of new media of communication, it is important to emphasize that the deployment of communication media does not consist simply in the establishment of new networks for the transmission of 'information between individuals whose basic social relationships remain intact; on the contrary, the deployment of communication media establishes new forms of interaction and new kinds of social relationships between individuals.

Much of what follows in the present chapter is about trying to understand the contemporary complexities of an ongoing transformation of interaction in modern society, and it draws on a growing body of literature, to which Thompson is one of the major contributors, that is concerned precisely with media and changing social relationships. This literature provides a valuable addition to the existing strands of academic work in sociology (see especially Goffman 1959; 1963; 1967) and social psychology (for an overview, see Duck 1999) that have a tendency to focus largely on the face-to-face dimensions of human interaction (an exception is Goffman 1981 on radio talk).

'Prior to the early modern period in Europe', observes Thompson (1995: 86), 'the exchange of information and symbolic content ... for most people ... took place exclusively within the context of face-to-face situations.' Pre-modern cultures tended to be characterised by 'communities of high presence-availability', in which interaction involved being in 'close physical proximity' to others: 'The corporeality of the agent, the limitations upon the mobility of the body in the trajectories of the *durée* of daily activity, together with the physical properties of space, ensured that this was so' (Giddens 1984: 123). However, the rise of mediated interaction was facilitated by the emergence of modern technical means by which individuals have increasingly been able to make themselves 'available' to others who are physically absent. Today, there is the possibility of constructing a simulated or virtual co-presence, a 'mediated proximity' (Tomlinson 1999), of the sort that was outlined briefly at the end of the previous chapter. This does not mean, of course, that face-to-face interaction is disappearing in the late modern age (just as places have not disappeared as a consequence of the time–space transformations of modernity). There is what Deirdre Boden and Harvey Molotch (1994) name a continuing 'compulsion of proximity', understood as physical proximity, in social life (and see Urry 2002, who asks why it is that people still feel the need to engage in corporeal travel in order to meet face-to-face). Face-to-face and technologically mediated communications are now being combined in a novel 'interaction mix'.

Face-to-face interaction, then, is to be found in circumstances of physical immediacy, where 'the participants ... share a common spatial–temporal reference system' (Thompson 1995: 82). Sharing a common locality enables them, for instance, to use what are known in pragmatics (see Levinson 1983) as 'deictic expressions' (ethnomethodologists call them 'indexical' expressions). The significance of an utterance like 'here', 'there', 'this' or 'that' is often dependent on a visual reference in the physical setting. Having said that, it is worth bearing in mind how the phenomenon of deixis may sometimes be evident in the context of a printed text or else in, say, live television commentary on a public event where the commentator and viewers share access to the same media setting (Marriott 1995). In addition, participants in face-to-face interaction routinely employ and have mutual access to 'a multiplicity of symbolic cues' including speech, 'gestures' and 'changes in intonation', and for this reason it could be said that face-to-face communication is already mediated in a basic fashion by spoken and body language. Actions are 'oriented towards specific others' and there is the potential to engage in 'a two-way flow of information and communication' (Thompson 1995: 83). Certain situations of face-to-face interaction, such as the formal lecture or speech to a physically co-present audience, do serve to limit the possibilities for dialogue, but in informal, private conversations in day-to-day life, it is ordinarily expected that the communications will be 'two-way'.

For Thompson, mediated interaction appears to serve as a broad category, as in his general reference to the rise of mediated interaction, whilst also referring, more particularly, to modes of communication such as letter writing (a cultural and technological practice that has origins which pre-date the advent of modernity) and telephone conversations. Indeed, this is the potential source of confusion that I signalled above. In each of these two overlapping senses of the term, the interaction is marked by a 'separation of contexts', by which he means a physical separation between the participants, and a 'narrowing of the range' of symbolic cues. Depending on the medium being used, those symbolic cues will vary. For example, somebody who is composing a letter to an absent other does not have the option of using talk or facial expressions to convey information. 'Similarly, communication by means of telephone', writes Thompson (1995: 83), 'deprives the participants of the visual cues associated with face-to-face interaction while preserving and accentuating the oral cues.'

Like face-to-face interaction, mediated interaction in the second, restricted sense is oriented towards specific others and is potentially dialogical. A letter is addressed, and a telephone call made, to some person or organisation in particular. On receiving a letter, it is possible for us to write back in response. When talking on the telephone, the two interlocutors usually speak in turn. With regard to the dialogical features of interpersonal communication, conversation analysts make a helpful general point about the importance of 'turn-taking' practices for the sequential organisation of talk-in-interaction (for instance, Sacks *et al.* 1974; Schegloff 1986; Hopper 1992; Sacks 1995), often referring specifically to data that is generated from recordings of telephone conversations.

Finally in Thompson's typology, there is mediated quasi-interaction, a further subdivision of his broad category of mediated interaction. This is a term that he reserves for referring to 'the kinds of social relations established by the media of mass communication (books, newspapers, radio, television, etc.)' (Thompson 1995: 84). A crucial difference from letter writing and telephone conversations is that the actions of authors, journalists and those involved in the production of broadcast output get oriented towards an 'indefinite range of potential recipients'. The flow of communication is also 'predominantly one-way' or monological. Readers of books and newspapers, and the listeners and viewers consuming radio and television, are too numerous to be known on an individual basis, which is why they have to be imaginatively projected in advance by media producers. Media consumers are not required and not permitted, at least within the framework of the mediated quasi-interaction itself, to respond in a way that is directly audible or visible to the producers, although they may occasionally employ other means of communication to express their feelings and opinions. For example, they can write letters of appreciation or complaint and nowadays they are frequently encouraged to telephone (and email) their comments on various matters to media organisations.

Given Thompson's own description of 'mass communication' as monological, as predominantly one-way, it may appear somewhat strange that he sees it as involving any sort of social interaction at all. He attempts to explain this apparent contradiction in the extract reproduced below:

> Since mediated quasi-interaction is monological in character and involves the production of symbolic forms for an indefinite range of potential recipients, it is best regarded as a kind of quasi-interaction. It does not have the degree of reciprocity and interpersonal specificity of other forms of interaction, whether mediated or face-to-face. But mediated quasi-interaction is, none the less, a form of interaction. It creates a certain kind of social situation in which individuals are linked together in a process of communication and symbolic exchange. It is a structured situation in which some individuals are engaged primarily in producing symbolic forms for others who are not physically present, while others are involved primarily in receiving symbolic forms produced by others to whom they cannot respond, but with whom they can form bonds of friendship, affection or loyalty.
>
> (Thompson 1995: 84–5)

The last few words in this quotation are of particular interest because we are probably more used to thinking of 'bonds of friendship, affection or loyalty' as being formed in the context of face-to-face communication with known others (and perhaps then maintained through mediated interaction in the narrow sense of letter writing and telephone conversations), yet his argument clearly suggests that such bonds are also possible in, say, 'electronically immediate' relationships between a television presenter and distant audience members. This would be one example of the 'new kinds of social relationships between individuals' (Thompson 1994: 34) that are distinctive to modernity. Relationships of that kind are, he argues, 'non-reciprocal in character ... since mediated quasi-interaction is non-dialogical' (Thompson 1995: 219), although the physically absent audience members might come to feel, over time, that they have 'got to know' the person appearing on screen (Horton and Wohl 1986).

Mix

I will be returning to those points about 'non-reciprocal intimacy at a distance' (Thompson 1995: 219) in due course, but before doing so it is appropriate for us to consider a couple of other issues, which have to do with a qualification and a criticism regarding Thompson's application of the typology. First, an important qualification made by Thompson (1995: 85–6) himself, having identified the three types of interaction, is that there are often mixtures of those different forms in people's everyday routines:

> For example, individuals may have a discussion with others in the room while they are watching television, thus combining face-to-face interaction and mediated quasi-interaction ... a television programme may involve face-to-face interaction between members of a panel and members of a studio audience, although the relation between these individuals taken together and the diverse recipients of the TV programme remains a form of mediated quasi-interaction. It would be easy to adduce more complex variations (for example, some individuals phone in questions to members of a studio panel, whose responses are heard or seen by listeners or viewers, and so on).

These examples are crucial because they help to show how face-to-face, mediated and mediated quasi-interactions are not to be understood as completely separate. Thompson is insisting here that they may actually co-exist in plural or 'hybrid' forms. So, as was emphasised earlier, the historical rise of technologically mediated communication has not simply led to the decline of co-present interaction in physical settings, a state of affairs that is implied in a common-sense expression like 'television has killed the art of conversation'. Instead, it would be far better for us to say that, in conditions of modernity, 'the "interaction mix" of social life has changed' (Thompson 1995: 87).

A second issue arises out of a sympathetic critique of Thompson's work on social interaction. James Slevin (2000: 89) accuses him of not making any 'mention of the internet', despite the fact that 'internet use had already gained considerable momentum' by the mid-1990s when he published his book on media and modernity. To be fair to Thompson, although it is indeed the case that the internet is not named as such, he does include a footnote on the 'use of computer technology in combination with telecommunications systems' allowing for 'the possibility of two-way communication ... which is "many-to-many" in character' (Thompson 1995: 278). In this passing reference to a particular kind of computer-mediated communication, it is recognised that the participants may be creating situations of interaction that are quite difficult to map on to his existing typology. Nevertheless, in attempting to apply the typology in an analysis of the internet, Slevin (2000: 79) suggests that use of the medium 'gives rise to all three ... interactional situations' (and, we should add, to a mixing of forms of interaction).

According to Slevin, apart from the obvious example of radio and television programmes being transmitted via the internet (for a discussion of 'webcasting', see Hendy 2000), the use of 'webpages' is the 'nearest match' to what Thompson names mediated quasi-interaction, 'yet even here, individuals and collectivities can respond by creating their own pages' (Slevin 2000: 80). More generally, much computer-mediated communication conforms to what Thompson calls mediated interaction, in its narrower sense: 'The internet clearly contributes to the repertoire of possibilities for the two-way flow of actions and utterances in the form of e-mail ... and chat options between individuals privately' (Slevin 2000: 79). Like Thompson, though, Slevin acknowledges that mediated interactions between participants on the internet are not just 'one-to-one'. There are also 'many-to-many dialogical domains' for public communications, like IRC chat channels: 'Although telephone chat systems have already demonstrated the need for such forums in modern societies, the scale and the possibilities opened by the internet are unprecedented' (Slevin 2000: 80).

In addition, Slevin (2000: 79) recognises that mediated interaction via the internet can be combined with, and may give rise to, certain face-to-face situations:

> For example, two individuals may be having a discussion in a room while at the same time taking turns to type messages to a distant friend. ... Similarly, members of a project team responsible for building a website might e-mail each other and arrange to meet ... to discuss the project's progress.

Here, he clearly echoes Thompson's remarks on the mixing of interaction types in daily living. Slevin reminds us, too, of problems associated with treating the internet as if it had a 'cyberian apartness' (Miller and Slater 2000) from the everyday. To focus all our attention on what happens in the 'virtual realms' (Mitchell 1995) of cyberspace would be to 'miss out on the intricate ways in which internet use interlaces with face-to-face discourse' (Slevin 2000: 79).

Intimacy

We can now return to ideas about mediated 'intimacy at a distance', which were touched on at the close of my initial account of Thompson's typology. In fact,

Thompson (1995) is not the first theorist to use this phrase, having borrowed it from the work of Donald Horton and Richard Wohl (1986). They are the co-authors of a remarkable piece on mass communication and 'para-social interaction', originally published back in the mid-1950s at a time when television, the medium at the centre of their analysis, was very much in its infancy. I refer to their writing as remarkable because, although it does have certain limitations, it starts to open up a general way of thinking about media and changing social relationships that still has considerable currency today. When introducing the concept of mediated quasi-interaction, Thompson (1995: 278) admits that his own term 'is similar to the expression' employed by Horton and Wohl, noting how 'in an early and insightful article ... they suggested that mass communication gives rise to a new type of social relationship which they call "para-social interaction"' (social 'para-interaction' is actually a more precise term for the kind of relating which Horton and Wohl have in mind here, because all human relationships, including those technologically mediated by broadcasting, are best thought of as fully 'social').

Horton and Wohl (1986: 186) theorise what they see as the basic form of interaction between television performers and audience members as a 'simulacrum of conversational give and take'. In looking at styles of screen performance, they are particularly interested in a 'special category of "personalities"' or 'personae', typically known only for their appearances on television (see also Langer 1981). These personae appear, for instance, as various sorts of show host and presenter, as 'quiz-masters', 'announcers', 'interviewers' and so on. On occasion, such a performer 'is seen engaged with others; but often he [*sic*] faces the spectator, uses the mode of direct address, talks as if he [*sic*] were conversing personally and privately' (Horton and Wohl 1986: 185–6). There is what Thompson has called a separation of contexts between the place of the performance and the places of viewing. The personae's actions are oriented towards an indefinite range of potential recipients and the communication is effectively monological. Nevertheless, Horton and Wohl are proposing that there is the simulation of a face-to-face encounter for audiences (the performance is an 'objectively perceptible action' in which viewers can be 'implicated imaginatively'). Indeed, while watching a persona's screen performance, the television viewer has access to those multiple symbolic cues, of spoken and body language, that are evident in most co-present, face-to-face situations (although any physical contact between the participants in a quasi-interaction or para-interaction is obviously quite impossible).

Furthermore, the simulation of a face-to-face relationship with the television personality is not to be understood simply as a one-off mediated encounter. Rather, the appearances of these public figures are serialised. 'The persona offers, above all, a continuing relationship', write Horton and Wohl (1986: 187), since her or his scheduled performances on television are 'regular and dependable ... integrated into the routines of daily life.' John Langer (1981: 354–5), a media analyst, helps us to build on that basic observation by comparing what he labels television's 'personality system' with the 'classical paradigm of the star system' in Hollywood cinema:

> Whereas the star system operates from the realms of the spectacular, the inaccessible ... presenting the cinematic universe as 'larger than life', the personality system is cultivated almost exclusively as 'part of life' ... the personality system works directly to construct and foreground intimacy and immediacy; whereas contact with stars is unrelentingly sporadic and uncertain, contact with television personalities has regularity and predictability; whereas stars are always playing 'parts' ... television personalities 'play' themselves ... personalities are distinguished for their ... 'will to ordinariness', to be accepted, normalized, experienced as familiar.

In the passage reproduced above, we are reminded of the differences between cinema and television as audio-visual media, and of the key features of broadcast output as a whole (principally its ordinariness, familiarity and predictability), which are related in this case to thinking about the self-presentations of television personalities (for later discussions of intimate performances and modes of address found in British broadcasting during the 1980s and 1990s, see Wilson 1993; Lury 1996).

Today, perhaps especially on breakfast and daytime television, it is not too difficult to find examples of the 'will to ordinariness' at work. So in the UK, we could look at the down-to-earth and 'homely' styles of presentation that are routinely employed by Eamonn Holmes and Fiona Phillips on *GMTV*, or else by the husband-and-wife team, Richard Madeley and Judy Finnigan, on *This Morning* and subsequently on their afternoon magazine show, *Richard and Judy*. In Australia, *Mornings with Kerri-Anne* features a similar performance of the ordinary. These presenters, in 'playing themselves', seem to want to come across to their audiences as nothing special and, precisely, as 'part of life'.

Langer's claim that the personality system of television functions to 'foreground intimacy' resonates with the central argument made by Horton and Wohl, who believe a 'bond of intimacy' may be formed between personae and their distant audience members. Since the relationship between persona and audience member is 'inevitably one-sided', it falls chiefly on the television performer to attempt to create this feeling of intimacy at a distance (of course, fan mail and other forms of feedback channelled outside the mediated quasi-interaction can also serve to sustain that relationship):

> There are several principal strategies for achieving this. ... In addition to creating an appropriate tone and patter, the persona tries as far as possible to eradicate, or at least to blur, the line which divides him [*sic*] and his [*sic*] show, as a ... performance, from the audience both in the studio and at home. The most usual way of achieving this ambiguity is

for the persona to treat his [*sic*] supporting cast as a group of close intimates. Thus all the members of the cast will be addressed by their first names, or by special nicknames, to emphasize intimacy. ... Furthermore, the persona may try to step out of the particular format of his [*sic*] show and literally blend with the audience. Most usually, the persona leaves the stage and mingles with the studio audience in a question-and-answer exchange.

(Horton and Wohl 1986: 188–9)

With reference to popular entertainment programmes shown in the USA during the 1950s, Horton and Wohl manage to identify particular ways of seeking to draw in television viewers that are still evident in contemporary broadcasting. Here, they recognise the importance of the host's face-to-face interactions with regular fellow performers and with members of a physically co-present audience in the studio. These performance techniques are intended to create the impression that there is 'a kind of participation' or 'fellowship', which is open by extension to those people who are watching the show from elsewhere.

What Horton and Wohl do not manage to provide is any convincing evidence, based on empirical audience research, of how viewers actually respond to the offers of 'intimacy' that are made in the performances of television's personae. Apart from a passing reference to a letter published in a newspaper advice column, in which the author of the letter confesses to having 'fallen in love' with a television personality, they base their theory of mediated relationships on observations of what appears on the screen, and on occasionally problematic assumptions about audience behaviour. However, in a recent longitudinal study of viewers in the UK (Gauntlett and Hill 1999), there are relevant data suggesting that, through the passage of lifetime (Scannell 1988), television presenters may indeed come to be seen by some as 'familiar companions'. For instance, when asked what would be missed most if there was no longer any television to watch, a participant in the study states: 'I would miss most of all the feeling of having company ... I have "friends" on radio, too, but seeing the people I like is even better' (in Gauntlett and Hill 1999: 115).

Sociologist Graham Allan (1989: 1) points out that, in his discipline, as a rule: 'There has been relatively little serious analysis of friendship as a form of personal relationship occurring in industrialised societies ... friendship is treated as being rather peripheral ... despite its significance in ... everyday life.' When friendship and intimacy do receive the serious consideration they deserve (see also Allan 1979; Jamieson 1998), little is said about the role played by media in friendship relations, and even less about the sort of intimacy at a distance with media figures that Horton and Wohl begin to explore. Joshua Meyrowitz (1985), though, has taken up their line of inquiry, discussing relations with what he terms 'media friends'. Whereas Horton and Wohl's focus is on the potential for intimacy with television personalities who have 'no traditional performance skill' (beyond the ability to present themselves to viewers as ordinary and 'likeable'),

Meyrowitz (1985: 119) is interested, too, in the media performances of public figures like politicians, musicians and sporting celebrities, who are 'now judged not only on the basis of their "talent" but also on the basis of their personalities'.

A good example of this trend in recent years would be the growth of what is known, often pejoratively, as 'personality politics', which means that politicians are more and more 'image conscious', increasingly concerned with their media appearances and 'public relations'. That concern may extend to performing not just as competent public servants but also, rather like television personalities, as ordinary and personable individuals (see Fairclough 2000 on Tony Blair's verbal presentation of self as a 'normal person'). In Thompson's words, political leaders, with the assistance of their PR advisors, 'seek to employ the means of communication at their disposal in order to manage their visibility before others – and especially others, in the modern age of television, who are spatially remote':

> But mediated visibility is a double-edged sword. While new media of communication have created new opportunities ... enabling political leaders to appear before their subjects in a way and on a scale that never existed before, they have also created new risks. ... Hence the visibility created by the media may become the source of a new and distinctive kind of fragility.
>
> (Thompson 1995: 140–1)

The fragility to which he refers is bound up, for instance, with the continual danger of making 'gaffes', or of having previously concealed aspects of private life enter into the public domain to become the subject of 'media scandals' (Lull and Hinerman 1997). Taking the case of former American president, Bill Clinton, we could think about the threats to his political and personal credibility that resulted from a widely publicised affair with White House intern Monica Lewinsky (for further discussion of this political sex scandal, see Thompson 2000).

Grief

The justification Meyrowitz (1985) offers in support of his claim, that some people can form bonds of intimacy with media friends, has to do with what happens on occasions when a well-known figure of this kind dies unexpectedly or is murdered. In these circumstances, he argues (partly on the basis of personal experience), a strong public response often follows, and he believes the theoretical framework developed by Horton and Wohl (1986) might help us to understand that response:

> The framework explains ... why it is that when a 'media friend' such as Elvis Presley, John Kennedy or John Lennon dies or is killed, millions of people may experience a sense of loss ... the death of John Lennon,

for example, was strangely painful to me and my university colleagues who had 'known' him and grown up 'with' him ... such mediated relationships lead to a ... new genre of human grief. ... In order to banish the demons of grief ... people take to the streets or hold vigils. ... Ironically, but appropriately, the media provide the most ritualized channels of mourning. Radio and television present specials and retrospectives. And many people use the telephone to contact real friends who shared the intimacy with the para-social friend.

(Meyrowitz 1985: 120)

More recent expressions of 'grief' following the deaths of media figures include reactions to the murder of a BBC television presenter Jill Dando, and, on a far larger scale, to the unexpected death of Diana, Princess of Wales in a car accident.

Robert Turnock (2000: 35), in his study of British television viewers' responses to news of Diana's death and coverage of the subsequent funeral, poses the question: 'How is it possible to grieve over someone that you have never met?' He is careful to point out that not all of the people featured in his research data reported feelings of grief, yet others do seem to have experienced great upset over her death. Consider, for instance, the following brief extract from a written account:

My family and I watched the entire funeral. My husband has his own business, but he was shut for the day as a mark of respect ... we just felt it was the appropriate thing to do. ... We watched BBC1 until she reached her final resting place around 2.15 p.m. We stayed at home in our breakfast room, drinking tea and crying. It did not feel right to go out on such a sad day.

(in Turnock 2000: 99)

Clearly, a central issue in this account is the suspension or interruption of routine. Its author tells of her husband's business closing down for the day, of watching one television channel for hours on end, and of remaining indoors in their 'breakfast room' until the afternoon. The funeral appears to have 'shown up' as eventful for them 'against a background of uneventful everyday existence' (Scannell 1996: 160). More significant for our present discussion of grief, though, are the tears that they shed for a public figure they had never met 'personally', face-to-face.

Turnock's own answer to the question he poses revolves mainly around a reading of Diana as 'an ideal soap opera heroine', whose 'character' went through emotional 'ups and downs', making available 'melodramatic identifications' to audience members (see also Ang 1985; 1990, on *Dallas* and its viewers). 'Diana was very much like a regular cast member in a television serial', writes Turnock (2000: 47), appearing in media settings 'on a frequent basis between 1981 and 1997.' As one participant in the study reveals: 'She had seemed so much part of our lives for almost 20 years ... I have to admit feeling quite a profound sense of loss' (in Turnock 2000: 47).

It was an intriguing characteristic of Diana's 'celebrity' that, while she obviously occupied a quite extraordinary social position through her marriage into the British royal family, she frequently offered a 'performance of "ordinariness"' (Couldry 2001: 231) in media settings. Although Diana was in part a sign of wealth and 'glamour' appearing on the cover of many magazines, which might be thought to put her in the same bracket as a film star, she evidently possessed the will to ordinariness that Langer describes in his work on television's personality system. Perhaps the best example of this will at work is her performed 'sincerity' in a *Panorama* television interview originally broadcast on BBC1 in the UK, in which she speaks candidly and emotionally about, amongst other things, the break up of her marriage. She presents herself there as somebody who has 'suffered':

> A cold and heartless royal family apparently cast her aside, while her husband indulged in an extramarital affair. Her eating disorder ... was an explicit hint at the emotional and psychological turmoil inside. Her attempts to escape and find love were exposed in the tabloid press.
>
> (Turnock 2000: 45)

Of course, not all viewers will have interpreted her self-presentation on that occasion as 'a case of the real thing' (Scannell 1996: 74), but what she made available to audience members was the potential for non-reciprocal intimacy at a distance in a mediated quasi-interaction.

I want to make two final points here, before we leave the general subject of grief in 'mediated relationships' and the specific case of Diana's death. Each of these points returns us once again to a consideration of the time–space relations that are inherent in the constitution of social interaction. First of all, although the data analysed by Turnock are drawn solely from Britain, the cultural practices of 'mourning Diana' (see Kear and Steinberg 1999) were by no means confined to a single national context. As I have argued earlier in the book (in my discussion of eventfulness), the death of Diana can be thought of as a global news story. The instantaneous, transnational reach of this particular story enabled forms of 'mourning at a distance' (Duruz and Johnson 1999) on the other side of the world from the scene of the fatal crash in Paris. Jean Duruz and Carol Johnson (1999), in their review of some of the complex and highly varied responses of Australians to the news, refer to press reports of grieving mothers and gay men in Sydney, and of empty Melbourne dance clubs on the Saturday night when the funeral was televised live in Australia.

Second, back in the UK, there were embodied acts of what Nick Couldry (2000a: 37) calls 'pilgrimage and witnessing' following news of the death (see also Couldry 1999). Large numbers of people travelled physically to sign condolence books and lay flowers with others in public places, or even to be in attendance in central London near the event of the funeral itself (where, interestingly, the service could be viewed on outdoor television screens, creating a peculiar interaction mix). These corporeal mobilities are evidence of a kind of compulsion of proximity (Boden and Molotch 1994) that might have been helping participants 'to banish the demons of grief' (Meyrowitz 1985: 120). So while television and other electronic media facilitate the instantaneous 'presencing' of an eventful occasion in conditions of physical absence, this certainly does not rule out the possibility of co-present 'corporeal gatherings' to mark the loss of a media friend.

Pathologisation

Up to now, my commentary on the theory of media and interaction proposed by Horton and Wohl (1986) has been generally positive, and for good reason. Writing shortly after the arrival of television in daily life, they are able to identify some of the principal styles of screen performance for distant viewers, which are still apparent in broadcasting today. However, it was noted in passing that their work does have certain limitations. More specifically, I suggested that their assumptions about audience behaviour are occasionally problematic.

Our concern in this section will be with the problem of the 'pathologisation' of various social groups, whose members are seen to be especially vulnerable to an 'extreme para-sociability'. Horton and Wohl distinguish what they regard as deviant viewing activity from an assumed social norm. They observe that the interaction (or para-interaction) between personae and audiences can provide 'a social milieu in which the everyday assumptions and understandings of primary group interaction and sociability are demonstrated and reaffirmed' (Horton and Wohl 1986: 196). This is a point that will be developed further in the following section with particular reference to Paddy Scannell (1996: 4) on 'the sociable dimension of radio and television broadcasting'. The situation in 'normal social life', though, is contrasted by Horton and Wohl (1986: 196) with 'the formation of compensatory attachments by the socially isolated, the socially inept, the aged and invalid, the timid and rejected', in which they perceive a danger that the mediated relationship will become 'a substitute for autonomous social participation' and could therefore 'be regarded as pathological'.

Years later, Thompson (1995) actually reproduces much the same argument, in a slightly modified form, in his own account of non-reciprocal intimacy at a distance. He believes that this sort of intimacy has, on the one hand, 'attractions' for people who choose to engage with media figures, and yet, on the other hand, potential 'costs':

> It enables individuals to enjoy some of the benefits of companionship without the demands typically incurred in contexts of face-to-face interaction. It provides individuals with an opportunity to explore interpersonal relations in a vicarious way, without entering into a web

of reciprocal commitments. ... In one form or another, most individuals in modern societies establish and sustain non-reciprocal relations of intimacy with distant others. Actors and actresses, news readers and talk show hosts, pop stars and others become familiar and recognizable figures who are often discussed by individuals in the course of their day-to-day lives, who may be referred to routinely on a first-name basis and so on. But it is also clear that in some cases these non-reciprocal relations of intimacy may assume a much greater significance in the lives of particular individuals. They can become such an important aspect of an individual's life that they begin to overshadow other aspects, in such a way that forms of everyday interaction are redefined in their terms.

(Thompson 1995: 219–20)

His example of a particular individual whose everyday interactions are being 'redefined' in terms of intimate relations with a media figure is that of 'a 42-year-old married woman with three children', who finds herself in a 'one-sided love affair' with the singer Barry Manilow (Thompson 1995: 220–1). When she has sex with her husband, this woman imagines that she is making love with her idol, which is ultimately a 'source of confusion' and emotional 'pain' for her. For Thompson (1995: 225), she provides an illustration of what can happen when 'fandom' becomes an 'addiction': 'When this occurs, the individual may find it difficult to sustain the distinction between the world of the fan and the practical contexts of daily life.'

We should be cautious, though, about accepting the claims made by Horton and Wohl (regarding 'pathological' mediated relationships) and by Thompson (regarding the psychological costs of 'compulsive' fan activity) (see also Jensen 1992, for a valuable critique of 'fandom as pathology'). To begin with, I think it is worth us noticing how they identify, either explicitly or implicitly, certain types of people who are seen as the most likely to fall prey to the dangers of non-reciprocal intimacy at a distance (the 'isolated', the 'inept', middle-aged mothers and so on). In Joli Jensen's words, these groups 'can be distinguished from people like us (students, professors and social critics)' (Jensen 1992: 9). This is similar to the way in which, say, children have frequently been singled out in the past as 'others' who are especially vulnerable to the supposed 'negative effects of the media' (see Buckingham 1997). There is a distancing strategy being employed here, in which individuals in some social groups are 'defined ... in terms of their inability ... to conform to ... norms' (Buckingham 1997: 33).

Another, possibly more significant, reason for caution has to do with the way in which Horton and Wohl, and Thompson too, appear to privilege co-present, face-to-face interaction over technologically mediated communications, investing the former with greater 'authenticity'. Indeed, in my view Meyrowitz (1985) is, to an extent, guilty of the same mistake, when he draws a distinction between media friends and 'real friends'. Horton and Wohl fear that, in instances of so-called extreme para-sociability, relations of intimacy with distant others will become an inadequate 'substitute' for social contact in a shared physical setting, and Thompson worries about 'the practical contexts of daily life' getting over-shadowed by mediated quasi-interactions. We could ask, however, whether they would be so anxious if the opposite was the case, that is, if an intense engage-ment in face-to-face interactions resulted in minimal media use.

Whilst I have no difficulty at all in agreeing with Thompson that, on occa-sion, compulsive behaviour can be problematic for the individual concerned, such behaviour is not exclusive to mediated relationships. If the Barry Manilow fan in his discussion was having a long-term, secret and obsessive affair with her next-door neighbour, then this might also be a cause of confusion and pain when she sleeps with her husband. There is no need, in other words, to point to technologically mediated communication *per se* as the problem.

Sociability

Back in the opening chapter of this book, I promised to explore more fully, at a later stage, Scannell's ideas on 'broadcast output … as public discourse' (Scannell 1991). The time for that discussion has arrived and it will centre on the concept of 'sociability', since for Scannell (1996) this is the 'fundamental characteristic' of broadcasting. Sociability constitutes the 'basic communicative ethos' of radio and television, he contends (as we shall see in due course, it is also an important feature of mediated interaction via the telephone or internet). His understanding of the concept is derived from the work of a classical socio-logical thinker, Georg Simmel (1950). Although Simmel's writings were originally published some years prior to the establishment of broadcasting, they offer us a general definition of sociable interaction that is taken up and applied by Scannell in a detailed analysis of programmes.

For Simmel (1950: 45), 'sociability has no objective purpose … but the success of the sociable moment'. 'When people enter into each other's company for the sake of sociability', explains Scannell (1996: 22), 'they seek nothing more than the pleasure of each other's company.' By extension, he attempts to theorise the relationship between broadcasters and their audiences as, at root, a sociable one 'that lacks any specific … aim or purpose':

> This, of course, is not to deny that a very great deal of broadcast output has … aims and purpose. News intends to provide information. Adverts intend to persuade. But even when there is a manifest content with obvious strategic-purposive intentions … there is a necessary prior sociable commitment in the communicative form of every programme. The force of this claim is to undercut any ultimate strategic, manipula-tive or exploitative purpose in broadcasting. It is not to say such

motives do not pervade broadcasting's communicative ethos, but rather that they do not constitute it.

(Scannell 1996: 23)

This is quite a claim, and it is bound up with his broader rejection or 'setting aside' of the 'critical paradigm' (Hall 1982) in media and cultural studies, along with its focus on power and politics (strong indications of that rejection are already evident in Scannell 1992).

If broadcasting has a degree of 'institutional authority', then Scannell (1996: 24) believes that this authority is largely undermined by the fact 'that you cannot coerce listeners to listen' or viewers to view. In order for anyone to listen and watch, it is necessary to 'try to speak to them in ways that they would wish to be spoken to ... the appropriate expressive idiom for any broadcast is one that fits the contexts in which viewing and listening take place' (Scannell 1996: 24). Broadcast talk therefore has to be oriented to the day-to-day, predominantly private, circumstances in which audience members find themselves physically. Historically, this led to the emergence of what Scannell (1992), borrowing a phrase from his colleague, David Cardiff, terms the 'domestication of public utterance', of 'friendlier' modes of address and discursive styles in many areas of output (echoes of Horton and Wohl are audible here).

One area of programming is of particular interest to Scannell (1996: 25), though, because it is so directly concerned with the construction of sociability, 'namely chat shows, game shows and quizzes ... "people" programmes':

> The essential ingredient of all these programmes – their basic format – is an organized set of social interactions situated in a studio, or some other suitable public space. The members ... consist of (1) a host, (2) participant-performers, (3) a live audience and (4) absent listeners and viewers. The object ... is fun, having a good time.

Interactions between 'members' in categories one to three are carefully managed in an effort to achieve or 'bring off' sociable moments for members of distant audiences (in category four). This is done primarily through conversation in the form of what Simmel (1950: 52) refers to as 'talk for the sake of talking'. Of course, it might reasonably be objected here that the 'participant-performers' in such programmes can be talking with the aim of self-promotion, or else for the purpose of winning a prize of some sort, yet Scannell would insist that, above all, the conversation is being produced for 'absent listeners and viewers' whose motives for engaging with a programme of this kind are usually 'nothing more' than 'for relaxation' or 'for company'.

Paying close attention to the form of talk that is to be heard in this area of programming, Scannell (1996) traces the historical development of the genre on BBC radio from the mid-1930s through to the post-war period. He ends there by analysing a quiz show, *Have a Go!*, which reached the height of its popularity in Britain in the mid-1950s. A further continuation of his study of 'fun' in broadcasting, as far as the 1990s, is located in a subsequent analysis of the ITV television game show *Blind Date* (see Scannell 1999), which shares its format with an Australian programme that was called *Perfect Match*. Let us now consider what he has to say about these two popular entertainment programmes.

Have a Go! was recorded on location in the physical presence of live audiences at public venues in different towns and cities. A small number of local people, selected as participant-performers, 'engaged in a bit of chat with the show's host before answering a few simple questions that might win them a smallish sum of money' (Scannell 1996: 48). The host of this quiz show was a well-known radio personality of the time called Wilfred Pickles, 'a working-class Yorkshireman ... who became a household name during, and for many years after the war ... a typification of the working man – bluff, jovial, friendly and down to earth' (Scannell 1996: 38). We could note, then, that Pickles' 'regional' identity, identifiable in his northern accent and occasional use of dialect, was designed precisely to establish him as an ordinary, sociable persona.

Drawing on the vocabulary of phenomenology (Heidegger 1962) and anticipating the later study of *Blind Date*, Scannell (1996: 146) writes of the 'care-structure' of *Have a Go!*, which 'runs right the way through it from its gross ... organizational features down to the momentary inflection of a voice'. By care-structure, he means here the 'professionalism', effort and thought that has gone into producing the programme, apparently effortlessly, for absent listeners and viewers. Scannell's crucial argument, that this care or concern is 'there-to-be-found' in the detail of the talk itself, can be illustrated with reference to a brief extract from his transcription of one of the broadcasts. In the extract, reproduced below, the host is already involved in conversation with Florrie, the first contestant on the show:

21	*Pickles:*	Do you do a job too?
22	*Florrie:*	Yes I'm a bus conductress.
23	*Pickles:*	Are yer?
24	*Florrie:*	Yes.
25	*Pickles:*	An'ow long've you been doing that?
26	*Florrie:*	Twelve year.
27	*Pickles:*	Really?
28	*Florrie:*	Yes.

(in Scannell 1996: 146)

He points to how, if the exchanges on lines 23 and 24, and also on lines 27 and 28, were removed from the transcript, no relevant information about the contestant would actually be lost, leading him to pose the question of what these utterances are for.

Scannell's answer is that without the lines he identifies in the transcript, the 'mood of the interaction' would be lost. These exchanges are 'precisely mood-generating': ' "Are yer?" "Really?" … Suchlike things are hearable in … a way that discloses a concern, … nothing more (or less) than being engaged … in talk-with-another … to find and show that the other is somehow someway interesting' (Scannell 1996: 147). The potential pleasure to be had from listening to such a performance is the 'enjoyment of good company'. In other words, the host's style of talk with the contestant is geared towards constructing a mood of sociability. It is also geared towards presenting Florrie as a personality in her own right, if only for the brief duration of this contestant's appearance on the show (see Lury 1996, who discusses related aspects of 'the performance of ordinary people', by which she means non-professional performers, in broadcasting).

As with *Have a Go!*, Scannell (1999: 282) remarks that: 'The object of *Blind Date* is fun.' The programme-makers presume 'that there might be something entertaining in … inviting ordinary members of the public (male and female) to take part in a game in which someone will select … a partner from the opposite sex for a "blind date" ' (Scannell 1999: 286). He proceeds to advocate a particular approach to the Saturday evening programme, referring to this as a 'phenomenology of fun', which is focused on the show's care-structure or its managed efforts to make fun happen. 'There is of course a paradox here', Scannell (1999: 283) adds, because a 'key expectation that we have of fun is that it should be spontaneous.' So a difficulty that the programme faces is in appearing to distant audiences to have liveness, immediacy and spontaneity, when in fact it is pre-recorded and 'carefully planned'.

Nevertheless, his assertion is that the show gets produced in such a way as to give viewers a sense of it 'unfolding' in the live now of transmission. In addition, he draws our attention to the 'performative skill' of its long-time (recently retired) presenter, Cilla Black, whose talk and body language are central to the creation of 'a complex weave of interactions between herself as host, the studio audience, those who play the game each week and … viewers' (Scannell 1999: 286). Like Pickles, Black makes use of her regional background, speaking with a Liverpudlian accent as she engages in light-hearted, apparently informal banter with contestants (her entry into popular entertainment was as a singer associated with the Liverpool music scene of the 1960s).

When Scannell looks closely at the 'complex weave of interactions' Black is involved in, he returns to an interesting issue raised in passing by Horton and Wohl (1986), which is the role of the studio audience. At the beginning of each programme, then, she steps down on to the stage and speaks, directly and simultaneously, both to a live audience in the studio and to the absent viewers 'at home'. Scannell (1999: 283–4) asks whether the show is, is any sense, 'produced and performed' for the people watching in the studio, before replying that, in his opinion, it is not:

> I want to suggest that the studio audience is part of the show which is, first and last and in every particular, for the television audience. ... How so? Well, consider the well-known fact that studio audiences, in shows like this, are always rehearsed. They are advised when to applaud and cheer, and join in. Their behaviour is treated by the producers as part of the overall effect of the show, as something to be managed and controlled with viewers in mind. ... The studio audience is vital to creating the atmosphere of the show, its 'mood'. ... The studio audience in *Blind Date* is essential to the creation of a specific public mood – a collective willingness to have a good time, a shared disposition to laughter and fun.

This notion of 'mood' counts for him as highly significant in 'any phenomenological analysis' of culture.

At this point, though, it is necessary for us to pause and reflect on the approach that Scannell takes to the construction of fun, because he is challenged by David Morley (2000) over his arguments about sociability in broadcasting. Morley (2000: 110–11) recognises 'the elegance of many of his analyses of the dynamics of ... programme forms', but feels 'unable to share Scannell's desire to simply set aside ... power and politics':

> By the very way (and to the very extent that) a programme signals to members of some groups that it is designed for them and functions as an effective invitation to their participation in social life, it will necessarily signal to members of other groups that it is not for them and, indeed, that they are not among the invitees to its particular forum of sociability. Only a programme constructed within the terms of some form of cultural Esperanto could hope to appeal equally to all, without favour or division. Sociability, by definition, can only ever be produced in some particular cultural (and linguistic) form – and only those with access to the relevant ... cultural capital will feel interpellated by and at home within the particular form of sociability offered by a given programme.

We return, in the passage above, to a disagreement between Morley and Scannell that has to do with a much bigger theoretical split between critical and consensus views of society. The perspective adopted by Morley puts an emphasis on cultural difference (following his line of thought, it might perhaps be preferable to speak of 'sociabilities') and exclusion. For him, the key is 'which forms of sociability feel foreign to whom', since any particular collective production of 'the sociable' will have its 'constitutive outside' (Morley 2000: 112).

Indeed, Scannell does recognise on occasion that programmes like *Have a Go!* and *Blind Date* are not universally appreciated or interpreted as fun. For all his talk of radio and television constituting an inclusive 'world-in-common', he accepts that the pleasures (and displeasures) of listening and viewing are to some extent varied. In the case of *Have a Go!*, the BBC's own audience research revealed that the programme was found by many listeners 'to be entertaining, amusing, warm, cheering and fun', yet others felt 'its humour was common and vulgar' (Scannell 1996: 56). Clearly, class cultural distinctions helped to generate those different responses to the radio show and its mood (and phenomenology need not disregard social class, see Charlesworth 1999). Furthermore, in his concluding comments on *Blind Date*, Scannell (1999: 288) acknowledges that 'what is gathered as fun in the care-structure of *Blind Date* is particular to ... the contemporary world of modern, western societies'. The television programme's 'horizon', its taken-for-granted set of attitudes and assumptions, is historically and geographically specific.

Sociability is a concept that gets applied not only in the study of broadcasting, but also in academic work on other electronic media. In the remainder of this section, my attention shifts to that literature, as I now consider some of the forms of sociable interaction constituted within telephone and internet communications. Our principal concerns so far have been with the emergence of mediated sociability, and with its ongoing cultural and linguistic realisations. Those interests reappear in the material reviewed below.

Historical sociologist Claude Fischer (1991), for instance, tells the story of the telephone industry's 'discovery' of sociability (and see Frissen 1995). He writes: 'Industry leaders long ignored or repressed telephone sociability ... only after decades of customer insistence on making such calls ... did the industry come to adopt sociability as a means of exploiting the technology' (Fischer 1991: 113). In recent times, telephone companies have employed advertising slogans like 'Reach out and touch someone' and 'It's good to talk', encouraging calls that are made 'just to keep in touch' (Drew and Chilton 2000) with friends and family members, but for many years 'telephone visiting' of this sort was regarded as frivolous and unnecessary (as 'trivial gossip'), and therefore discouraged. Instead, the early marketing of telephone services typically prioritised functional, 'practical uses' of the technology, inherited from telegraphy, for the purpose of rapid information delivery.

Gender, as Ian Hutchby (2001: 82) reminds us, was an important factor in shaping the telephone as a 'technology for sociability':

> It took the telephone companies some time to realize that ... marketing strategies were not an accurate reflection of what was actually being done with the telephone. What was happening was that women in particular were appropriating the artefact for quite different ends, namely, informal chatting and the maintenance of social contacts.

This story provides a demonstration, for Fischer (1991), of how the initial designers and promoters of any communications technology do not always foresee its ultimate uses in ordinary social life. It also relates to my discussion, in the first part of the book, of some of the problems associated with a perspective known as technological determinism.

Ann Moyal (1989; 1992) in Australia and Lana Rakow (1992) in the USA each offer empirical evidence of women's routine appropriation of the telephone for sociable interaction. Distinguishing between 'instrumental' calls of a functional nature and 'intrinsic' calls involving interaction with friends and relatives (what she terms 'kinkeeping'), Moyal finds that, among the women questioned in her survey, the latter type of call is made more frequently and likely to be of a longer duration than the former type. She speaks of her respondents' creation of an extended 'psychological neighbourhood'.

Meanwhile, in Rakow's ethnographic account of telephone use in a small American town, she notes that 'the telephone is a gendered ... technology' (Rakow 1992: 33), not just in the sense that it is clearly identified there as 'part of women's domain', but also because gendered identities and social relations are partly constructed through the use, or non-use, of this technology. 'Most women reported to me that their husbands, fathers and boyfriends generally do not use the telephone for anything other than to conduct business or to get something done or arranged', comments Rakow (1992: 42). Whereas these men appear to 'shy away' from the telephone's potential for, or affordance of, mediated intimacy and sociability, the women in her study were 'attracted to it for just that characteristic' (Rakow 1992: 43).

What neither Moyal nor Rakow examine, though, is the complex organisation of talk in telephonic sociability. This is a task left to conversation analysts, who, as I mentioned above, have a particular interest in the ordering of talk-in-interaction. For example, Hutchby discusses the pioneering sociological work of Emanuel Schegloff (1986) on the 'core sequences' of conversation ('summons-answer', 'identification/recognition', 'greetings' and 'initial inquiries') that are found at the start of many mundane telephone interactions.

Hutchby (2001: 91–2) considers the following transcription of a telephone call opening provided by Schegloff:

1		*(ring)*
2	*Nancy:*	H'll*o*?
3	*Hyla:*	Hi:,
4	*Nancy:*	Hi::.
5	*Hyla:*	How *are* yuhh=
6	*Nancy:*	=Fi:ne how er you,
7	*Hyla:*	Oka:[y,
8	*Nancy:*	[*Goo*:d,
9		*(0.4)*
10	*Hyla:*	.mkhhh[hh
11	*Nancy:*	[What's doin',

On lines 1 and 2, we can see an instance of the summons-answer sequence. The interesting thing about this sequence, and what marks it out as different from a summons and answer in conditions of physical co-presence (say when an individual shouts across the street to someone they know and gets a reply), is that 'the summons is a purely technological one: the sound of the phone's ring' (Hutchby 2001: 96). 'The next two sequences, identification/recognition and greetings, are accomplished simultaneously in this call', writes Hutchby (2001: 92). Hyla's first utterance, a greeting on line 3, suggests she has identified Nancy as the answerer, while Nancy's 'return-greeting' on line 4 shows that 'reciprocal recognition has been achieved', all without names being exchanged (it is notable that nowadays, when many telephones are equipped with a 'caller recognition' device, the identity of the caller is revealed in an electronic display before the ring is answered). An initial inquiries sequence, which Schegloff also labels the 'howareyou' sequence, follows on lines 5–8, incorporating 'simple responses' and a subsequent 'terminating assessment' from Nancy (for examples of certain divergences from Schegloff's 'canonical model' of telephone call openings, see Drew and Chilton 2000, who analyse a series of 'regular and habitualised' calls made between a mother and daughter living apart).

After completing the core sequences, allowing for limited exceptions to the canonical model, participants in telephone talk are situated in the 'anchor position'. This means that they are ready for the introduction of a 'first topic' of conversation. Usually, that topic arrives in the next 'turn' from the person making the call, but in the transcript above, it is the person being called who, following a brief pause in the interaction, asks a question designed to 'elicit a topic' for discussion.

Finally here, I turn to the subject of 'sociability on the Net' (Misztal 2000). Like Scannell, Barbara Misztal (2000) draws on Simmel (1950). As part of her more general elaboration of a theory of 'informality' in contemporary culture, she attempts to conceptualise the sort of sociable relations that are sometimes found in computer-mediated communication (although, unlike the technologically mediated relationships described by Moyal, Rakow and Schegloff, these frequently involve interaction between strangers). Borrowing Simmel's perspective on the 'democratic structure' of sociability, she compares internet chat with face-to-face exchanges at a cocktail party: 'Sociability of computer-mediated communication and sociability at the cocktail party are distinguished by relatively egalitarian relations. ... In both cases, relatively widespread reciprocity illustrates that one's satisfaction cannot be totally disconnected from the cost of ... conduct for others' (Misztal 2000: 197). There are, of course, documented instances of 'flaming' in cyberspace (for example, see Wallace 1999), yet Misztal believes that the principles of 'netiquette' tend to guard against such outbursts. Taking part in sociable interactions, whether they are online or offline, requires a degree of concern for fellow participants (raising issues of 'face', to which we will be returning later), since 'the pleasure of the individual is closely tied up with the pleasure of the others' (Simmel 1950: 48).

Comparing internet and cocktail party conversation is interesting, but it ought to be noted that the cocktail party is a middle-class social situation in which, to quote from Morley's critique of Scannell, 'only those with access to the relevant ... cultural capital will feel ... at home' (Morley 2000: 111). In addition, pursuing the terms of his critique, specific forms of online and offline sociability exclude, or at least discourage, members of those groups who are 'not among the invitees'. These points about cultural difference and exclusion are well illustrated in a recent book by Lori Kendall (2002), who writes on life in (and out of) an internet forum that she calls *BlueSky*.

Whereas Misztal takes a cocktail party as her point of comparison with the sociability of computer-mediated communication, Kendall prefers to employ the metaphor of the 'local pub' or bar in an effort to interpret the everyday interactions between participants on *BlueSky*. She remarks on the gendering of this media setting or virtual environment: '*BlueSky* participants ... enact a form of masculinity congruent with computer culture, itself a largely masculine domain. ... Not all ... currently work with computers, but most have done so at some time' (Kendall 2002: 73). The collective production of sociability here also has its constitutive outside, as demonstrated by the way in which 'the style of interaction ... excludes most women' (Kendall 2002: 100), even though Kendall reports becoming a 'full participant' in the culture in the course of her own ethnographic investigation. As a consequence, she remains highly suspicious of claims that life in cyberspace is broadly democratic or egalitarian. In her view, it is 'a realm populated mostly by the white and middle class and is still largely dominated by men' (Kendall 2002: 221).

Conversationalisation

Language use figured as a significant topic in my review of work on sociability. I looked, for instance, at Scannell's ideas about broadcast talk (Scannell 1991; 1996) and at the core sequences of mundane telephone call openings (Schegloff 1986; Hutchby 2001). Another contemporary cultural theorist, who can help us to shed light on this general topic of media and language, particularly on the 'conversationalisation' of media and other public discourses, is Norman Fairclough (1992; 1994; 1995). Although he is not an advocate of the kind of conversation analysis done by Schegloff (instead, his approach is known as 'critical language study' or 'critical discourse analysis'), Fairclough does have an interest in the relevance of informal, conversational styles of talk in modern society. However, he is quite unwilling to set aside issues of power and politics in investigations of communication. Indeed, power is a fundamental concept in his mode of critical discourse analysis (see especially Fairclough 1989).

Outlining what he understands to be the principal discursive features of social change, Fairclough (1992: 204) identifies some of the ways in which 'conversational discourse has been and is being projected from its primary domain, in the personal interactions of the private sphere, into the public sphere'. This is seen, on the one hand, as a 'manifestation of increasing infor-mality' in social life today (for further discussion of the wider 'informalisation' process, see Chaney 2002). On the other hand, Fairclough (1994: 253) views the conversationalisation of public discourse as 'overlapping' with a 'partially independent' process of 'commodification': 'the reconstruction of, for instance, public services on the analogy of commodity markets'.

A concrete example of the overlapping processes in operation is an under-graduate prospectus produced by Fairclough's own university in the UK. His analysis of this document focuses on the pages informing prospective students of an American studies degree. He argues that the public service of higher education now constructs students as consumers, employing the 'promotional' discourses (Wernick 1991) typically found in advertising in order to market and 'sell' its 'commodities'. Accompanying that commodification of learning is the adoption of a conversational style often seen in modern advertising. In the case of the prospectus pages Fairclough analyses, this style incorporates relatively informal direct address to the reader. So, in the statement of entry qualification requirements that are imposed on applicants, the wording is 'you will need' rather than, say, 'you must have' or 'we require' (see Fairclough 1994: 256–7). Within the terms of his analysis, that direct address would be perceived as an instance of 'synthetic personalization … the manipulation of "interpersonal" … forms for strategic and instrumental purposes' (Fairclough 1994: 257).

In a specialised study of 'media discourse', Fairclough (1995) sets out a similar perspective on language use in broadcasting. There, he links the 'marketisation' of media, which has to do with 'increasing commercial pressures and competition' in the industry, with 'the tendency of public affairs media to become increasingly conversationalized' as the 'boundary between public affairs and entertainment' is relaxed (Fairclough 1995: 10–11). One of his many examples of conversationalisation in broadcast output is drawn from a news magazine programme in which the male host presents himself to the audience members as 'an ordinary bloke talking to ordinary people, sharing with them a common "lifeworld"', where conversationalisation is 'realized in a variety of linguistic features … items of colloquial vocabulary … and … conversational narrative' (Fairclough 1995: 10).

Fairclough does not regard the link between commodification, or marketisa-tion, and conversationalisation as inevitable. He concedes, implicitly to Scannell, that the growing use of informal language on radio and television may 'represent some degree of cultural democratization … raising the status of the language and experience of ordinary life', but insists (following Fowler 1991) that conversationalisation can have an 'ideological function' too, frequently serving to naturalise and legitimise dominant constructions of reality:

> To put the issue rather baldly, do conversationalized discourse practices manifest a real shift in power relations in favour of ordinary people, or are they to be seen merely as a strategy on the part of those with power

to more effectively recruit people as audiences and manipulate them socially and politically?

(Fairclough 1995: 13)

Ultimately, his answer is that the communicative style of broadcasting 'lies at the intersection of ... democratizing, legitimizing and marketizing pressures, and its ambivalence follows from that' (Fairclough 1995: 149).

Face

Earlier in the chapter, Erving Goffman's writings were cited as an important contribution to the literature on human communications (for commentaries, see Drew and Wootton 1988; Manning 1992). My starting point for this section and the next is a particular observation of his, that in circumstances of physical co-presence the participants in social encounters routinely carry out 'face-work' (Goffman 1967). The concept of face that he outlines there is taken up and developed by Penelope Brown and Stephen Levinson (1987) in their later analysis of 'politeness', and I want to show how these notions of face and politeness are also applicable in the study of mediated or mediated quasi-interactions. To support my case, I will refer to an investigation of 'broadcast troubles-talk' on a radio phone-in programme (Atkinson and Moores 2003), but in order to prepare the way for that discussion we need to comprehend something, first of all, about the thinking of Goffman, Brown and Levinson on 'attention to face' in interaction.

Following Goffman's lead, Brown and Levinson (1987) understand face to be the 'public self-image' of the participant in an encounter. It is 'something that is emotionally invested, and that can be lost, maintained or enhanced, and must be constantly attended to in interaction' (Brown and Levinson 1987: 61). Identifying two different aspects of face, they assume social actors to have, and (at least at the level of practical consciousness) to know each other to have, both 'negative face' and 'positive face'. The former is defined as the implicit desire of an individual not to be 'impeded' or put upon by others, related to what Goffman terms a person's 'defensive orientation', while the latter is bound up with a basic wish for her or his self-image to be 'approved of'.

Although Brown and Levinson assume people have a tendency to be 'heedful' of the 'face wants' of others in social interaction (see Goffman 1967: 14, who calls this 'a protective orientation toward saving the others' face'), they proceed to point out that there are various kinds of speech act which could 'threaten' face. They draw a distinction here 'between acts that threaten negative face and those that threaten positive face' (Brown and Levinson 1987: 67). For instance, acts with the potential to threaten an addressee's negative face include the speaker making a request, issuing an order or giving advice, while those potentially threatening an addressee's positive face include the speaker expressing disagreement or disapproval.

When speakers perform, for whatever reason, a potentially 'face-threatening act', they do so 'baldly, without redress' or else with 'redressive action'. In the first of these, the speech act is carried out 'in the most direct, clear, unambiguous and concise way possible' (Brown and Levinson 1987: 69), whereas, in the second, there is an attempt to minimise any potential 'face damage' by indicating that the face wants of an addressee have still been taken into account in the design of the utterance. Goffman would say 'a standard of considerateness' has been upheld. Redressive action is directed towards either negative or positive face, and this brings us to the crucial arguments Brown and Levinson make about tactful, cooperative 'politeness strategies'.

'Negative politeness' involves attending to and 'redressing' an addressee's negative face, her or his basic claim to freedom from imposition. A typical strategy is the use of 'hedging' devices, which will be discussed below with reference to a specific instance of phone-in talk. 'Positive politeness', on the other hand, 'is redress directed to the addressee's positive face' (Brown and Levinson 1987: 101). Examples of positive politeness offered by Brown and Levinson are the paying of compliments and the use of 'in-group identity markers' to construct solidarity (such as forms of familiar address or colloquial discourse styles). Laughter, if it is appropriately positioned in the interaction, may also be a way of doing positive politeness, since it can indicate a sharing of values.

In my view, Brown and Levinson (building on Goffman) provide some valuable theoretical tools with which to approach talk-in-interaction, whether that talk is found in face-to-face behaviour (Goffman 1967) or in technologically mediated communication. However, if we are to borrow these tools for the purposes of media analysis, then criticism of their work should be taken on board. Most importantly, there is a difficulty with the way in which 'politeness theory purports to be universal' (Jaworski and Coupland 1999: 296). Attempts to apply this theory always require sensitivity to cultural contexts and variations. For example, the linguist Shoshana Blum-Kulka (1997: 54), referring to findings from her own empirical research on language use among Jewish families in Israel, remarks on how 'an emphasis on sincerity and truthfulness in interpersonal relations overrides the importance of avoiding infringement of the other, licensing (especially in the private sphere) high levels of directness'. To assume, therefore, that particular sorts of speech act are, in the abstract, necessarily threats to face or expressions of politeness, would be problematic. As Adam Jaworski and Nikolas Coupland (1999: 296) comment, similar utterances 'may be perceived as an imposition in one group but as an act of camaraderie in another'.

There is actually an interesting parallel between the licensed 'directness' of interpersonal communication observed by Blum-Kulka and elements of the broadcast talk that I will now present as my illustration of the operations of face and politeness in media settings (drawing on Atkinson and Moores 2003).

In both cases, then, an emphasis is put 'on sincerity and truthfulness'. My concern here is with transcribed extracts from a radio phone-in programme in the 1990s called *Live and Direct*, which was hosted each weekday on Talk Radio in the UK by Anna Raeburn, who is one of the best-known 'agony aunts' to have worked in British broadcasting (see Barnard 2000). This show falls within a genre that Andrew Crisell (1994) names 'the confessional phone-in', in which callers disclose personal problems on air and make a request for help, before being given advice by the host. Since the electronically mediated communication, via broadcasting and telephone, involves practices of 'troubles-telling' (Jefferson and Lee 1992), in addition to requests and advice giving, the mediated encounters between host and callers might have certain 'face implications' (although Raeburn's prior 'soliciting' of the troubles-telling clearly lessens the weight of any initial imposition when someone rings up and discloses a problem).

The title of the programme captures its intended immediacy and spontaneity, and the fact that callers are linked directly to the studio by telephone. At the same time, the word 'direct' could well be related to the host's style of 'straight talking' at the microphone. She has a directness that is bound up with her presentation of self to audiences as sincere and truthful, as well as ordinary and trustworthy. So, in one of the monologues by which the programme gets introduced (see Atkinson and Moores 2003: 133), Raeburn offers listeners 'an honest plaster' for emotional wounds, committing herself to speaking 'the uncomfortable truth as I see it' (as well as openly admitting, 'I'm human too ... just as fallible just as vulnerable just as bashed about and world weary as you are'). This directness, as she acknowledges in her monologue, might not appear to be 'polite', yet even when the listener is warned 'you may not hear (.) what you want to hear' (in Atkinson and Moores 2003: 133) it can be argued that she is still doing positive politeness of a sort. There is a popular saying that only close friends are able to 'tell it like it is'. By employing such a strategy on occasion, the host is not simply posing a threat to the negative face of callers, but also 'paying them the compliment' of being a sincere, honest friend. In other words, Raeburn's straight talking must be interpreted in the context of 'a continuing relationship' (Horton and Wohl 1986) she looks to develop with her audience members. Indeed, there is evidence in transcriptions of the phone-in talk that at least some callers relate to the host as a 'regular and dependable' presence in their lives. For example, a woman tells the host: 'I enjoy listening to you so much and I feel now as though I'm talking to a friend Anna (.) I feel that close to you' (in Atkinson and Moores 2003: 135).

Compliments paid to the host live on air have the potential to 'enhance' her positive face, as do displays of modesty in response to callers' expressions of approval. Such a dynamic may be seen in the following transcribed extract from an interaction, on which I will be concentrating, between Raeburn (R) and a caller named Paula (P):

1	R:	how then can I help you
2	P:	well I it it just really is a voice of
3		sanity
4	R:	(laughs) oh my dear you couldn't have
5		chosen a worse person go on
		[ ]
6	P:	(laughs)
7	R:	(laughs again)
8	P:	I could believe me

(in Atkinson and Moores 2003: 141)

The host's denial that she has 'a voice of sanity', on line 4, might be read as 'doing being modest' (and as 'doing being ordinary', see Sacks 1984; 1995). On lines 2 and 3, Paula compliments Raeburn, who then chooses to make light of it. A joke is made at the host's own expense (lines 4 and 5) and the caller, as a regular listener who is familiar with the presenter's persona, is able to share in the humour. It is worth noticing, too, the host's use of 'my dear' on line 4, which is a form of familiar address that Brown and Levinson associate with positive politeness.

Before moving on to consider the next transcribed extract, it is necessary to reflect further on what conversation analyst Gail Jefferson (1984) would term the organisation of laughter in the extract above. At a difficult moment in the telephone call, after Paula has narrated her personal problem, partly in tears (her husband has had a succession of strokes that have left him hospitalised), Raeburn seems to be using laughter on line 4 not only to display modesty but also as a way of releasing some of the tension that has built up. What interests me more, though, is the 'turn' at laughing taken by the caller on line 6, followed on line 7 by the host's act of laughing again. As Jefferson (1984: 348) remarks, 'recipient laughter by reference to a prior speaker's laughter is a recurrent phenomenon in ordinary conversation'. Laughter is often sequenced, coordinated and 'methodical'.

I have previously noted Raeburn's investment in honesty. She presents herself as somebody who is prepared to tell the truth, even when it is 'uncomfortable', and the following transcription (Atkinson and Moores 2003: 142) serves as an illustration of that sincere, direct approach. The host 'baldly' issues and repeats a forthright declaration to Paula on lines 1 and 2, and she subsequently goes on to depict a painful situation into which the caller could be placed in the future (lines 4 to 6):

1	R:	you will adapt you will adapt because you
2		haven't got any flippin' option
3	P:	that's right
4	R:	and you'll have days when you come home
5		shut (.) the front door and burst into
6		tears
7	P:	yes

A couple of things ought to be mentioned here, since they back up an earlier argument about the need to analyse straight talking in context. While there is a potential threat to the caller's negative face, given the directness of the host's speech, the colloquial term 'flippin' on line 2 is an in-group identity marker (identifying Raeburn with the ordinary 'lifeworld' of audience members) that could be viewed as an expression of positive politeness, as might her willingness to tell it to Paula 'like it is'. Furthermore, it is noticeable that the caller states agreement on line 3 with the advice given and utters a 'supportive minimal response' (Holmes 1995) on line 7. These actions appear to indicate that she is not offended by the host's words.

However, the highly sensitive nature of the problem leads the host to modify her discourse later, when she gets round to talking about the inevitable death of Paula's husband, by employing 'hedges', metaphor and euphemism:

```
1     R:    it wouldn't be responsible for him to be
2           home with you if he's having strokes at
3           that rate
4     P:    no
5     R:    and if they are I mean the (.) pure
6           meaning of stroke as I understand it is a
7           brain death and if he's having little  ones
                           [        ]
8     P:                  that's right
9           yes=
10    R:    =then he can continue for a long time but
11          it is like a light being threatened in a
12          wind it's it blows ov it blows out and
13          almost out and then it comes back again =
14    P:    =that's right (.) yes =
15    R:    =and it diminishes slowly (.) so I think
16          that the only thing you can do is to
17          prepare yourself for what I would call (.)
18          I hope without offending you
19    P:    yes oh yeah=
20    R:    =the long day's dying
```

                                    (in Atkinson and Moores 2003: 143)

Hedging devices, as Janet Holmes (1995: 74) explains, are frequently used as expressions of negative politeness, since they serve to 'attenuate or reduce the strength of the utterance', to 'damp down its force or intensity or directness'. In Brown and Levinson's terms, they are a form of redressive action taken by the speaker, intended to limit the potential damage of a face-threatening act to an addressee's negative face. Looking at this passage of talk, examples of hedging ('I mean', 'as I understand it', 'what I would call (.) I hope without offending you') can be found on lines 5 and 6, and lines 17 and 18. Also, in referring to a candle flame on lines 11 to 13 and line 15, or in using the phrase 'the long day's dying' on line 20, Raeburn is treading carefully with poetic language.

Friendliness

While she does not cite Goffman (1967) or Brown and Levinson (1987), communications researcher Nancy Baym (2000) offers an analysis of computer-mediated interaction that clearly connects with their way of thinking about face and politeness. Her study is of messages that are 'posted' by members of an internet 'newsgroup' which is devoted to a discussion of television soap operas. Taking into consideration the specific topic of discussion there, it is perhaps not surprising that the majority of 'posters' identify themselves as women (on the feminine cultural competences called on by soap opera as a genre, see, for instance, Brunsdon 1981). This is, then, one sector of cyberspace that appears not to be, as Kendall (2002) put it, 'dominated by men'. A significant part of Baym's study is about 'the creation of friendliness' among newsgroup partici-pants. She gives her analysis of this phenomenon an ethnomethodological twist by insisting that friendliness in social interaction is 'not a given' but rather a 'communicative accomplishment'. For Baym (2000: 121), being friendly is 'something a group does rather than something a group is' (Baym 2000: 121).

If friendliness is an accomplishment, we need to ask how it is accomplished in particular situations, including mediated situations of the kind observed by Baym. In the specific case of the newsgroup in which she participated, a degree of disagreement, potentially a threat to face, was inevitable as posters were giving their varied opinions on the stories and characters in soaps. Her interest, though, is in 'the behaviors they use to construct disagreements that attend to the ethic of friendliness' (Baym 2000: 123). This is precisely what Brown and Levinson would term the politeness strategies of group members.

An example of the strategies that are employed is when participants preface disagreements with 'partial agreements', so as to build 'social alignment' or soli-darity before taking issue with a previously expressed view. Those partial agreements involve making statements like 'I thought the same thing, too' and 'at first, I'll admit, I thought Nat was being very stupid' (see Baym 2000: 125–6, for the dialogues from which these statements are lifted). Another discourse strategy Baym (2000: 124) points to is the use of 'qualifiers' to frame disagreements: 'Qualification leaves room for the poster to turn out to be wrong ... reducing the threat to the other's position.' The following passage is from an exchange concerning developments in an American serial, *All My Children*, and it includes a number of these qualifiers, which Baym (2000: 124) highlights for us:

> *I may be wrong*, but *I thought* Brooke did invite Carter Jones. *I actually thought* he *may* be covering the event as a reporter. Seeing as how

Brooke started the homeless shelter, *I would think* that would give her some say in who may attend a fund raiser.

Qualifications or hedges of this sort are designed to 'mitigate' any offence to other group members taking part in the discussion. They constitute face-work in an electronically mediated interaction.

Doubling

To conclude this chapter, I return to ideas about 'doubling' that first arose towards the end of the last one. In thinking there about media and the transformation of localities, we encountered Scannell's conception of the doubling of place (Scannell 1996). My argument here is that, when place gets doubled in practices of electronic media use, it is necessary for us to recognise how social relationships can be pluralised too (see also Moores 2004). There are opportunities in late modern societies, at least for those with the economic and cultural means to access relevant communication technologies, for relating instantaneously to a wide range of spatially remote others, as well as to any proximate others in the physical settings of media use. Both these modes of relating to others merit our careful consideration, as does the complex interplay between them. Indeed, the notion of a 'doubling of interaction' provides another way of theorising the changing interaction mix of social life (Thompson 1995).

My initial point of reference for this exploration of pluralised relationships (and realities) is research done in the USA by James Lull (1980; 1990) on the 'social uses of television' in household cultures. He has helped to pioneer an approach that bridges the established academic division between studies of 'mass' and 'interpersonal' communications, asking about the part played by television viewing in 'family communication patterns': 'Television and other mass media ... can now be seen to play central roles in the methods which families and other social units employ to interact' (Lull 1990: 29). In this regard, his work can be compared with that of Meyrowitz (see Gumpert and Cathcart 1986, to which both Lull and Meyrowitz are contributors), although Lull's writings are based on detailed empirical investigations of audiences and the theoretical positions he adopts are rather different.

Like Baym (2000), Lull is interested in the perspective of ethnomethodology, referring, for example, to the collected writings of Harold Garfinkel (1984). The broadly conceived objects of study in that strand of social theory, which in Lull's words 'influenced me greatly', are the 'ethnomethods' of lay individuals:

Ethnomethods are the common, often taken-for-granted actions that people construct in order to organize and make meaningful the most routine aspects of everyday life. The ethnomethodological approach focuses on how social actors accomplish these fundamental operations of everyday life, including, of course, the construction of routine communication activity. Any human behavior can be considered ethnomethodologically: walking, talking, viewing television.

(Lull 1990: 11)

In his ethnomethodological consideration of television viewing (for a similar perspective on talking, one of the other social practices listed above, see Miller and McHoul 1998), Lull is also borrowing certain insights from the 'uses and gratifications' tradition of media inquiry (Blumler and Katz 1974; Rosengren *et al.* 1985). A key question within that tradition is how media function as resources that are appropriated by people in their day-to-day lives so as to gratify 'needs'. He is able to pursue this problem a stage further by taking 'the household group', rather than simply 'the individual viewer', as his main unit of audience analysis.

Lull (1980; 1990) presents us with a 'social uses typology', in which the emphasis is on 'relational uses' of television in the domestic environment. It is in this presentation of his findings that we see evidence of a pluralisation of relationships or a mixing of interactions. For instance, a relational use to which television is routinely put is what he names 'communication facilitation' (that is, the facilitation of interpersonal communication between family members, or else between family members and visitors from outside). Far from killing the art of conversation, Lull (1990: 37–8) is proposing that television's 'characters, stories and themes' serve as topics for opening conversations:

> The medium is used as a convenient resource for entertaining guests in the home. To turn on the set ... is to introduce instant common ground. Strangers in the home may then indulge in 'television talk' – verbal responses to television programs ... allow audience members to discuss topics of common experience which probably have little personal importance. Television viewing under these circumstances provides ... an exercise in conversational form for the interlocutors. In this way, viewers become better acquainted but invest minimal personal risk.

From our point of view in the current chapter, it could be said that he is describing an 'intermingling' of mediated quasi-interaction, or para-interaction, at a distance with face-to-face communication in the immediate surroundings of the living room (yet the precise scene painted in the extract will not be reproduced in all living rooms, since the cultural conventions associated with 'entertaining guests' are varied). Incidentally, his understanding of television use in everyday life, as creating 'instant common ground' and 'topics of common experience' for mundane talk, fits neatly with Scannell's assertions about the sociable function of broadcasting.

Media situations 'overlay' (Kendall 2002) local physical settings, with symbolic materials from the one being appropriated for 'affiliation' purposes (Lull 1990) in the other (and vice-versa, because 'talk on television' often incorporates styles of lay expression, see Livingstone and Lunt 1994). This over-laying of physical location with 'media place', and the consequent doubling of interaction, is also captured in Schegloff's remark, quoted in the previous chapter, that 'there are two "theres" there' in moments of mobile phone use (Schegloff 2002: 287). I now want to go back to his notes on mobile phones (or cell phones) and changing social relationships, and, in particular, to a brief story that he tells. His story is 'set' on a train carriage in New York and, to be precise, on an occasion of telephonic talk-in-interaction too:

> A young woman is talking on the cell phone, apparently to her boyfriend, with whom she is in something of a crisis. Her voice projects in far-from-dulcet tones. Most of the passengers take up a physical and postural stance of busying themselves with other foci of attention (their reading matter, the scene passing by the train's windows, etc.), busy doing 'not overhearing this conversation'. ... Except for one passenger. And when the protagonist of this tale has her eyes intersect this fellow-passenger's gaze, she calls out in outraged protest, 'Do you mind?! This is a private conversation!'
>
> (Schegloff 2002: 285–6)

He does not state it explicitly but his narrative describes, in my view, plural and competing information flows, and therefore plural and competing definitions of the situation.

Schegloff's protagonist, who is physically on a train journey, a 'moving-between-places' (Casey 1993), protests that she is having a 'private conversation'. Whilst her assertion is in some ways surprising, given that she is speaking 'in far-from-dulcet tones' and so her voice is audible to other passengers in the same 'railroad car' (and while this assertion is also a possible source of humour in the narrative), there are still signs that could support such an indignant expression of personal experience: 'this young woman is talking to her boyfriend, about intimate matters, in the usual conversational manner – except for the argumentative mode, and this also, perhaps especially, makes it a private conversation' (Schegloff 2002: 286). Curiously, almost all of the fellow passengers collaborate to support this woman's view, 'doing "not overhearing this conversation"'. They cannot help overhearing the argument, at least a single side of it, yet they pretend not to hear, busily looking down at their 'reading matter' or out of the carriage windows, thereby avoiding eye contact with the mobile phone user so as not to intrude openly on another's intimate business (a case of what Goffman 1963 calls 'civil inattention'). Of course, there is a single passenger who, as Schegloff's tale implies, refuses to accept the performed pretence, perhaps as a result of being irritated by the intrusion of private talk into a public setting. What I am proposing is that, at the point where eye contact is made, the two 'theres' there (the two sets of interaction and the situations they define) end up 'colliding' with each other.

Just one more example of the doubling of place and interaction will suffice, and it is taken from the work of internet researcher Nina Wakeford (1999). She chooses to investigate the intersection of online 'landscapes', 'frequently described as "cyberspace" or "the virtual" ', with 'a "real" place' (Wakeford 1999: 180–1), an internet café in London where she was employed for several months as a 'cyberhost' providing assistance to customers. Her concern in looking at these social settings is principally with the constitution of gender relations, offline as well as on.

Contrary to utopian visions of cyberspace having liberated people completely 'from the restrictions of embodiment', and having created a 'gender-free or even gender-equal' virtual environment, Wakeford (1999: 179–80) insists, in line with the thinking of Kendall (2002), that 'traditional images and experiences of gender persist in most Internet fora'. In any case, her argument continues, also roughly in line with Kendall's, with an observation that the 'landscapes of computing' are 'not restricted to' the realms of the virtual (and see Slevin 2000). The setting of the internet café, then, serves as 'a translation landscape of computing where the Internet is … interpreted for "ordinary people" who consume time on the machines, and/or food and drink' (Wakeford 1999: 180). Indeed, it is a physical environment in which bodies are very much present. What makes the café setting that she worked in particularly interesting is the attempt by its owners to encourage customers to 'see the Internet as a place where women could participate' (Wakeford 1999: 180). However, while women are to be found in the café floor area in significant numbers, either as customers or cyberhosts, Wakeford reports that the business' everyday operation still depends on a team of mainly male technical support staff and 'system administrators' with 'expert knowledge', located on the top floor of the building.

Chapter 3 began by outlining Thompson's typology of interactions and his thoughts on the changing interaction mix of social life. With particular emphasis on the pioneering work done by Horton and Wohl on intimacy at a distance (an influence on Thompson), it was observed that there are now some quite distinctive sorts of relationship between physically absent others. I was critical of these theorists, though, for their pathologisation of certain social groups, and for the way in which they ultimately privilege the face-to-face over technologically mediated communications. Scannell's phenomenology of fun in broadcasting was then examined, leading to a more general exploration of the cultural and linguistic dimensions of mediated sociability, with a focus on forms of sociable interaction found in telephone and internet dialogues. Following case studies of politeness strategies used in mediated and mediated quasi-interactions, the chapter concluded with my reflections on the doubling of social relationships. One of the advantages of this notion of doubling or pluralisation, and also of ideas about a simultaneous mixing of interactions, is that they allow for a consideration of how physical and mediated proximities intersect, having various relational consequences.

4

SIGNIFICATION

So far, in the second part of this book, I have already touched on a number of theoretical approaches to the study of interaction that could be said to deal, at least implicitly, with the making of meanings in social life. From the perspective of ethnomethodology and conversation analysis, for instance, the significance of an expression or utterance depends to a large degree on its evolving contexts. For conversation analysts this includes, principally, its position within ordered sequences of talk-in-interaction, such as those typically found in telephone call openings. To take another example, Paddy Scannell's phenomenological approach to broadcasting and its care-structures is generally designed to disclose 'the output of radio and television in its meaningfulness' (Scannell 1996: 148). My main focus in the current chapter, though, will be on issues of signification or meaning construction, as well as on related issues of taste and cultural value (which are more closely associated with and more explicitly addressed by a critical, cultural studies perspective on media and communications in modern society). I begin and end here by referring to the work of Roland Barthes (see especially Barthes 1973; 1984), starting with an account of his influential, but ultimately flawed, analysis of French popular cultural images in the 1950s and 1960s, and finishing with a discussion of some personal reflections that he offers much later on the medium of photography. In between these sections, my commentary charts a series of conceptual developments in 'social-semiotic theory' that serve to draw our attention to different dimensions of signification, textuality and social context.

Connotation

In his early writings, Barthes is concerned to develop a kind of analysis that he calls 'semiology', more usually referred to nowadays as semiotics. He takes his lead for this project from a speculative proposal made many years before, in the first part of the twentieth century, by Ferdinand de Saussure (1983) in the discipline of linguistics. 'It is ... possible', says Saussure (1983: 15), 'to conceive of a science which studies the role of signs as part of social life.' Like Claude Lévi-Strauss (1977) in social anthropology, Barthes' interest is in applying some of the principles of Saussurean linguistics to the wider study of cultures, helping to bring into existence that 'general science of signs, or semiology' (Barthes 1968: 9) foreseen by Saussure. For Barthes, the growth of mass communication in the modern world provides a justification for such an approach, since he argues there is a pressing requirement to understand the role of media in contemporary 'systems of signification'.

For an initial explanation and illustration of the cultural theory of the 'sign' in semiotics, we might usefully look at an essay by Barthes (1977) on what he terms the 'rhetoric' of the image. His example in the essay is a French advertising poster used to publicise food products sold by a company named 'Panzani': 'Here we have a Panzani advertisement: some packets of pasta, a tin, a sachet, some tomatoes, onions, peppers, a mushroom, all emerging from a half-open string bag, in yellows and greens on a red background' (Barthes 1977: 33). In considering this photographic image, he identifies, on the one hand, a 'denotation' or 'literal message'. The photograph (a 'signifier') denotes a certain scene (the 'signified'), which is described for us by Barthes in the quotation above.

All signs, as Saussure points out, are 'bipartite', divided in two. They involve a link between signifier and signified, and Saussure (1983: 67) insists that in language the relation between them is 'arbitrary': 'There is no internal connection, for example, between the idea "sister" and the French sequence of sounds *s-ö-r*.' Indeed, this arbitrary linkage can be demonstrated by thinking about the way in which other languages have a different sequence of sounds for the same basic 'idea'. A photographic signifier, by contrast, does typically bear a close resemblance to its signified at the level of denotation. Semioticians would say that the relationship is 'motivated', although there is still a separation between the material image and the objects that are represented.

On the other hand, in the extract reproduced below, Barthes (1977: 34–5) identifies a lengthy series of additional, 'symbolic' messages at the level of 'connotation':

> First (the order is unimportant as these signs are not linear), the idea that what we have in the scene ... is a return from the market. A signified which itself implies two euphoric values: that of the freshness of the products and that of the essentially domestic preparation for which they are destined. Its signifier is the half-open bag which lets the provisions spill out over the table, 'unpacked'. ... A second sign is more or less equally evident; its signifier is the bringing together of the tomato, the pepper and the tricoloured hues (yellow, green, red) of the poster; its signified is Italy or rather Italianicity. This sign stands in a relation of redundancy with the connoted sign of the linguistic message (the Italian assonance of the name Panzani) and ... there is no difficulty in discovering at least two other signs: in the first, the serried collection of different objects transmits the idea of a total culinary service ... as

though Panzani furnished everything necessary for a carefully balanced dish and ... as though the concentrate in the tin were equivalent to the natural produce surrounding it; in the other sign, the composition of the image, evoking the memory of innumerable alimentary paintings, sends us to an aesthetic signified ... the 'still life'.

The denotative sign, then, serves as 'the support of' these various symbolic messages. Expressing it the other way round, 'a system of connotation ... takes over the signs of another system in order to make them its signifiers' (Barthes 1977: 37). As Barthes (1973: 114) puts it elsewhere, connotative signs (the realm of what he terms 'myth') are part of a 'second-order semiological system', and so 'that which is a sign ... in the first system becomes a mere signifier in the second'.

Myth is a central concept in Barthes' early work (Barthes 1973; 1979), and it equates roughly with the concept of 'ideology' that is found in the vocabulary of Marxist theory. In order to understand his use of this term, we must now turn to a further image that he describes and analyses:

I am at the barber's, and a copy of *Paris-Match* is offered to me. On the cover, a young Negro in a French uniform is saluting, with his eyes uplifted, probably fixed on a fold of the tricolour. ... I see very well what it signifies to me: that France is a great Empire, that all her sons, without any colour discrimination, faithfully serve under her flag, and that there is no better answer to the detractors of an alleged colonialism than the zeal shown by this Negro in serving his so-called oppressors ... there is a signifier, itself already formed with a previous system (a black soldier is giving the French salute); there is a signified (it is here a purposeful mixture of Frenchness and militariness).

(Barthes 1973: 116)

This is, according to Barthes at least, the connotation of the photograph of the young black soldier on the magazine cover, which he looks at while waiting for a haircut. His assertion is that such a connotation has a mythical or an ideological function, giving colonial relations of power the appearance of an eternal and 'harmonious' state of affairs. He offers us a broad definition of myth as the transformation of history into nature, pointing to how 'myth organizes a world ... wallowing in the evident', so that, for instance, 'French imperiality ... goes without saying' (Barthes 1973: 143). Indeed, his definition is strikingly similar to the way in which the Marxist philosopher Louis Althusser (1984) writes about ideology as the imposition of 'obviousnesses'.

Within British, and Australian, media and cultural studies, there have been several attempts to borrow the style of cultural criticism that Barthes developed, in an effort to 'demythologise' contemporary popular cultures (see, for instance, Masterman 1984; Easthope 1986; Fiske *et al.* 1987). Perhaps the most interesting attempt to pursue his particular line of semiotic inquiry is a book by Rosalind Coward (1984), which provides a feminist critique of myth. Rather like Barthes, she examines images in food advertising and on magazine covers, but I want to take her analysis of television nature programmes as my example of the critical perspective she adopts. If Barthes is proposing that myth gives historically specific social arrangements the appearance of 'the natural', then Coward (1984: 213) observes how the nature programme's commentary seems to do precisely this by being 'often intensely anthropomorphic', by which she means 'that all sorts of human ... attributes are projected on to the behaviour of animals'. 'We encounter', writes Coward (1984: 212), 'the "dominant" male defending his "territory"; the hierarchies between males in their access to females; ... females ... assuming submissive postures ... endless examples of home-making and parental provision.' Of course, to naturalise gender relations and inequalities is to represent them as beyond challenge or social change.

These 'readings' of images and sounds (of 'media texts', in the jargon of semiotics) are engaging, and are clearly intended by Barthes and Coward to contribute to a politicisation of culture. However, I want to argue that there is a basic problem with the sort of semiotic approach they are advocating. It is neces- sary for us to ask, quite simply, about the status of their interpretations, since there is a danger of them assuming that the connotations they identify are gener- ally available to all those people who come into contact with the texts. Neither Barthes nor Coward actually seeks to investigate the interpretations that are made by 'lay readers'. In response to my criticism of their work, it might well be objected that when we are dealing with matters of myth or ideology, meanings are so naturalised (and therefore 'unconscious', in the psychoanalytical sense in which Althusser uses this term) that they are difficult for most people to express in words because they go 'without saying'. The purpose of semiotics, for writers like Barthes and Coward, is to make readers discursively conscious of myth so that it can be contested. Furthermore, even if we were able to get people to talk about the media images and sounds they encounter in everyday life, it is impor- tant for us to remember that their words would still constitute a text to be read.

Nevertheless, my own preference is for an approach to signification that allows for the possibility of multiple, socially patterned interpretations, and which sets out to explore empirically these potentially varied constructions of meaning. I will soon be referring to some research of this kind on the 'decoding' of television programmes by viewers. In preparation for that discus- sion, though, we need to consider an alternative perspective on meaning construction, which is associated in particular with the linguistics of Valentin Volosinov (1986).

Multiaccentuality

Writing in the Soviet Union in the late 1920s, Volosinov (1986) elaborates a distinctive 'social semiotics' of language (see Hodge and Kress 1988) from the perspective of Marxism. Quite unlike Barthes and other structuralist or post-structuralist academics, he does not take his lead from Saussure (neither is Volosinov influenced by Freud's psychoanalysis, as Althusser was via the work of Lacan 1977). In fact, his approach to language is at odds with what he labels the 'abstract objectivism' of Saussurean linguistics.

Whereas Saussure (1983) delimits his object of study by dividing '*langue*' from '*parole*' (that is, by separating 'language as a structured system' from instances of speech, giving the former pride of place in his linguistics), Volosinov (1986: 21) insists: 'The sign may not be divorced from the concrete forms of social intercourse.' Although Saussure (1983: 15) encourages us, as we saw earlier, to understand 'the role of signs as part of social life', Volosinov argues that the emphasis on trying to abstract a 'linguistic structure' actually prevents him from coming to terms with the construction of meanings in 'living' interaction. Any attempted abstraction of this sort 'is not adequate to the concrete reality of language', which is in practice 'a continuous generative process implemented in the social-verbal interaction of speakers' (Volosinov 1986: 98).

Similarly, while Saussure's conceptualisation of language as 'a social institution' rests on the assumption that there will be shared meanings within a common 'linguistic community', Volosinov (1986) puts an emphasis instead on the 'multiaccentuality' of the sign. He focuses, then, on the 'intersecting of differently oriented social interests within one and the same sign community':

> Class does not coincide with the sign community, i.e. with the community which is the totality of users of the same set of signs. ... Thus various different classes will use one and the same language. As a result, differently oriented accents intersect in every ideological sign. Sign becomes an arena of class struggle. This social multiaccentuality of the ideological sign is a very crucial aspect.
>
> (Volosinov 1986: 23)

In other words, he chooses to emphasise the contestation of, or struggle over, meaning in language use. His definition of 'accent' is therefore much wider than that which is typically found in the field of sociolinguistics. It may be the case that a powerful group in society (for him, the 'ruling class') 'strives to impart a supra-class, eternal character to the ideological sign ... make the sign uniaccentual' (Volosinov 1986: 23). This is what Barthes would call the production of bourgeois myth. Yet the potential plurality of meanings cannot, Volosinov asserts, ever be completely closed down in the interests of a single social group.

I want to come back now to each of these closely related points that are made by Volosinov as he rejects two of Saussure's central claims about language. Let us start with his call to study utterances in the context of 'social intercourse', a call that anticipates much later developments in discourse pragmatics (see Blum-Kulka 1997). In an essay on language as discourse, he gives

107

'an intentionally simplified example' to illustrate his case that an utterance is related to its immediate social situation:

> Two people are sitting in a room. They are both silent. Then one of them says, 'Well!' The other does not respond. For us, as outsiders, this entire 'conversation' is utterly incomprehensible. Taken in isolation, the utterance 'Well!' is empty and unintelligible. Nevertheless, this peculiar colloquy of two persons, consisting of only one ... word, does make perfect sense, is fully meaningful and complete. In order to disclose the sense and meaning of this colloquy, we must analyze it. But what is it exactly that we can subject to analysis? Whatever pains we take with the purely verbal part of the utterance ... we shall still not come a single step closer to an understanding of the whole sense of the colloquy. ... What is it we lack, then? We lack the 'extraverbal context' that made the word ... a meaningful locution for the listener. This extraverbal context of the utterance is comprised of three factors: (1) the common spatial purview of the interlocutors ... (2) the interlocutors' common knowledge and understanding of the situation ... (3) their common evaluation of that situation.
>
> (Volosinov 1976: 99)

He goes on to explain that, around the time the single word was spoken, 'both interlocutors looked up at the window and saw that it had begun to snow; both knew that ... it was high time for spring to come; finally, both were sick and tired of the protracted winter' (Volosinov 1976: 99). There is a jointly seen, known and evaluated context that makes this socially situated speech act meaningful for the participants directly involved in the interaction.

It is worth noting here how Volosinov is interested, to a certain extent, in shared meanings (in the example given above the participants have a 'common evaluation' of the situation), yet he differs from Saussure in his belief that meanings are not automatically shared amongst all those people who speak a language such as Russian or English. He wants to see meaning construction as a more localised accomplishment, although his philosophy of language does acknowledge the existence of 'genres of speech performance in human behavior' (Volosinov 1986: 96; and see Bakhtin 1986) that operate across similar contexts. 'Village sewing circles, urban carouses, workers' lunchtime chats, etc., will all have their own types' or genres of talk, writes Volosinov (1986: 97). In addition, via the concept of multiaccentuality, he is insistent on retaining a connection between situated acts of language use in local contexts and the structured divisions, and inequalities, of modern societies. Indeed, I would suggest that this is precisely what serves to distinguish his perspective not just from Saussure's but also from approaches to 'deixis' or 'indexicality' in pragmatics and ethnomethodology.

Still, Volosinov's thoughts on multiaccentuality and the sign as an arena of social struggle might be hard to understand initially, and so we could turn to

Stuart Hall (1982) for a couple of helpful illustrations of this argument. Hall notes that, historically, the meanings of terms like 'the nation' and 'the people' have shifted and been disputed, as they got 'articulated' by very different social interests and in various kinds of political project. He also cites another instance of the 'different accenting of the same term': 'In the discourse of the Black movement, the denigratory connotation "black = the despised race" could be inverted into its opposite: "black = beautiful"' (Hall 1982: 78–9). Similarly, in the field of sexuality and sexual politics, it is possible for us to recognise the multiaccentuality of a term such as 'gay', which has been used both as a term of homophobic abuse and as a positive assertion of identity ('glad to be gay').

Hall links the ideas of Volosinov with those of a Marxist writer and political activist from the same period named Antonio Gramsci (see Gramsci 1971). His proposal is that whilst each of them has a clear conception of class and power, they share a general view of the cultural domain (the domain of meaning construction) as a complex, contradictory and contested site. In the words of Tony Bennett (1986: xiii), Gramsci's theory of 'hegemony' involves seeing popular culture 'as a force field of relations shaped ... by ... contradictory pressures and tendencies'. Volosinov and Gramsci provide cultural studies with an important alternative to the theory of 'ideological state apparatuses' advanced by Althusser (1984) in the early 1970s, which tends to present signification as 'too uni-accentual' (Hall 1982: 78) and the reproduction of capitalist 'relations of production' as too smooth or harmonious a social process (secured chiefly through the 'interpellation of individuals as subjects' in ideology).

Decoding

Building on those remarks made by Volosinov in the 1920s about the 'social multiaccentuality of the ideological sign' (Volosinov 1986: 23), as well as on the concept of connotation employed by Barthes (1973; 1977), Hall (1980a) suggests the possibility of developing a social semiotics of 'television discourse'. This approach attempts to account not only for the ways in which television images and sounds represent the world (we saw how that was Coward's main interest in her analysis of nature programmes), but also for the different interpretations or 'accentuations' given to televisual texts by their readers. He does not set out there to generate a 'grand model' of relations between broadcasting and its audiences (his original paper, written in the 1970s at a time when the critical paradigm was just emerging, has a more 'polemical thrust' against certain traditional forms of mass communication theory and research, see Hall *et al.* 1994). Nevertheless, he lays the foundation for subsequent investigations into the encoding and decoding of television messages (see especially Brunsdon and Morley 1978; Morley 1980; 1992; Morley and Brunsdon 1999).

What is now usually known, despite his own modest intentions at the point of writing, as Hall's 'encoding/decoding model' raises political questions about signification in social context. As he puts it in an interview years later, these have to do precisely 'with the construction and reconstruction of meaning, the way meaning is contested' (Hall *et al.* 1994: 254). He asks how the 'moments' of television 'production/circulation' (involving the encoding of 'a meaningful discourse' or 'message form' that is itself a 'determinate moment' in mass communication) and consumption (involving the decoding of that discourse) are dynamically related to one another. Reflecting on practices of encoding, his observation is that:

> A 'raw' historical event cannot, in that form, be transmitted by, say, a television newscast. Events can only be signified within the aural-visual forms of the televisual discourse. In the moment when a historical event passes under the sign of discourse, it is subject to all the complex ... 'rules' by which language signifies. To put it paradoxically, the event must become a 'story' before it can become a communicative event.
>
> (Hall 1980a: 129)

Since Hall takes as his example in this passage the encoding of an eventful happening in television news discourse (a discourse designed to routinise event-fulness, see Scannell 1996), it might be useful to compare briefly the perspective that he offers with Scannell's line on the broadcasting of public events, which I discussed at some length in a previous chapter.

While Scannell (1996) would no doubt be able to agree that an event is always necessarily 'storied' in a particular fashion by television, his emphasis remains on the role of broadcast talk and imagery in helping to create the event's aura, and in enabling audience members to be in two places simultane-ously. In contrast, rather than focusing on the experiential or phenomenological dimensions of broadcasting, Hall (1980a) is concerned above all with its ideo-logical operations. He employs what Scannell (1998), following Ricoeur (1974), characterises as a 'hermeneutics of suspicion'. For Hall, the televisual representation and narration of happenings tend to entail the construction of dominant, 'preferred meanings', through which the social world may appear in ways that suit the interests of the powerful. When he writes about such a 'preferring', however, his case is not that the broadcasters are intentionally 'biased', taking the side of dominant groups in society. They typically claim to be working within a professional code of impartiality. Rather, the producers of television news discourse are, he contends, adopting a taken-for-granted set of ideological assumptions about how the world is to be represented.

This is not the end of the story for Hall (1980a: 133), though, because 'at the connotative level' meaning is never entirely 'fixed' and so signification has a degree of fluidity to it. Even if encoding is understood as a preferring of specific constructions of meaning, and even if it has 'the effect of constructing some of the limits and parameters within which decodings will operate' (Hall 1980a: 135), it cannot 'guarantee' a singular decoding. In Volosinov's terms, the 'intersecting of differently oriented social interests' (Volosinov 1986: 23) in practices of decoding means that there will be a potential plurality of readings. According to Hall (1980a: 135), such interpretations should not be thought of simply as 'private, individual ... readings' because they are likely to be patterned by social differences and, therefore, to 'exhibit ... significant clusterings'.

Summing up my discussion of Hall's paper, I want to stress that he, like Volosinov before him, has no desire to put forward any general point about 'the infinite playfulness of language' (in the style of a poststructuralist theorist such as Derrida 1976) or else about the complete 'openness' of texts 'which can be decoded in any way' (Hall *et al.* 1994: 263). There are definite, if complexly articulated, determinations of meaning (and operations of power, see Gray 1999) that are identified by Hall, both in the encoding and decoding of television messages. What we are being encouraged to look at is how different sorts of viewer in different social positions, drawing on varied interpretative resources, make sense of a programme in particular ways.

Ultimately, the issues raised at the end of the last paragraph require empirical investigation, and David Morley (1980; 1992) presents us with findings from his qualitative research on the decodings of a popular news magazine programme in the UK, in which he sought to apply Hall's thinking. Referring to the transcripts of 'focused interviews' with groups of people from various occupations and levels of the education system (each group was first shown a recording of the programme), Morley demonstrates that there are, indeed, multiple and socially patterned interpretations (the 'significant clusterings' anticipated by Hall 1980a). In some cases, the groups are reported to have produced versions of a 'negotiated' or 'oppositional' decoding. However, whereas Volosinov (1986) seems to see a direct correspondence between class position and meaning construction in his notes on multiaccentuality, Morley (1992: 118) concludes that 'class position ... in no way directly correlates with decoding frameworks'. Instead, he suggests it is a question of how the social positions of viewers provide them with access to a certain range of codes and 'cultural repertoires', on which they then draw when it comes to reading an encoded television text. So while several of the groups in his decoding research could be described, in socio-economic terms, as working-class, this did not automatically lead to those groups making sense of the news programme in the same way. For instance, interpretations are inflected by a discourse of conservative populism, left-wing trade union politics or else an involvement in black youth cultures.

Following the research he conducted, Morley's own criticisms of the project (see Morley 1981; 1986; 1992) identify a number of theoretical and methodological problems that he encountered there. From my perspective in this chapter, there are two especially important points raised by his auto-critiques. The first of these has to do with the immediate contexts in which viewing takes place:

> This is a relatively simple matter in so far as ... I recruited groups of individuals for interview in the context either of colleges in which they were studying, or of other public locations where they came together,

already constituted as groups. While this approach had the obvious advantage of giving me ease of access to groups of people who already functioned as groups, at the same time this strategy had the disadvantage that I was not talking to people about television in the context in which they normally watch it.

(Morley 1992: 133)

Of course, when referring above to the context in which people 'normally watch' television, he has in mind the private settings of household living.

Second, his initial 'critical postscript' on the project calls for the development of 'a model of text/audience relations' that would be adequate to the task of dealing with 'the relevance/irrelevance and comprehension/incomprehension dimensions of decoding' as well as with 'the acceptance or rejection of substantive ideological themes' (Morley 1992: 127). It is the latter dimension of decoding, whether people ' "agree or disagree, or partly agree" with the ideological propositions of the text' (Morley 1992: 127), that originally interested Hall and Morley. What Morley's call directs us towards, though, is a greater concern with patterns of preference in media use, and also with the social distribution of cultural competences that enable consumers to like or dislike (and to find intelligible or unintelligible) specific types of media output. Later, we will return to these matters of taste, broadening the scope of our discussion to include more general practices and patterns of cultural consumption in day-to-day life.

Export

Now, I intend to pursue the theme of decoding, introduced in the preceding section, in relation to particular issues of media and globalisation that were discussed in the first part of the book. John Thompson (1995: 38), citing the work of Morley (1992) and others, praises qualitative audience researchers for showing us how 'the ways in which individuals make sense of media products vary according to their social background and circumstances, so that the same message may be understood in differing ways in different contexts'. In elaborating a social theory of media and modernity, which, as we have already seen, recognises the extended availability of media messages in time and space, he invites us to consider the consequences of this insight into media reception and interpretation for our thinking about global communications today:

> While communication and information are increasingly diffused on a global scale ... appropriation of media products is always a localized phenomenon, in the sense that it always involves specific individuals who are situated in particular social-historical contexts, and who draw on the resources available to them in order to make sense of media messages and incorporate them into their lives ... the practical contexts

of everyday life. The globalization of communication has not eliminated the localized character of appropriation but rather has created a
new kind of symbolic axis in the modern world, what I ... describe as
the axis of globalized diffusion and localized appropriation.

(Thompson 1995: 174)

To explore in greater detail the 'axis' described here by Thompson, we can turn
to the findings of research projects focusing on local appropriations of television
programmes (soap operas rather than a national news broadcast) that have been
distributed transnationally.

A classic example of an American television 'export' is the prime-time soap
opera, *Dallas*. In economic terms, this programme has been highly successful
outside as well as within the USA, making a large profit for its producers and
distributors (allowing for the fact that it 'failed' in Japan, see Liebes and Katz
1990). The programme was exported to countries in various parts of the world
during the late 1970s and early 1980s, 'ranging from Turkey to Australia, from
Hong Kong to Great Britain', when it was regarded by certain cultural
commentators 'as yet more evidence of the threat posed by American-style
commercial culture against "authentic" national cultures and identities' (Ang
1985: 1–2). *Dallas* was sometimes seen, then, as a symbol of media and cultural
imperialism, but we need to be wary of any automatic assumption that its global
commercial success is evidence of a transnational, imperialistic 'export of
meaning':

> Labelling something imperialistic is not the same as proving it is. To
> prove that *Dallas* is an imperialistic imposition, one would have to
> show ... that there is a message incorporated in the program that is
> designed to profit American interests overseas, ... that it is accepted
> uncritically by the viewers and allowed to seep into their culture.
>
> (Liebes and Katz 1990: 4)

What Tamar Liebes and Elihu Katz are proposing in this passage is that 'the
decoding of *Dallas*' (see also Katz and Liebes 1985), the localised appropriation
of a programme 'diffused on a global scale' (Thompson 1995: 174), requires
empirical investigation.

At least according to the ratings figures, the programme was watched in large
numbers by people in several Western European countries (Silj 1988: 77–9), and
Ien Ang (1985) investigates viewers' experiences of watching *Dallas* in the
Netherlands. Having 'placed a small advertisement in a Dutch women's magazine', in which she invited readers to write to her with their reactions to the
programme, Ang (1985: 10–11) provides us with what she calls a 'symptomatic'
analysis of the letters that were sent, arguing that 'the letters must be regarded as
texts'. Her reading of the soap opera and of the readings made by these Dutch
viewers suggests neither that the programme incorporates a message 'designed to

profit American interests overseas' (Liebes and Katz 1990: 4), nor that, as a result of the show's popularity there, the Netherlands has become 'Americanised'. Rather, she discovers that this tale is interpreted by many of her letter-writers (those with the necessary 'melodramatic imagination') as a 'family tragedy', which has an 'emotional realism' at the connotative level. While the fictional world of the Ewings, the wealthy family at the centre of the narrative, bears little literal resemblance to the life circumstances of the Dutch viewers, they are still able to find the fiction to be psychologically 'lifelike': 'it appears that what is experienced as "real" indicates above all a certain structure of feeling which is aroused by the programme: the tragic structure of feeling' (Ang 1985: 47).

More extensive research into decodings of the programme is presented by Liebes and Katz. Their empirical study involved interviews with groups 'each … consisting of three married couples of like age, education and ethnicity' and, for the most part, these groups were assembled in Israel, 'chosen from among Israeli Arabs, newly arrived Russian Jews, veteran Moroccan settlers and members of kibbutzim' (Liebes and Katz 1990: 6). In each case, an interview was recorded at the home of one of the couples, following a collective viewing of a broadcast episode of *Dallas*. The main rationale for this method of investigation is that it can reveal 'mutual aid' in the interpretation of a television text, enabling the generation of what the researchers term 'ethno-semiological data': 'it is precisely … group-influenced thoughts and statements in which we are interested' (Katz and Liebes 1985: 189).

Analysing the responses of the different groups, Liebes and Katz consider a range of issues. For instance, they look at variation in the ways in which viewers jointly 'retell' the episode that has just been watched (see also Liebes 1998), and at differing degrees of 'critical distance' from the screen fiction ('distancing' is defined here as 'discussion of the program … as formula, as a story governed by aesthetic and business constraints', as opposed to discussing the programme as if its characters were real people, see Liebes and Katz 1990: 36). From our point of view in this section of the chapter, though, the most interesting findings relate to mutual aid in 'moral evaluation'. Some of the groups certainly appear to treat *Dallas* as a sign of 'America', but this does not necessarily mean that a positive judgement is being made. Liebes and Katz (1990: 88) include the following extract from an interview with an 'Arab group':

Halil: One can deduce from the serial that there is a disintegration of family ties in American society, in capitalist society and in all Western society. There's no respect, no patience, none of the things which are considered good and which, to our mind, are the basic principles.

Sharifa: [*Dallas*] portrays the family falling apart.

Taking a similar line, members of a kibbutz group say of the characters, 'I tell myself how terrible it would be if I were one of them' and 'I live better than they do ... with all that they have money, my lifestyle is higher than theirs' (Liebes and Katz 1990: 88). This is evidently a rejection, not an acceptance, of American or Western 'material values'.

John Tomlinson (1991: 50) notes the importance of the work done by Liebes and Katz, in the context of debates about cultural imperialism, since for him it shows particular audiences outside the USA to be 'more resistant to manipulation and "invasion" than many critical media theorists have assumed'. When referring here to 'critical media theorists', he has in mind the writings of Herbert Schiller, which were discussed earlier in this book, and of other political economists of communication. However, Ramaswami Harindranath (2000: 150) identifies a problem with what, from his perspective, is the 'rather reductionist and crude notion of culture' employed by Liebes and Katz, accusing them of having 'reified' ethnicity in their research design and theoretical framework. In his own investigation of how groups of viewers in the UK and India responded to documentaries they were shown, Harindranath offers a rather more complex and nuanced account of cultural differences (and similarities). He seeks to avoid 'the conflation of culture and ethnicity implicit in ... Liebes and Katz', and argues, for example, that it would be a 'fundamental error' to assume 'all Indians share the same cultural resources' (Harindranath 2000: 160). His findings suggest that level of education (specifically, whether or not respondents have experience of higher education) is one of the crucial factors cutting across the national contexts, helping to shape interpretations of television programmes.

The next study that I deal with (Miller 1992; 1997) is also concerned with how a soap opera produced in the USA, in this case *The Young and the Restless*, is locally appropriated after being exported overseas, in this instance to Trinidad. As the researcher, anthropologist Daniel Miller (1992: 163), explains by way of introduction: 'My own entry into this ... came during fieldwork in Trinidad when, for an hour a day, fieldwork proved impossible since no one would speak with me, and I was reduced to watching people watching a soap opera.' By using the term 'reduced', Miller seems to be indicating that, to begin with, he found the local fascination with a television programme a frustrating distraction from the serious business of anthropological research. In time, though, he came to realise that the appropriation of an imported media product raises fundamental issues to do with the constructive role of consumption in day-to-day life (and his previous work does include reflections on theories of culture and consumption, see Miller 1987).

Indeed, Miller's main conclusions are 'that at the level of consumption we can observe ... the recreation of the soap opera as Trinidadian' (Miller 1992: 179), and also that 'authenticity has increasingly to be judged *a posteriori* not *a priori*, according to local consequences' (Miller 1992: 181). His point, then, is that the popularity of *The Young and the Restless* in Trinidad does not signal the destruction of some traditional, authentic local identity by the forces of global capitalism. For him, the intriguing question is how an imported fiction, through its incorporation into Trinidadian popular culture, gets to be seen locally as 'True True Trini' (just as, in his later research on internet use in Trinidad to be discussed further in the final chapter, he asks how the internet comes to be a site for doing being Trini).

Miller's answer is that the textual themes and preoccupations of the programme actually connect with a strong sense of 'bacchanal' in Trinidad, a term which has local connotations of scandal and of confusion or disorder, usually caused by scandal. Hearing references to the show in daily conversations, his claim is that it has a cultural salience (in Ang's terms, an emotional realism) for regular viewers. As one of these followers of the soap opera comments: 'The same thing you see on the show will happen here' (Miller 1992: 169). The term bacchanal is even included in the chorus of a Trinidadian calypso that is concerned with the unfolding plot of this television soap. 'It may be made in the United States by people who have barely heard of Trinidad', writes Miller (1997: 32), 'but in its consumption it becomes more genuinely Trinidadian than anything which is locally made.'

My last example of the interpretation of a serialised fiction that is distributed transnationally comes from Marie Gillespie's ethnographic research on the experiences of young Punjabi Londoners living in the district of Southall, which we touched on briefly at an earlier stage in the book. Like Miller, she is interested in talk about television in everyday life, and one of the programmes that her writing focuses on (because of its popularity with the young people she studied) is the Australian soap opera *Neighbours* (Gillespie 1993; 1995). Her argument, again rather like Miller's, is that at the point of consumption there is a connection forged between the preoccupations of a 'foreign' (at least in terms of its production) fiction and the local circumstances of viewing:

> The central and interrelated concerns of *Neighbours* are family and kinship relations, romance and courtship rituals, and neighbourly relations in the community, which are also the central and immediate concerns in the lives of young people in Southall. They use *Neighbours* to compare and contrast their own social world with the one represented in the soap. The productive tension between perceived similarities and differences enables them to negotiate the relations between parental and peer cultures and to articulate their own emergent systems of norms and values.
>
> (Gillespie 1993: 26)

Furthermore, she goes on to assert that there is a close link between the soap opera's narrative form, which privileges the verbal over the visual and revolves around the talk of characters, and the significance of gossip for 'Punjabi youth' in this part of London.

Gossip in Southall, especially amongst adults, is regarded by the young people in Gillespie's study as a threat to their personal freedom, as a result of its potential to damage family honour or '*izzat*'. It is seen by them as an important way in which adults seek to maintain the surveillance of, and therefore exercise 'social control' over, the routine behaviour of youths (of girls in particular because *izzat* depends, crucially, on 'the chastity of daughters'). As Gillespie (1995: 152) explains below, one of the characters in the soap opera has a specific relevance in this regard for these young people:

> The connection between soap gossip and Southall gossip is most force-fully demonstrated by the local appropriation of Mrs Mangel, the key gossip character in *Neighbours* at the time of the fieldwork. She is seen to embody everything that one would despise in a neighbour. ... She talks behind people's backs with malicious intent. She is an interfering busybody who twists and distorts events in order to put people down. While purporting to uphold the moral values of the community, she shows a prurient interest in any aberration of social or moral codes of behaviour. Among young people the term 'Mangel' has entered everyday usage as a term of abuse for anyone who gossips: 'Oh, she's a right Mangel!' can be heard commonly ... appropriation of the Mangel metaphor is revealing of a specific local response to *Neighbours* ... the anxieties of young people in Southall are projected onto the Mangel character as the embodiment of the significant threat that gossip poses to their lives.

In fact, Gillespie notes that even when, towards the end of her ethnographic research, this character disappeared from the story to be replaced by another 'key gossip character', the term 'Mangel' remained in widespread usage in Southall.

Before leaving this discussion of the export and appropriation of cultural goods, there is an additional point of connection between the writings of Miller and Gillespie that should be mentioned here. It has to do with the meanings, in Trinidad and in Southall, of a different kind of artefact altogether, Coca-Cola or 'Coke'. In the context, once again, of debates about globalisation and cultural imperialism, the soft drink is a good case to consider since we know that for some it represents, alongside examples such as *Dallas* and McDonald's, the imposition of American culture on consumers outside the USA.

According to Miller (1997: 34–5), Coca-Cola is perceived by his informants as 'a black sweet drink from Trinidad', rather than 'as a mark of foreign domi-nation'. The reasons for their perception are bound up with the social organisation of the production, as much as the consumption, of the drink on this Caribbean island. He explains that Coca-Cola is actually manufactured and bottled locally under a franchise agreement (the only imported element 'is the concentrate'). In turn, its consumption gives the drink a distinctively 'local flavour', as Coke is the 'preferred mixer' taken with rum, which is 'undoubtedly ... the national drink of Trinidad' (Miller 1997: 34). While recognising that this does not negate 'the obvious point that Coke remains a global commodity', Miller (1997: 35–6) urges us to see how 'the global is always experienced within a given locality'.

Meanwhile, for Punjabi youth in Southall, Coca-Cola does have a symbolic association with the USA. Indeed, when Gillespie invites teenagers in her study to talk about television advertisements for the drink, they respond enthusiastically to the idealised images of 'kids in America' (as they do to representations of American youth in the television series, *Beverly Hills 90210*). On the face of it, their responses would seem to 'prove' the case that Americanisation is taking place. It might be said, then, that the encoded, ideological messages here are being decoded 'full and straight' (Hall 1980a), accepted without negotiation or opposition. Attention to the local circumstances of interpretation, though, reveals a more complex situation that facilitates our understanding of why the identification with images of American teenagers is made. Gillespie (1995: 194) observes that the 'word most consistently used to describe American teenagers is "free"', and 'when considered against the background of social constraints under which girls especially live ... emphasis on freedom ... becomes easier to appreciate'. Even a trip to the American food outlet, McDonald's, located in a neighbouring London district, signifies an escape from surveillance by adults. As one young woman comments: 'It's good to get out of Southall, go down Hounslow with me mates and sit in McDonald's, get a Big Mac and a Coke ... and check out the guys' (in Gillespie 1995: 200).

Acknowledging the complexities of consumers' local decodings of global commodities, as Miller and Gillespie have done, is essential for the development of an adequate transnational cultural theory. However, I think we ought to be careful not to take a step too far and conclude that, because the interpretations of television programmes or soft drinks are creative and context-specific, there is no longer any need for us to worry about the economic power of global capitalism. In my view, political economists of communication are right to be worried about it. A future, major challenge in this area is to develop an adequate transnational cultural politics, which is sensitive to the axis of globalised diffusion and localised appropriation.

Acts

The work on decoding or interpretation that we have considered so far focuses, in the main, on the meanings of television output (a news magazine programme, soap operas and Coca-Cola advertisements) for audiences. What that research emphasises, to continue to borrow the jargon of semiotics, is the reading of media texts. Building on this foundation, I want to add a further dimension to our understanding of signification by thinking about the meaning of 'acts' of media consumption in their own right. My key point of reference here will be Janice Radway's study of popular romantic fiction readers, who frequent a bookshop in the suburb of an American city (see Radway 1987).

Ultimately, although she distinguishes analytically between their interpretation of narratives and the sense that they make of the very act of media use (her concern, of course, is with book reading rather than television viewing), those two things need to be thought about together in order for us to elaborate a satisfactory social-semiotic theory of media and communications.

Reflecting on her initial encounters with the readers, most of whom were 'married mothers', Radway (1987: 86) quickly comes to realise that the preoccupation she has with literary texts and readers' interpretations is not going to be enough to cope with what they have to say about their reading practices in day-to-day life:

> I would have to give up my obsession with textual features and narrative details if I wanted to understand their view of romance reading … it became clear that romance reading was important to the … women first because … picking up a book enabled them to deal with the particular pressures and tensions encountered in their daily round of activities … the early interviews were interesting because they focused so resolutely on the significance of the act of romance reading rather than on the meaning of the romance.

For example, the meaning of 'the act of romance reading' for one of the women, who actually worked in the bookshop, is summed up by her statement that 'my body is in the room but the rest of me is not (when I am reading)' (in Radway 1987: 87). Radway picks up on that will to escape everyday routine, temporarily and imaginatively if not physically (a non-electronic instance of the doubling of place), which is echoed in the comments of several of the women interviewed. She looks to explain the social circumstances that give rise to escapist reading of this particular sort.

'Escapism' is often employed as a derogatory, pathologising term in judging romance readers, but Radway insists that for the women in her study mental escape is a perfectly understandable desire (this is rather like Gillespie 1995 suggesting it is quite reasonable for young Punjabi Londoners to escape adult surveillance by going into McDonald's). For those who work at home, 'attending to the physical and affective needs of their families' (Radway 1987: 92), reading functions as a limited 'declaration of independence' from their roles as wives and mothers. It is a way of claiming time for relaxation and 'securing privacy' during days that are largely spent caring for husbands and children.

Having listened to the accounts given by her interviewees, then, Radway finds herself moving away from the text and its readings towards what could best be described as a sociological or social-psychological approach to situated acts of reading in daily life. Indeed, in a subsequent piece (Radway 1988) she advocates moving away altogether from the study of media 'reception', arguing instead for a much wider ethnography of the everyday (and only then investigating how media are 'integrated and implicated within it'). Still, in her book on romance, she does return to questions of narrative, genre and interpretation because she has to establish why it is that these women choose avidly to read popular romantic fiction rather than, say, crime novels or science-fiction (another genre associated especially with escape). Her answer is that romance offers the women an opportunity for 'compensatory' pleasures through identification with 'a heroine whose life does not resemble theirs in certain crucial respects' (Radway 1987: 90). The most crucial respect in which the heroine's life differs from theirs has to do with the fact that, by the end of the story, she is 'nurtured' by a hero who 'openly declares his love for … the heroine with a supreme act of tenderness' (Radway 1987: 150). Radway (1987: 94) observes that in their day-to-day lives, while they are responsible for regularly and selflessly nurturing others in the household, 'the contemporary family contains no role whose principal task is the … emotional support of the wife and mother' (see also Chodorow 1978, whose theory of gender and the family is drawn on here).

Thompson (1990: 312) provides a lengthy commentary on Radway's book, stressing the complex cultural politics of reading the romance for the women:

> If we focus on the activity of reading as distinct from the texts which are read, we can see that reading romances is, to some extent, a way of … protesting against a situation which the … women experience as unfulfilling. It is a way of coping with a situation that is structured in a manner which requires them to service the needs of others while their own needs are left unmet. In this respect, the activity of reading romance fiction has, for these women in these circumstances, a certain critical character. … But the critical character of the activity of reading is, in this case, probably overshadowed by the compensatory character of the texts which are read … which … serves to … fulfil vicariously their unmet needs, thereby enabling them to continue their day-to-day lives without altering in any fundamental way the social relations which characterize them. Just how the balance between these two aspects of romance reading – the critical and the compensatory – will work out over time is a question that Radway, quite reasonably, leaves open.

There are, in other words, what Bennett (1986) would call 'contradictory pressures' at work here in popular culture. As Radway (1987: 7) remarks in her introduction, she has arrived at 'the realization that … meaning … was multiply determined' by the act of reading, on the one hand, and by the decoding of a narrative fiction on the other.

Context

Clear parallels can be drawn between these conceptual (and political) concerns with book reading and the issues raised by Morley's research on practices of television viewing within family households in London (Morley 1986; 1992), the follow-up to his previous work on decodings of a news magazine programme. Like Radway, he finds that media use in the household is caught up with relations of gender and power, and divisions of labour and leisure (for a broader consideration of the politics of domestic consumption, see Jackson and Moores 1995). Most significantly, though, we could say that his qualitative study of families watching television is in many ways about 'social acts of viewing' in everyday contexts (and see Lull 1990, whose comparable analysis of the social uses of television was discussed at the close of the last chapter). An important conclusion Morley (1992: 146) reaches is that investigating such acts, at least in households like the ones he visited, means 'investigating something which men are better placed to do wholeheartedly, and which women seem only able to do distractedly and guiltily, because of their continuing sense of domestic responsibility'.

There is more, from Morley's revised perspective, than viewers' interpretations of 'what is on the screen', and 'that "more" is', in large part, 'the domestic context in which viewing is conducted' (Morley 1992: 158). 'I want to argue', writes Morley (1992: 157), 'that it is necessary to consider the context of viewing as much as the object of viewing.' This argument evidently resonates with what Radway has to say about the distinction between meaningful acts of reading and the meanings of romance texts for readers, yet it is necessary for us to remember that the act of reading a book is not quite the same as the act of watching television (since book reading routinely affords greater privacy than viewing does, and since the book tends to have a higher cultural status than the television set, allowing readers to trade on its 'instructional' value, see Radway 1987). Furthermore, when Morley draws our attention to the significance of viewing contexts, he also has in mind the physical places of cinema spectatorship or what Mark Jancovich et al. (2003) call 'cultural geographies of film consumption'.

I have already commented, in the opening chapter of this book, on some of the differences between film and television as audio-visual media. Morley (1992: 157–8) nevertheless makes an interesting theoretical link, advocating the development (following Corrigan 1983) of a 'phenomenology of "going to the pictures"' alongside his own emphasis on the meanings and experiences of domestic television use:

> Quite simply, there is more to cinema-going than seeing films. There is going out at night and the sense of relaxation combined with the sense of fun and excitement. The very name 'picture palace', by which cinemas were known for a long time, captures an important part of that experience. Rather than selling individual films, cinema is best understood as having sold … a certain type of socialized experience. … Any analysis of the film subject which does not take on board these issues of the context in which the film is consumed is, to my mind, insufficient. Unfortunately a great deal of film theory has operated

without reference to these issues, given the effect of the literary tradition in prioritizing the status of the text itself abstracted from the viewing context.

What we require is an understanding of how the immediate social environments of media consumption (intimately connected with wider contextual patterns of division and inequality in modern societies, see Volosinov 1986) contribute to shaping processes of signification.

Technologies

It is time now for me to introduce another conceptual distinction, and complicating factor, into our discussion of communication and the multiple dimensions of meaning construction. Up to this point in the chapter, the notion of 'the text' has been reserved exclusively for thinking about symbolic forms of media output or representation. Roger Silverstone (1990: 179), though, suggests 'an extension of the metaphor in relation to television as technology':

> However the relationship between television and its audience comes finally to be understood, it will need to take into account two kinds of mutually interdependent 'textualities': that of the content and that of the technology – the textuality both of message and of medium.

When he writes about 'message' and 'medium', I am reminded of the work of Marshall McLuhan (1964), but whereas McLuhan declares that the medium 'is' the message (dismissing the content of mediated texts or messages as relatively unimportant) Silverstone is arguing that it is necessary for us to recognise the existence of plural, 'mutually interdependent "textualities"'. Television programmes consisting of images and sounds can, as we have seen, be thought of as texts within the terms of semiotics. His contention here is that 'television as technology' should also be theorised as a type of text. Borrowing the language of computing, he adds that 'there is meaning in the texts of both hardware and software' (Silverstone 1990: 189).

This way of thinking about 'technologies-as-texts' is already present, in fact, in Barthes' writing on myth, because one of the objects of his textual analysis is a motor car (Barthes 1973). In the study of television and everyday life, too, Morley's research on family viewing involved him in reflecting on the cultural significance of a piece of technological 'hardware' such as the remote control device, 'which sits "on the arm of Daddy's chair" and is ... a highly visible symbol of condensed power relations' (Morley 1992: 147). Similarly, in a very different national context, the social anthropologist Ondina Leal (1990) tries to read the complex meanings of the television set as a 'material object' in the houses of people with varied class positions living in a Brazilian city (see

Dittmar 1992; and Dant 1999, for valuable overviews of literature on the meanings of material possessions and 'material culture'). For instance, she describes how television-as-technology, accompanied by the 'entourage' of decorative objects that typically surrounds it, 'represents the ... search for the social recognition of TV ownership' (Leal 1990: 24) among the working class. Indeed, this representation does not even depend on the set being switched on (and see Gell 1986), although the programmes on the screen may also serve to signify the presence of a modern, urban 'rationality' in the private sphere. The visibility of the technology from the street, facilitated by the positioning of the television as a piece of domestic furniture and by the practice of always keeping doors open, is the crucial factor according to Leal.

Returning to the UK, we could take a further example of that line of thought from the work of Charlotte Brunsdon (1995; 1997), who attempts to chart interpretations of satellite television dishes in the late 1980s and early 1990s. It may often be too cold and risky in Britain to leave the front door open, yet the dish aerial displayed publicly on the house front or rooftop announces the possession of a new media technology (just as, in the 1950s, the initial appearance of terrestrial television aerials made a comparable statement, see O'Sullivan 1991). Brunsdon concentrates her attention on the character of public debate about satellite dishes during that period, pointing to a 'taste war' fought out by 'anti-dishers' and 'dish-erectors', which is indicative of a wider conflict between different 'taste formations' (I will expand on matters of taste in the next section of the chapter). Looking at press reports, she notes how those in the former group overwhelmingly dominate coverage. They are represented as speaking on behalf of others as 'councillors, spokespeople for trusts or ... residents' associations' (Brunsdon 1997: 158), showing a concern for what they believe to be the protection of the built environment from 'alien protuberances perversely attached to the outside of houses' (Brunsdon 1997: 160). Members of the latter group, meanwhile, are 'always particular individuals' speaking personally about their feelings, with 'the half-expressed desire for another order, ... more fun for the kiddies, less boring' (Brunsdon 1997: 163).

These accounts offered by Morley, Leal and Brunsdon treat the technology of television and its associated hardware (remote control devices, satellite dish aerials) as cultural signs of a sort. In Brunsdon's case, especially, there is a focus on what might usefully be termed the multiaccentuality of technology-as-text, since the anti-dishers and dish-erectors fiercely contest the meaning of a material object. However, it is not only the medium of television that may be approached in this fashion. Silverstone *et al.* (1992) helpfully extend the metaphor of the text to yet other information and communication technologies, including the telephone, the computer and the video (for an illustration of data generated by the empirical research they carried out, see Hirsch 1992; 1998). They examine the ways in which those 'artefacts ... achieve significance ... through their appropriation' (Silverstone *et al.* 1992: 21). Rather than going into the detail of their work, though, my commentary now turns to a brief selection of other projects that explore the significance of telephones, computers or video recorders in specific settings.

Analysing 'mental maps of the home' drawn by research participants, Silverstone *et al.* (1991: 215) report that the static domestic telephone 'tended to disappear, to become "invisible", so taken for granted does it appear to have become in many households'. A more 'visible' relative of this naturalised household device is the mobile phone or cell phone. Members of the Sussex Technology Group (2001), and Richard Ling and Birgitte Yttri (2002) in Norway, perceive the display of that new communications technology in public places to be part of a presentation of self to others. Owners of mobiles are 'aware that to use the phone to communicate with people at a distance is also to communicate something to the people in the immediate physical locale' (Sussex Technology Group 2001: 208).

Ling and Yttri provide us with evidence from focus-group interviews of some people's anxieties over the 'size and vintage' of the object. For example, they quote the words of a mother whose daughters are too embarrassed to be seen holding their father's mobile phone when they are out:

> My 13 year old is allowed to use her father's, but she refuses. It belongs in a museum. It is two years old and one cannot be seen with it. I was on a ferry from Denmark with my two daughters last weekend. I said to one of them that she could call home and say that we would be landing at such and such a time. 'With that telephone? Are you crazy?' It was a point-blank refusal. She had to change the card over to her own telephone. She would not touch the other one in public. She would have to hide to do that.
>
> (in Ling and Yttri 2002: 163)

Mobiles considered to be just 'too big' and 'too old' are referred to by younger interviewees as 'bricks'. At the same time, Ling and Yttri (2002: 164) note that 'there is a fine balance to be struck' because the overly conspicuous display of a small, up-to-date model (worn, say, on a belt) might also be thought of as 'not very cool': 'one needs to know the appropriate way to carry the device and where to include it in one's dress'. Here, the technology is regarded as an aspect of clothing and style.

If Leal was interested in the television set as a material object, then Elaine Lally (2002) has a similar concern to comprehend what she names the 'social life of the computer' in contemporary households, grounding her cultural theory of the technology's 'domestication' in interviews with members of several computer-owning households in Sydney. She attempts to understand how this mass-produced commodity can come to be experienced as a personal possession that is highly 'integrated into the lives' of its users. Of course, even prior to the point of purchase technologies like the home computer are put through a process of 'pre-domestication' (Silverstone and Haddon 1996) in the moments of their design and advertising (we could perhaps say that they have been encoded for domestic use), but Lally's attention is mainly directed towards the incorporation of computers into ongoing practices of 'home-building'. One aspect of her study, which is particularly reminiscent of Leal's, involves mapping the position of the technological artefact 'in relation to other household objects' (Lally 2002: 175). On occasion, that relationship is competitive, as when computer use displaces activities such as television viewing, typewriting or traditional gaming, yet computers are also 'often surrounded by other "collaborating" objects such as furniture and small moveable objects like books, disks and pieces of paper' (Lally 2002: 177).

A crucial issue facing household members, who may themselves be in a degree of competition, is where to locate the computer physically (for instance, Hirsch 1998 writes on the problems of initially finding a 'place for the modem' in the family home). In their wide-ranging study of 'children in the information age', one of the topics discussed by geographers Sarah Holloway and Gill Valentine (2003) is the choice of whether or not to put a computer in a child's bedroom. As Holloway and Valentine (2003: 102) note, a primary motivation for the purchase of a personal computer by parents is the enhancement of children's 'educational ... and future employment prospects': 'For the same reasons parents often invest in children's bedrooms in order to provide an appropriate space for them to "work"' (and see Livingstone 2002, who reflects on the increasingly common practice of families 'living together separately' with media technologies). They find that, particularly in 'higher ... socio-economic status households' in their UK sample, children do frequently have access to their own computer screens, although they add that this decision to locate the new technology in the bedroom context can give rise to parental anxieties over 'inappropriate', non-work uses. Such fears are not only to do with the dual significance of computers as educational and recreational technologies (Murdock *et al.* 1992), but also with a sense many parents have that the online world is 'a potentially risky space' (similar anxieties surrounded the arrival of domestic video technology years before, as outlined in Wood 1993). Holloway and Valentine (2003: 115) report on how, partly as a consequence of these fears, some parents prefer 'placing the computer in a family room', since it allows for greater supervision and 'serves to reduce the risks of improper use either by their children, or in the actions of others online towards their children'.

Gender difference, in addition to the generational divide between parents and children, may play a role in determining the household uses and meanings of an object like the computer or the video recorder. So Lally discovers, as Morley did in his work on television in the family, that opportunities to access technology are not always equally available to men and women. 'Mothers ... say that they do not have time to sit down at the computer', writes Lally (2002: 159), 'particularly when it comes to learning new skills.' She also asks whether the home computer is culturally coded 'pink or blue', colours which are themselves arbitrary signifiers of femininity and masculinity, referring to earlier research in cultural studies carried out by Ann Gray (1987; 1992) on the 'gendering' of video as a leisure technology.

Gray (1987: 42), who interviewed women in their homes, makes the important point that the 'gender specificity of pieces of domestic technology is deeply implanted in the "common sense" of households':

> As such it is difficult for the researcher to unearth. One strategy I have employed which throws the gender of domestic technology into high relief is to ask the women to imagine pieces of equipment as coloured either pink or blue. This produces almost uniformly pink irons and blue electric drills, with many interesting mixtures along the spectrum. The washing machine, for example, is most usually pink on the outside, but the motor is almost always blue. VCRs and, indeed, all home entertainment technology would seem to be a potentially lilac area, but my research has shown that we must break down the VCR into its different modes in our colour-coding. The 'record', 'rewind' and 'play' modes are usually lilac, but the timer switch is nearly always blue, with women having to depend on their male partners or their children to set the timer for them. The blueness of the timer is exceeded only by the deep indigo of the remote control.

Picking up on those observations, Lally (2002: 159) answers her own question by stating that 'the home computer, like the VCR, is neither completely pink nor blue but is lilac in parts, blue or pink in others'. In fact, she extends her analysis beyond the text of the hardware to consider the gendered significance of computer software, commenting on the 'coding' of various games packages by her interviewees.

When Gray remarks in the extract above that the women she talked with tended to depend on others to set the video timer for them, it is certainly not her intention to suggest that they suffer from technological incompetence (despite the fact that several speak of themselves as 'not being technically minded'). On the contrary, she reminds us that these are the skilful users of other, usually labour-related and sometimes complex, technologies in the domestic sphere. It is a matter, then, of differently distributed cultural competences and, on occasion, of what Gray (1992: 169) calls a 'calculated ignorance' too: 'there are decisions made ... to remain in ignorance of the workings of the VCR, so that it is their ... partner's job to set up the timer'. In such cases, the 'latent servicing element' in the technical know-how is both recognised and resisted.

Tastes

At the close of the preceding discussion of technologies, we touched on the topic of cultural competences and their social distribution, which is central to the current section of the chapter. Initially, I want to explore that topic in relation to the taste (and distaste) for a specific type or genre of media output, returning once more to audiences for soap opera and concentrating on what has been termed 'the relevance/irrelevance and comprehension/incomprehension dimensions of decoding' (Morley 1992: 127). This will then serve as my access point into a broader debate about tastes, values and practices of 'distinction' (Bourdieu 1984).

Brunsdon (1981: 36) seeks to theorise the kinds of 'cultural competence that ... soap-opera narrative ... demands of its social reader'. She identifies three categories of required knowledge. In addition to the first two sorts of competence (generic and serial-specific knowledge), her third category is 'knowledge of the socially acceptable codes and conventions for the conduct of personal life', on which she comments below:

> It is the culturally constructed skills of femininity – sensitivity, perception, intuition and the necessary privileging of the concerns of personal life – which are ... called on ... in the genre. The fact that ... this type of cultural capital ... is ideologically constructed as natural does not mean, as many feminists have shown, that they are the natural attributes of femininity. However, under present cultural and political arrangements, it is more likely that female viewers will possess this repertoire of both sexual and maternal femininities which is called on to fill out the range of narrative possibilities ... discourses of ... femininity which are elaborated elsewhere, already in circulation and brought to the programme by the viewer.
>
> (Brunsdon 1981: 36–7)

The first thing to notice in the passage reproduced here is that her implicit understanding of encoding and decoding seems to differ somewhat from Hall's original conception (Hall 1980a). While she shares the same general concern to treat the encounter between television and its viewers as 'interdiscursive' (since the 'relation of the audience to the text will not be determined solely by that text, but also by positionalities in relation to a whole range of other discourses ... of motherhood ... and sexuality for example', see Brunsdon 1981: 32), her focus in this piece is on issues of cultural preference, salience and intelligibility rather than directly on matters of ideology. However, she does recognise, of course, that the traditional skills of femininity are 'ideologically constructed as natural'.

Second, leading on from the last point, it is important to stress that Brunsdon is not adopting an essentialist position on the 'natural attributes of femininity'. From her feminist perspective, gendered identities, preferences and competences are seen to be constituted in historically and socially specific ways. In other words, she is not proposing that women, as a consequence of their biological difference from men, have an innate taste for soap operas as opposed to, say, television news and current affairs programmes. It has to do, instead, with the particular articulations of gender and genre in popular culture (links that were traced many years ago by Hobson 1980, in her notes on the masculine and feminine 'worlds of television'). Indeed, if we accept the argument that connections between genre and gender are always provisional and 'culturally constructed', then our model of 'text/audience relations' must be flexible enough to cope with shifting cultural formations and articulations over a period of time. Today, it may be the case that those soap operas scheduled in a prime-time evening slot are changing form to a certain degree as their producers introduce narrative features from other kinds of programme, developing story lines familiar from crime series, for instance (these sorts of change are discussed by Geraghty 1991; and also by Gledhill 1997, who each reflect on whether the soap opera can still be regarded as a feminine genre).

Third, it is interesting that, at one moment in the extracted passage, Brunsdon borrows sociologist Pierre Bourdieu's concept of 'cultural capital' (Bourdieu 1984). Her use of that term in this specific context (she appears to be employing it as a substitute for the general idea of cultural competence or knowledge) is actually at odds with the precise sense in which he employs the concept in his sociology of culture. As I explain more fully below, Bourdieu sees cultural capital (he is borrowing from the language of economics) as being accumulated principally by those people in powerful social groups who display 'legitimate taste'. They 'discriminate' between what, from their particular perspective, are considered to be 'the beautiful and the ugly, the distinguished and the vulgar' (Bourdieu 1984: 6), and they are skilled in understanding, for example, the aesthetic codes of 'fine art' (Bourdieu 1993a). Although Bourdieu has surprisingly few things to say about television in his sociological studies of taste and value (Frow 1995), he would presumably regard competent viewers of soap operas as accumulating little in the way of cultural capital, because the sort of knowledge they develop is not traditionally legitimated by an institution like the formal education system. There are theorists who write of 'popular cultural capital' and 'popular discrimination' (Fiske 1987; 1991), and of 'subcultural capital' (Thornton 1995), but these ideas are something of a departure from Bourdieu's original thinking.

It is important for us to recognise, after all, that one of the reasons why Brunsdon, and several other feminists in media and cultural studies, were motivated to study soap opera in the first place is because the pleasures of the genre for its audiences had been so denigrated and undervalued (see Brunsdon 1984; 2000). However, by insisting that regular soap followers are employing skill, knowledge or competence in their appreciation and enjoyment of the programmes, she is attempting to counter accusations that these viewers are somehow mindless and 'stupid'. Her implicit case is that, on the contrary, it is critics of the genre who fail to comprehend its encoded meanings, since they lack the necessary cultural know-how to decode it as relevant and intelligible drama.

Let me expand next on the argument Bourdieu is making, that alongside the unequal distribution of economic capital in modern society there is a cultural 'economy' with its own measure of value and accumulation of wealth (yet the orders of financial and 'symbolic wealth' are certainly not disconnected, and on occasion cultural capital may bring financial returns). In an interview in which he is pressed to defend his use of the key concepts of cultural capital and distinction, Bourdieu (1993b: 1) begins by extending the economic metaphor, referring to the notions of 'profit' and 'market':

> That is why it needs to be pointed out that there is such a thing as cultural capital, and that this capital secures direct profits, first on the educational market, of course, but elsewhere too, and also secures profits of distinction … which result automatically from its rarity, in other words from the fact that it is unequally distributed. … The dominant definition of 'distinction' calls 'distinguished' those behaviours that distinguish themselves from what is common and vulgar. … The profit of distinction is the profit that flows from the difference, the gap, that separates one from what is common. … And this direct profit is accompanied by an additional profit that comes from seeing oneself – and being seen – as totally disinterested.

The 'additional profit' that he mentions at the end of his statement has to do with the way in which legitimate tastes or, more exactly, institutionally legitimated tastes, pass themselves off as 'gifts of nature' rather than as 'products of learning' (Bourdieu 1984: 29). They are an expression of social interests and power relations in competitive market conditions. At this point, then, his reflections on taste appear to overlap with Barthes' observation that myth transforms the historical into the natural. Even though they are operating out of different disciplinary traditions and focusing on different aspects of culture, it might still be possible to compare their work and conclude that Bourdieu is deconstructing the myth of 'innate good taste'.

When investigating tastes, Bourdieu (1984: 11) proposes that the sociologist is 'in the area *par excellence* of the denial of the social'. The social 'acquisition of legitimate culture within the family circle … tends to favour an enchanted experience of culture which implies forgetting the acquisition' (Bourdieu 1984: 3). Bourgeois preferences appear in that social milieu, and in many other institutional locations beyond it, as 'obviously' better than those choices made within the zone of 'popular taste', with the latter often provoking a sense of distaste and disgust, a 'horror or visceral intolerance … of the tastes of others' (Bourdieu 1984: 56).

Clearly, Bourdieu's approach to tastes in the economy of contemporary culture is political as well as academic. His purpose is to show how cultural value judgements are far from 'innocent' (to that end, he engages in a detailed empirical survey of patterns in French cultural consumption in the 1960s). Instead, he suggests that the 'judgement of taste' is intimately bound up with the production and reproduction of social divisions. The emphasis in his work is on the division between dominant and subordinate classes, and also on what he perceives to be a struggle between different fractions of the dominant class. Broadly speaking, these are its intellectual and entrepreneurial fractions, whose members have invested primarily in either cultural or economic capital (Wynne 1990).

Whilst offering his critique of the naturalness of legitimate taste, Bourdieu does not neglect the characteristics of what he calls popular taste. So whereas the former is marked by an 'aesthetic disposition' that favours the cool contemplation of designated cultural objects and performances (appreciating works of art and literature or classical music, but also 'the choice of a vintage or a cheese or the decoration of a holiday home in the country', see Bourdieu 1984: 56), popular preferences are related to 'ordinary dispositions'. Those tend, according to him, to involve the 'subordination of form to function'. He believes, for instance, that there is 'hostility of the working class and of the middle-class fractions least rich in cultural capital towards every kind of formal experimentation' (Bourdieu 1984: 32) in what could generally be labelled the arts. Such varied dispositions or types of 'habitus' are linked, in his view, to the conditions of existence of different social classes. What facilitates the formation of an aesthetic disposition is a 'distance from necessity' that is not so evident in working-class life, where often a 'submission to necessity ... inclines ... people to a pragmatic, functionalist "aesthetic"' (Bourdieu 1984: 376) governing routine tastes and consumption choices.

Despite his strong emphasis on class differences, I should add that Bourdieu does also make occasional comments about the ways in which gender relations intersect with social class. Here, reflecting back on his work on taste, he touches on a specific feature of working-class masculinity:

> I try to explain the attachment to the values of masculinity, physical strength, by pointing out for example that it's characteristic of people who have little to fall back on except their labour power and sometimes their fighting strength. I try to show in what respect the relationship to the body that is characteristic of the working class is the basis of a whole set of attitudes, behaviours and values, and that it is the key to understanding their way of talking or laughing, eating or walking. I say that the idea of masculinity is one of the last refuges of the identity of the dominated classes.
>
> (Bourdieu 1993b: 4)

There is a parallel to be drawn at this point with Paul Willis' ethnography of masculine 'shopfloor' and 'counter-school' cultures in a British town (Willis 1977). Like Bourdieu, Willis is interested in what he sees as the highly contested processes of social reproduction, and in the embodied cultural dispositions and 'set of attitudes' found within working-class life (especially in the institutional settings of the factory and the school). In particular, his analysis highlights an investment in physical strength and 'practical ability' rather than a respect for the formal education system: 'As a big handwritten sign, borrowed from the back of a matchbox and put up by one of the workers, announces on one shopfloor ... "An ounce of keenness is worth a whole library of certificates" ' (Willis 1977: 56). At the same time, we need to be aware of criticisms of his research put forward by Angela McRobbie (1991: 22), who wonders quite rightly about what all of this means for working-class women and girls, and the sphere of the family 'in which fathers, sons and boyfriends expect to be, and are, emotionally serviced' (for further discussion of these issues of class and femininity, see Griffin 1985; Skeggs 1997).

An interesting application of Bourdieu's perspective is the research on 'Australian everyday cultures' carried out in the 1990s by Bennett et al. (1999). Combining quantitative and qualitative methods of inquiry, they look to map the cultural choices of contemporary Australians across a range of practices. Their findings demonstrate that those expressions of preference are 'pre-eminently social', and show the likes and dislikes of consumers to have a 'definite pattern'. For example, in the account that they provide of tastes in 'home decoration' (comparable portraits of Norwegian households are available in Gullestad 1993), quite distinctive domestic styles and dispositions are identified. Taking a series of 'case histories', Bennett et al. (1999: 25) claim that these 'allow us to see how the factors of gender, class and education interact with one another both in the choices people make about their homes, and in how they speak about those choices'.

'What does it mean', ponder Bennett et al. (1999: 24), 'to prefer one colour scheme to another?' Their answer, in the case of an 'upwardly mobile' woman named Gillian who holds a senior position in health management, is 'quite a lot'. She states her desire for a house with 'cool colours', initially suggesting to the interviewer that she 'just happens' to like them, but it later transpires that this ideal choice is, in large part, a way of distancing or distinguishing herself from the kind of family home she and her husband grew up in: 'The gaudy veneer and laminex surfaces of a 1970s working-class décor are something she wants to "get away from" ' (Bennett et al. 1999: 28). Gillian therefore exhibits a strong sense of distinction in this seemingly innocent expression of taste (for instance, describing the decorative style that she associates with her social background as 'disgusting by anybody's standards').

Another question posed by Bennett et al. (1999: 24) has to do with the 'significance attached to the paintings that people choose for their homes'. In the case of Dorothy, who works part-time as a cook in a childcare centre, and lives close to Brisbane with her husband and children, the whole business of 'what to like' in a picture is 'very much connected to that of what to do with it in a family context':

Interviewer: Can you define your taste in art?

Dorothy: Things that are real. I don't like any things that are sort of like Picassos or something like that. I don't like them because you don't look at them and see something real. ... I know that Graham would like paintings of draughthorses and if I was looking at paintings, I'd especially look at draughthorse ones, because he had that when he was a boy.

Interviewer: Because he's from a farming background … isn't he?

Dorothy: Yes. And he has had draughthorses all his life when he was growing up. And he would dearly love one with a big draughthorse and I'll just keep looking until I find one and I'll eventually get him one.

(Bennett *et al.* 1999: 34–5)

She shows us what Bourdieu terms a 'hostility … towards … formal experimentation', favouring a 'functionalist "aesthetic"' and mimetic modes of visual representation (issues that are also discussed in Murdock 1989).

Bennett *et al.* (1999: 11) recognise that 'Bourdieu's … investigation of a range of domains of cultural practice is immensely rich', leading them to adopt much of his approach, and yet they have 'some major theoretical differences with him' too. I will mention just two of these points of difference. A fundamental disagreement with Bourdieu is over the manner in which he theorises class: 'his account of class oscillates between a conventional ranking according to relation to economic capital … and a stratification by occupation … how these two very different models of class translate into each other … is never clear' (Bennett *et al.* 1999: 12). In earlier work, one of the co-authors of the Australian study, cultural theorist John Frow (1987; 1995), also suggests that there is still an essentialism of a sort operating in Bourdieu's conceptualisation of class and culture. Frow (1995: 31) is critical of 'a binary construction of the concepts of a "high" and a "popular" aesthetic understood as something like class languages, fixed and ahistorical class dispositions with a necessary categorical structure' (having said that, the evidence of home decoration preferences outlined above does seem to support Bourdieu's basic argument about the logics of legitimate and popular taste). At any rate, it is an ambition of Bennett *et al.* to develop a 'more adequately theorised model' of social class, which would allow for the possibility that there is now a degree of 'cultural declassification' (DiMaggio 1987) in modern societies.

Further problems arise for Bennett *et al.* (1999: 201) as a result of what they read as the 'remarkable insularity' of Bourdieu's investigation:

It is difficult to come away … without the impression that the tastes of the French in the … 1960s were almost entirely forged within their own national institutions. Apart from the occasional reference to the uptake of 'Californian sports', or an interest in an influential foreign film, the cultural output of the rest of the world was of no apparent interest to Gallic appetites … thirty years after Bourdieu's original research, it is impossible to imagine that the same indifference to global culture could still prevail even in France, let alone a country like Australia which has traditionally looked outwards for its cultural pleasures.

We are returned again, via their critique, to issues of global communication that were discussed at length earlier in this chapter. Data from the 'Australian everyday cultures' research do seem to indicate a shift, particularly among the young, to 'preferring American cultural materials' in the areas of television, film, literature and music. Nevertheless, it is reported that 'although Australians appear to be inhabiting cultural worlds which are more and more likely to be dominated by overseas products, there seems to be very little change in a belief in the importance of Australia in biographical self-awareness' (Bennett *et al.* 1999: 225). A majority of the participants in the study, then, state a feeling of attachment to 'Australian culture' (although this is, in itself, a highly complex category, since Australia has 'traditionally looked outwards'). Of course, thinking back to what Miller (1992) argued about the construction of meanings and identities in Trinidad, such a feeling is not necessarily in contradiction with the fact that Australians are found to have a growing taste for media products imported from the USA. The declining influence of many nation-states in circumstances of globalisation does not automatically lead, in all cases, to a reduction in national sentiment.

Fallacy

Having dealt with a series of developments in what could broadly be labelled social-semiotic theory, and with attempts to map patterns of taste and cultural value, I want to draw my discussion of signification to a close with two final sections that might lead us to qualify, in specific ways, our thinking about the making of meanings. Shortly, I will be considering the analysis of photography provided by Barthes (1984) in the last book that he wrote. There, he adopts a position on visual representation that is markedly different to the kind of semiotics we encountered in his early writings. He explores the personal significance of certain photographs for him and looks, ultimately, for a 'just image' (more than 'just an image') that can reveal 'the truth of the face' of somebody he has loved and lost. Barthes (1984: 8) chooses to focus, then, on photographs 'I was sure existed for me', arriving at the 'curious notion' that there might be 'a new science for each object': 'A *mathesis singularis.*' This is quite a departure from the general science of signs proposed by Saussure (1983), explicitly shifting analysis to the level of individual readings. In advance of my commentary on Barthes on the medium of photography, though, it is important for us to spend a little longer reflecting on the cultural studies perspective on meaning construction, which has permeated a fair proportion of the work covered in the preceding pages. Joke Hermes (1993; 1995), in her research on readers of women's magazines in the Netherlands, gives an added twist to debates in that field. She feels it would be a 'fallacy' to assume that media texts are always treated as meaningful by their audiences or users.

'I suggest', writes Hermes (1993: 493), 'that from time to time, all of us (some perhaps more often than others), engage in virtually meaningless media use.' Her suggestion arises chiefly out of the experience of talking with a large number of magazine readers:

> The goal of the eighty lengthy interviews with women and men was to reconstruct how women's magazines become meaningful. The interviews were a success in terms of social interaction. Although interviewing is tiring work, I enjoyed it. I was made most welcome by very diverse people, a majority of whom appreciated women's magazines and read them regularly. Informants were talkative enough – but they did not have much to say about women's magazines. Interpreting the interviews presented serious problems. ... Although some readers ponder what they have read and remember specific articles to some extent, most readers did not. Many could not give specific examples and usually references were vague. Quite often informants would hunt for a copy of a magazine if they wanted to say something about it. Generally speaking, although many readers have generic knowledge of women's magazines, the practice of reading women's magazines apparently does not call for reflection or involvement of a readily communicable kind.
>
> (Hermes 1995: 11–12)

As she proceeds to explain, her interviewees tend to describe the texts they read as 'easily put down'. This 'putdownable' character is linked to what she comes to understand as their use in an ' "in-between" activity' that 'does not require much attention' (Hermes 1995: 32).

Referring to the pioneering work of Radway (1987) on romance readers, Hermes admits to an initial disappointment at not being able to follow in her predecessor's footsteps, declaring that she 'would have liked nothing better'. Her disappointment is allied to a puzzlement over how 'my women's magazine readers have so much less to say than Radway's romance readers ... when ... I ... employed much the same interview strategy' (Hermes 1995: 14). Those romance readers, in their imaginative flights from the quotidian, were frequently gripped by what we might term 'unputdownable' or, at least, hard to put down stories. They engaged in a form of committed consumption. In contrast, although the people that Hermes speaks to clearly pick certain magazines to read in preference to others, they display 'far less concentration' and 'much more detachment' in this aspect of their everyday media use (see also Couldry 2000b, who offers additional comments on the putdownable qualities of particular media materials in circumstances of 'textual proliferation').

Now, Hermes is surely right to distinguish between romantic fiction and women's magazines as genres usually demanding different modes of attention from their readers, but I think it is also fair to say that the project she pursue. has important similarities to Radway's (as well as to the work of others located both inside and outside of cultural studies). In the end, having asked whether her interviewees are in a condition of 'everyday meaninglessness' when they read magazines, Hermes pulls back from this rather stark suggestion and seeks to identify the implicit significance of these reading practices. She believes that the significance resides principally in what Radway would see as the act of reading in contexts of daily living. So the inability of the research participants to recall very much at all about the detail of the texts should not be taken, ultimately, as a sign that there is 'no meaning' being produced. Rather, it is the practical activity of media consumption itself that is meaningful, even if the significance is (as Gray 1987 put it when discussing domestic technologies) 'deeply implanted' in 'common sense' and therefore not 'readily communicable'. Indeed, like Gray, Hermes tries to reconstruct those common-sense meanings from fragments in her interview transcripts.

Hermes draws, amongst other things, on Hermann Bausinger's 'social-phenomenological' theorising of media use (see Bausinger 1984), which was cited near the beginning of this book in my account of the concept of dailiness. She takes from him the basic principle that 'media are an integral part of the way everyday life is conducted' (Hermes 1995: 24), and in doing so situates meaning making in relation to day-to-day routines and rituals. Moving in that direction involves 'radically decentring the media text', enabling her then to discover various descriptive and interpretative repertoires or 'recurrent phrases and themes' running through the transcribed talk (and see Potter and Wetherell 1987, from whom she borrows her method of discourse analysis).

For instance, alongside 'the easily put down repertoire', Hermes finds 'the repertoire of relaxation' that is evident, too, in the words of women interviewed by Radway. In fact, there is yet another connection that can be made here with Radway, because Hermes points to the way in which, although they typically struggle to remember specific articles in the magazines, her readers sometimes employ the discourse of 'learning' and 'the repertoire of practical knowledge' when justifying their reading practices. This repertoire of practical knowledge, which has to do with picking up useful 'tips' from a magazine, might appear to take us back in the direction of the media text, but what she emphasises is the routine and taken-for-granted appropriation of such information in the accomplishment of ordinary tasks.

Authentication

Given his leading role in the formation of semiotics, a perspective from which it is usual to argue (as Hall did) that images never simply offer a faithful reflection of 'the real', it is perhaps surprising to hear Barthes (1984: 88–9) identify himself, after all, as one of 'the realists': 'The important thing is that the photograph possesses an evidential force.' He claims, then, that photography's crucial

135

ɔwer of authentication', and this assertion follows a series of
s on the medium. I will briefly summarise and contextualise
re.

arthes develops an analysis of photographs that leads him to
..ɔn between two Latin terms, *studium* and *punctum*. The first of
_ terms is used to refer to the 'kind of general interest' that he has in a
range of photographic images, since it is 'by *studium* that I am interested in so
many photographs ... it is culturally ... that I participate in the figures, the
faces, the gestures, the settings, the actions' (Barthes 1984: 26). For example,
he takes a 'so to speak, polite interest' in the genre of news photography. In
turn, his second term is defined directly in opposition to this. It describes an
involuntary response to that element of specific images which 'rises from the
scene, shoots out from it like an arrow and pierces me':

> A Latin word exists to designate this wound, this prick, this mark made
> by a pointed instrument: the word suits me all the better in that it also
> refers to the notion of punctuation, and because the photographs I am
> speaking of are in effect punctuated, sometimes even speckled with
> these sensitive points; precisely, these marks, these wounds are so many
> points. This second element which will disturb the *studium* I shall
> therefore call *punctum*; for *punctum* is also: sting, speck, cut, little
> hole. ... A photograph's *punctum* is that accident which pricks me (but
> also bruises me, is poignant to me).
>
> (Barthes 1984: 26–7)

So, to cite a particular instance, when he looks at a news photograph taken during
the Nicaraguan revolution, what makes Barthes (1984: 23) pause is the striking
juxtaposition of 'two helmeted soldiers' in a ruined street and 'behind them, two
nuns'. Similarly, the *punctum*, for him, is often a 'detail' or a number of minor
details in a picture (the bare foot of a soldier's corpse, a low belt and pair of
strapped shoes worn in a portrait of 'a family of American blacks', and so on).

Silverstone (1999: 52–3) reminds us that this sort of conceptual division is
present in some of Barthes' previous reflections on reading literature (see
Barthes 1975), in which he distinguishes between pleasure (*plaisir*) and bliss
(*jouissance*). Rather like the *punctum*, *jouissance* is thought of by Barthes as an
unexpected, 'asocial' response, a 'bliss which can erupt ... out of certain texts
that were nonetheless written to the glory of the dreariest, of the most sinister
philosophy' (Barthes 1975: 39). We should be cautious, however, when it
comes to talk of the asocial. Certain middle-class cultural competences are no
doubt required in order for the reader to be in a position to experience such
moments of 'ecstasy'. I would also want to add, in passing, that the way in
which Barthes conceives of *punctum* in relation to *studium* reminds me very
much of Scannell's later discussion of broadcasting (Scannell 1996), where
eventfulness is theorised as a temporary disturbance or punctuation of dailiness.

After providing several illustrations of his individual sense of being pierced or 'wounded' by parts of images, Barthes moves on to tell us a deeply personal story in which he recalls 'going through some photographs' of his mother, shortly after her death. He explains how, initially, 'I was not sitting down to contemplate them, I was not engulfing myself in them' (Barthes 1984: 63), and yet, after sorting them for a while, he became frustrated at not being able to ' "find" her' in the images. Then, on gazing at a picture of his mother as a child where she was photographed with her brother in a winter garden scene, 'I found it ... the truth of the face I had loved' (Barthes 1984: 67). In this moment, he feels that photography gives him a just image ('authentication') and a sentiment 'as certain as remembrance'. Still, he sees no reason to put the private, family picture in his book on photography, because the precise meaning of the text for Barthes (its 'evidential force') is not generally available:

> I cannot reproduce the Winter Garden photograph. It exists only for me. For you, it would be nothing but an indifferent picture, one of the thousand manifestations of the 'ordinary' ... at most, it would interest your *studium*: period, clothes, photogeny; but in it, for you, no wound.
>
> (Barthes 1984: 73)

Following the discovery of that image, he resolves to approach photography 'in relation to ... death' (for more on this important aspect of his analysis, see Barthes 1985).

Photography, for Barthes, is defined above all by its capacity to produce a 'that-has-been' effect. In the passage reproduced below, he starts by reflecting on the image of a young man in a prison cell, who is sentenced to death by hanging for the attempted assassination of a US secretary of state in the nineteenth century:

> The photograph is handsome, as is the boy: that is the *studium*. But the *punctum* is: he is going to die. I read at the same time: This will be and this has been; I observe with horror an anterior future of which death is the stake ... the photograph tells me death in the future. ... In front of the photograph of my mother as a child, I tell myself: she is going to die ... I shudder ... over a catastrophe which has already occurred. Whether or not the subject is already dead, every photograph is this catastrophe.
>
> (Barthes 1984: 96)

The wound or *punctum* for Barthes, in this case, is not a particular detail of the photograph. Instead, it has to do with time (specifically, with what we have called the irreversible passing away of human lifetime) and our being towards death (Heidegger 1962; Giddens 1984).

Chapter 4 started with an explanation and critique of Barthes' early, ground-breaking work on connotation and myth. Whilst his analysis of images is valuable in opening up issues of signification in popular culture, I favoured the social semiotics developed by Volosinov, which stresses the importance of contextual factors in meaning construction (and of what he calls the multi-accentuality of the sign). It was shown how the ideas of Barthes and Volosinov helped to inspire Hall's thinking, in the critical paradigm of media and cultural studies, on the encoding and decoding of broadcast discourse. This thinking led, directly or indirectly, to subsequent empirical research on interpretations of television texts, including on local readings and appropriations of programmes that were distributed transnationally. My account of social-semiotic theory then moved on to writings that highlight situated acts of media use in daily life, and what Silverstone terms the textuality of information and communication technologies. A key feature of this body of academic literature is its concern to relate signifying practices to patterns of cultural difference and power in contemporary society. Much the same concern also permeates work by Bourdieu and others on the unequal distribution of cultural capital. However, the focus there is less on the meanings of particular symbolic forms or technological artefacts than on a social hierarchy of tastes and a politics of cultural distinction. From these approaches to the social variability of interpretation and value, my discussion returned ultimately to Barthes (to his late writing on the poignancy and evidential force, for him personally, of specific photographic images).

5

IDENTITY

In this concluding chapter, I focus on issues of self and collective identity, engaging with arguments about the emotional, experiential and performative dimensions of contemporary social life, and what might broadly be termed the symbolic construction of 'community' (Cohen 1989) in modern societies. At various points over the coming pages, these issues are explored in relation to media and their uses, although my point of departure here will be a more general account of the formation of the self offered by Anthony Giddens (1991). Ultimately, he attempts to link the intentionality of personal lives with the extensionality of globalising processes, insisting that his account, despite its strong emphasis on self-identity, is not primarily a 'work of psychology'. Rather, it puts a sociological stress on the ways in which personal feelings are bound up with modernity's institutional features (giving rise, in particular, to those unique conjunctions of 'trust' and 'risk' that were mentioned briefly at an earlier stage in the book). For Giddens (1991: 2), then, self and society are now interconnected in a 'global milieu', where 'mechanisms of self-identity ... are shaped by – yet also shape – the institutions of modernity'.

Trust

Borrowing certain ideas from psychoanalysis, and especially from that strand of it which has come to be known as 'object relations' theory (Winnicott 1965; 1974), Giddens (1991) explains how the development of 'basic trust' (Erikson 1950) is crucial for self-formation. Basic trust is usually established in a child's relationship with its early caretakers and has to do with 'the emotional acceptance of absence: the "faith" that the caretaker will return, even though she or he is no longer in the presence of the infant' (Giddens 1991: 38). That trust or faith develops in the context of what has been called 'potential space' (and see Silverstone 1993: 581, who prefers to think of it as the opening up of a 'space for potential', in which 'the separation of "me" from "not me" can take place'). In this space, 'transitional objects' such as blankets or soft toys (the precise objects will be historically and socially variable) are often significant for the child, both as 'defences against anxiety' and as 'links with an emerging experience of a stabilised world of objects and persons' (Giddens 1991: 39). Roger Silverstone (1993; 1994) suggests media of communication, above all television, should also be understood as transitional objects of a kind, which can subsequently occupy the space vacated by an infant's 'first "not-me" objects'. We return to that intriguing analysis of television later.

Giddens (1991: 39–40) proceeds to extend these ideas about basic trust in familiar others by introducing his own concepts of 'emotional inoculation' and 'protective cocoon':

> The trust which the child ... vests in its caretakers, I want to argue, can be seen as a sort of emotional inoculation against existential anxieties – a protection against future threats and dangers which allows the individual to sustain hope and courage in the face of whatever debilitating circumstances she or he might later confront. Basic trust is a screening-off device in relation to risks and dangers in the surrounding settings of action and interaction. It is the main emotional support of a defensive carapace or protective cocoon which ... individuals carry around with them as the means whereby they are able to get on with the affairs of day-to-day life.

When he says above that basic trust is a 'screening-off device', which enables individuals to protect themselves against anxieties and 'to get on with ... day-to-day life', this connects with his observations on how ontological security is sustained in part by a 'bracketing out' of the 'chaos' lurking on 'the other side of what might appear to be quite trivial aspects of ... action and discourse' (Giddens 1991: 36). There, he refers us to Harold Garfinkel's sociological experiments with trust and the conventions of ordinary language use in everyday social situations (Garfinkel 1984).

What Garfinkel did was simply to instruct a number of student volunteers to question any taken-for-granted assumptions made in face-to-face, conversational communications with their friends or relatives. For example, in the dialogue reproduced below, a student named Ray repeatedly asks for clarification of what would normally be accepted as quite routine enquiries:

> Hi, Ray. How is your girl friend feeling?
>
> What do you mean, 'How is she feeling?' Do you mean physical or mental?
>
> I mean how is she feeling? What's the matter with you? (He looked peeved.)
>
> Nothing. Just explain a little clearer what do you mean?
>
> Skip it. How are your Med School applications coming?
>
> What do you mean, 'How are they?'
>
> You know what I mean.

I really don't.

What's the matter with you? Are you sick?

(in Garfinkel 1984: 42–3)

As Giddens (2001: 87) notes in a commentary on those experiments, the reason why a social actor is likely to get so upset by such 'breaches' of the conventions of ordinary talk is precisely because they call into doubt 'unstated cultural assumptions about what is said and why', assumptions that serve in turn to underpin the order of daily interaction and allow mundane conversation to be meaningful for the participants. This student is, irritatingly but successfully, disrupting (and thereby highlighting) an aspect of practical consciousness employed in instances of 'small talk'. If, in their everyday dealings with others, people were unable to screen off or bracket out at least a fair spread of the whole 'range of possibilities' open to them in interpreting talk, then Giddens (1991: 36) proposes that the result would be a chaos involving the loss of any cooperatively produced 'framework of reality'.

The writings of Giddens on basic trust, and of Garfinkel on experiments designed to breach trust conventions, are taking us back in many ways to my discussion of day-to-day routines in the opening chapter, where we initially encountered the notions of ontological security and practical consciousness. Giddens believes that the cyclicity of routine and continuity of care are important in the life of an infant. In adult life, too, he sees everyday rituals continuing to be 'coping mechanisms' for dealing with fundamental anxieties of human existence, perhaps the most fundamental of which has to do with knowledge of our own finitude. Of course, a completely unwavering 'commitment to established routines' could be a sign of compulsive behaviour, yet his view is that routine also provides 'a central element of the autonomy of the developing individual': 'the practical mastery of how to "go on" in the contexts of social life is not inimical to creativity, but presumes it and is presumed by it' (Giddens 1991: 40–1).

As I will explain in due course, Giddens builds on this basic conception of the self and of social action, which centres on the dynamic between feelings of security and anxiety, applying it in a much wider discussion of experiences in the distinctive conditions of (predominantly late) modern existence. Problems can sometimes arise when social or cultural theories rely too heavily on a 'transhistorical', psychoanalytical model of 'subjectivity' (as in the rather different case of Lacanian film analysis, see Hall 1980b for a critique), but Giddens is committed to comprehending senses of security and anxiety, or trust and risk, in their contemporary specificity. Let me give just one example of that commitment at this stage, to help prepare the way for a fuller discussion to follow.

Inattention

Like Garfinkel's breaching experiments, the example I have in mind is concerned with a feature of daily social interaction, although our focus here is on body language rather than speech. Giddens (1990; 1991; 2001) approvingly cites the work of Erving Goffman (1963) on civil inattention in public settings (a concept first mentioned in passing in my notes on the doubling of place and social relationships in practices of media use). One of the highly distinctive characteristics of modernity, at least for the city dweller, is the experience of passing hundreds, maybe even thousands, of strangers each day while physically moving around, as compared with life in pre-modern cultures where the figure of 'the stranger' was far less common. Goffman (1963: 84) describes the behaviour that is frequently found in this 'unfocused interaction' between unknown others:

> Where the courtesy is performed between two persons passing on the street, civil inattention may take the ... form of eyeing the other up to approximately eight feet, ... and then casting the eyes down as the other passes – a kind of dimming of lights ... we have here what is perhaps the slightest of interpersonal rituals, yet one that constantly regulates the social intercourse of persons in our society.

An equivalent instance would be the actions of strangers who share a lift or elevator. It is usual in such a local situation for prolonged eye contact to be avoided, for the gaze to be averted, since staring may well be interpreted as a hostile act (for confirmation of this important point about avoidance of eye contact, along with a recognition that a degree of discrete 'monitoring' of others is necessary, see also Bauman 1990: 67).

Sociologist Barbara Misztal (1996), drawing on a further key concept of Goffman's that we have met previously, discusses civil inattention as a sort of reciprocal tactfulness or face-work (Goffman 1967). Similarly, Giddens (1990: 81) reads it as a 'demonstration of ... polite estrangement ... an implicit reassurance of lack of hostile intent'. For him, the crucial thing about this polite estrangement is that it 'serves to sustain attitudes of generalised trust' in public places where there is inevitably a level of risk, making it 'an elemental part of how modernity is "done" in everyday interaction' (Giddens 1991: 46). He tells us that the ritual was not performed in pre-modern contexts, so on those rare occasions when people encountered a stranger they could 'stare in a way that would seem rude or threatening in a modern social environment' (Giddens 1991: 47).

Practices of civil inattention, which construct an 'implicit contract' for 'mutual protection', provide a helpful illustration of how, according to Giddens (1990: 81), 'apparently minor aspects of bodily management' may be connected to 'some of the most pervasive features of modernity' (in this case to the anonymity and associated dangers, as well as the opportunities, of urban cultures). At the same time, though, his example drawn from Goffman tends to assume a fairly unitary experience of contemporary city living. He does note that, when a person walks through a 'tough neighbourhood' with which she or he is unfamiliar, there could be a lack of trust in the intentions of others. However, I think Giddens fails to appreciate fully the differing degrees of security and anxiety that might be felt by people in different social positions. Without wanting to be reductive, it seems to me that these feelings of safety and danger must surely be related, in complex ways, to divisions of class, gender, generation and ethnicity (and see Tulloch 2000). In other words, experiences of being in the physical presence of strangers in cities today are likely to be highly varied and uneven (for a broader critique of Giddens along similar lines, see Anthias 1999). Indeed, this critical point connects with Giddens' own admission that his theory of self and society does 'not try to document those inequalities' (Giddens 1991: 6).

Reflexivity

There is a good deal more to say yet on trust and modernity, and we will be returning to this topic shortly in a section of the chapter that focuses on experiences of risk (we also return below to relations with 'familiars' and strangers). In that section, the dynamic between feelings of security and anxiety is examined in the context of technologically mediated communication. First, though, it is necessary for us to consider a further element in Giddens' account of selfhood. Up to this moment in our discussion of his work, I have not specified exactly what he means by the term 'self-identity'. Doing so now requires me to turn to his concept of 'reflexivity', since self-identity 'presumes reflexive awareness' and is defined by Giddens (1991: 53) as 'the self ... reflexively understood by the person in terms of her or his biography'.

'A person's identity', asserts Giddens (1991: 54), 'is ... to be found in ... the capacity to keep a particular narrative going.' Like others in the humanities and social sciences who are interested in issues of self or subjectivity (for example, see Ochberg 1994; Plummer 1995; Sarup 1996; Finnegan 1997), he argues that self-identity is 'storied' (indeed, it might be possible to theorise collective identities in much the same way, see especially Bhabha 1990). There is a 'narrative of the self', through which a coherent, yet always revisable and contestable, biography may be constructed.

Such stories can be told to others, but often they are located in what cultural studies theorist Richard Johnson (1986: 300–1), names the 'forms of inner speech and narrative':

> Are we not all continuous, resourceful and sometimes frenetic story-tellers? Narrative form is not only universal in culture's objective manifestations, in texts that impinge on us from 'outside'. We tell stories 'inside' our heads, in the imaginative world ... which accompanies our every action. We are not merely positioned by narratives we read; we position ourselves by our constant internal narrations. We use 'realist' forms of narrative to plan the future ... 'fictional' or fantastical forms to escape, divert or take a pleasurable break. We construct stories about our individual and collective pasts. As well as

repressing embarrassing or traumatic moments, we relive them imagi-
narily. Such memories and histories are important in constructing a
sense of who we presently are. This is one way in which we secure
some subjective continuity ... how we struggle – individually or
collectively – for some integrity.

There are two things in particular that I want to highlight in this passage. One
is the way in which Johnson evidently distances himself from certain structuralist or poststructuralist perspectives. When he claims that individuals are
'not merely positioned by narratives' in texts 'that impinge on' them (insisting
'we position ourselves', too, in 'our constant internal narrations'), his clear aim
is to reinstate a degree of agency to a 'theory of the subject' from which experience and social action have been evacuated, or else explained away as the
illusory effects of ideology and public discourse (a more recent critical commentary on the 'repudiation of experience' in poststructuralism is provided by
Pickering 1997).

Second, though, Johnson does recognise that publicly circulated narrative
forms help to give structure to private stories of the self. Valentin Volosinov
(1986) remarks on how 'inner speech' is dependent on 'semiotic material'.
Johnson's view is the same in the sense that he believes a realist, fictional or
'fantastical' form gets appropriated in the organisation of an inner narrative, and
Giddens (1991) actually makes a similar, if brief and underdeveloped, point
about the possible implications of media entertainment for 'reflexive biographies'. Referring to soap operas, his assertion is that, even if the content of
these continuous serials is occasionally disturbing, 'what matters' most is the
form: 'in these stories one gains ... a feeling of coherent narrative' (Giddens
1991: 199). He seems to be suggesting that this sense of narrative coherence
and continuity over time can be made use of by regular viewers, enabling them
to gain some 'reflexive control' over their own 'life circumstances' through the
personal stories they tell themselves.

The two aspects of Johnson's argument foregrounded in my comments
above, as well as Giddens' ideas on the narrative of the self, are echoed (and
pursued) by John Thompson (1995) in his account of self and experience in a
'mediated world'. He starts by arguing that an unfortunate legacy of the critical
social and cultural theory elaborated within 'a broadly "structuralist" tradition'
is an 'impoverished conception' of selfhood (Althusser 1984 would serve as a
classic example of this problematic tendency). In that body of work, states
Thompson (1995: 210), 'the self is viewed largely as a product ... of the
symbolic systems which precede it'. There, emphasis is put on the subjection of
individuals to the symbolic order of language and culture, and subjectivity is
usually theorised as highly fragmented (for one of the better attempts to
advance a poststructuralist theory of the subject, which at least recognises the
problem of evacuating agency completely, see Henriques et al. 1984). Instead,
drawing principally on the philosophical tradition of hermeneutics (for instance,

Ricoeur 1974), Thompson's preference is to see the self as 'a symbolic project that the individual actively constructs ... out of the symbolic materials which are available to him or her, materials which the individual weaves into a coherent account of who he or she is' (Thompson 1995: 210). Self-identity is understood here as a creative enterprise. However, Thompson adds a crucial word of caution, reminding us that the materials creatively accessed by individuals in the 'symbolic project of the self' are 'distributed unevenly'. Interestingly, he backs up his qualification concerning social inequalities by citing Pierre Bourdieu's sociology of culture, which we met in the previous chapter.

Furthermore, for Thompson (1995: 212) the key feature of self-formation in the modern period is the growing importance of what he calls 'mediated symbolic materials': 'increasingly the self becomes organized as a reflexive project through which the individual incorporates mediated materials (among others) into a ... biographical narrative'. This subjective dimension of social change brings with it, in his opinion, both 'new options' and 'new burdens':

> The growing availability of mediated experience ... creates new opportunities, ... new arenas for self-experimentation. An individual who reads a novel ... is not simply consuming a fantasy; he or she is exploring possibilities, imagining alternatives, experimenting with the project of the self. But as our biographies are opened up by mediated experience, we also find ourselves drawn into issues and social relations which extend well beyond the locales of our day-to-day lives. We find ourselves not only to be observers of distant others and events, but also to be involved with them in some way. ... We are called on to form a view about, to take a stand on, even to assume some responsibility for, issues and events which take place in distant parts of an increasingly interconnected world. ... Most individuals try, as best they can, to steer a path between the claims and responsibilities arising from the practical contexts of their day-to-day lives, on the one hand, and those stemming from mediated experience, on the other.
>
> (Thompson 1995: 233–4)

The main burden that Thompson identifies in the extract has to do with an individual's response to the plight of others on a global scale. Those others could be the victims of, say, famine, poverty or genocide. Via broadcasting, then, listeners and viewers are able to witness various disconcerting representations of 'distant suffering' (Boltanski 1999). Of course, as Thompson (1995: 229) acknowledges, an understandable emotional reaction to the spectacle of human suffering is to maintain a distance, either by changing channel (a different type of inattention to the one detailed earlier) or by choosing to attend to more pressing local demands: 'Who has not felt the need, from time to time, to turn away from the images that appear on the TV screen, to close off temporarily the realm of experience opened up by this medium?' Yet there are also some indications that a precarious sense of 'global responsibility' may be emerging, with media exerting a 'moral force' (raising quite complicated issues concerning 'the compassion of the audience' and the phenomenon known as 'compassion fatigue', see Tester 2001).

' "How shall I live?" ' becomes a central question in what Thompson terms the 'reflexive project' of self-identity, to be 'answered in day-to-day decisions about ... what to wear and what to eat – and many other things' (Giddens 1991: 14). These decisions are often taken in response to more specific 'questions that were unprecedented in premodern times; for example, "How do I raise my child?" or "How do I treat my spouse?" ' (Grodin and Lindlof 1996: 6). Indeed, another such (distinctively modern) question would be about how to respond to the suffering of unknown others witnessed on television. The answers are not always straightforward. They may be a matter of debate, open to revision and potentially the cause of uncertainty. In all of these examples, not just the last one, the interpretation or appropriation of mediated symbolic materials can play a crucial role in any decision-making process. Communication researchers Debra Grodin and Thomas Lindlof (1996) point to self-help books, talk shows and advertising as just a few of those media genres that are concerned with, and to some extent constitutive of, dilemmas of 'how to live' (with what to wear and eat, how to conduct family relations and so forth).

All human cultures involve some 'reflexive monitoring of action' in the sense that social actors routinely monitor what they do in the course of doing it, whether at the level of practical or discursive consciousness. Still, Giddens (1990; 1991) is at pains to stress that there is a distinctive 'reflexivity of modernity'. This radicalised and 'thoroughgoing' reflexivity applies not only to the construction of self-identities and social relationships, but also to the institutional dimension of modern society. A telling instance of institutional reflexivity is to be found in the realm of modern science, where it was once thought that scientific knowledge would progressively bring greater certitude to life. It turns out, though, that modernity's reflexivity, which is characterised by 'the susceptibility of most aspects of social activity, and material relations with nature, to chronic revision', actually serves to undermine certainty of knowledge because no matter 'how cherished, and apparently well established, a given scientific tenet might be, it ... might have to be discarded altogether ... in the light of new ideas or findings' (Giddens 1991: 20–1).

Risk

I shift our analytical focus now to the concept of risk, which is closely related to the ideas about uncertainty outlined above. Risk is a key word in the vocabulary of Giddens' later work (Giddens 1990; 1991; 1999) and it is even more central to Ulrich Beck's sociological theory of second modernity or 'world risk society' (Beck 1992a; 1992b; 1999; Beck and Willms 2004). Each of these theorists (whose thoughts on reflexivity and risk have evolved in remarkably similar ways, as demonstrated by their dialogue in Beck *et al.* 1994) observes that there is something unique about a number of the risks currently facing humanity. In my commentary below, I will try to explain why they believe this is so, making reference to relevant illustrations of contemporary risk and 'risk-anxiety'. However, I go on to propose (see also Cottle 1998) that insufficiently detailed attention is given by those social theorists to the role of mediated symbolic exchanges in constituting experiences of risk (of trust and security too). As Myra Macdonald (2003: 105) argues, media discourses are significant 'in helping to structure perceptions of where risk lies'.

According to Giddens (1991: 4), modernity incorporates a new element of risk and a novel 'risk culture':

> Modernity reduces the overall riskiness of certain areas and modes of life, yet at the same time introduces new risk parameters largely or completely unknown to previous eras. These parameters include high-consequence risks: risks deriving from the global character of the social systems of modernity. ... However much there is progress towards international negotiation and control of armaments, so long as nuclear weapons remain, or even the knowledge necessary to build them, and so long as science and technology continue to be involved with the creation of novel weaponry, the risk of massively destructive warfare will persist.

When he begins the passage reproduced here by noting how the 'overall riskiness of certain areas' of social life is reduced in the late modern age, his point is that, for instance, modern medicine and health care have drastically improved the life expectancy of most people living in the 'developed world'. Yet the 'new risk parameters' associated with an accumulation of nuclear weapons, to pick up on Giddens' own example, are of a sort that could not have been imagined in earlier historical periods. For the first time in history, there is the development of a technical capacity to destroy human societies altogether.

We might wonder how individuals are able to cope emotionally with such an unprecedented, 'high-consequence risk' as the threat of global nuclear annihilation. Giddens (1990: 132) assumes that most people manage to do so pragmatically by bracketing out the risk-anxiety and getting on with their regular daily business: 'While it would be difficult to deem irrational someone who was constantly and consciously anxious ... about the possibility of nuclear war ... this outlook would paralyse ordinary day-to-day life.' In addition, he suggests that there is often the emergence of a sense of 'fate'. It would perhaps be better for us to say 're-emergence', since this kind of sense was common in pre-modern cultures where catastrophic events were frequently presumed to be in the lap of the gods. This serves to relieve the individual of 'the burden of engagement with an existential situation which might otherwise be chronically troubling' (Giddens 1990: 133). People may manage the anxiety and 'cocoon' themselves, then, by falling back on the security of routine and predictability in everyday life, or else by deeming the situation to be beyond their control and therefore not worth worrying about unduly. Of course, there are other possible responses as well, including that of 'radical engagement', where people mobilise to protest against perceived sources of danger and in a concerted effort to alter the political climate (as in campaigns for nuclear disarmament).

Although the threat of a nuclear holocaust brought about by military conflict must be the ultimate contemporary risk, it is far from being the only one. Indeed, it could be argued that there are far more tangible fears associated with additional 'manufactured risks' (Giddens 1999) and 'manufactured uncertainties' (Beck and Willms 2004) in late or second modern times. 'At a certain point ... very recent in historical terms', writes Giddens (1999: 26–7), 'we started worrying less about what nature can do to us, and more about what we have done to nature' (yet there are obviously those in less affluent parts of the world who do still worry, with good reason, about 'the risk of famine when the harvest is bad'). When referring to what has been 'done to nature' he has in mind risks that are, or at least strongly appear to be, socially produced, like the threats of global climate change, nuclear power generation, so-called 'mad cow disease' and genetically modified crops.

Beck takes as his paradigmatic case of contemporary, manufactured risk the consequences of an accident in the 1980s at Chernobyl, a nuclear power station in what was then the Soviet Union. In an interview, he tells the story of the unfolding happening from his own perspective in Germany:

> We were suddenly exposed to a danger that was physically imperceptible and which could only be experienced through mediation, through the media, which meant through the contradictory statements of experts. ... To get answers to the most everyday questions, like 'Can I let my kid play in the sandbox? Can I buy mushrooms?' ... we were dependent on the minute to minute statements of experts who were simply blinding in their contradictoriness. And underneath it all was the horrifying thought that maybe food itself might now be poison.
>
> (Beck and Willms 2004: 117)

A number of important factors converge in this instance. While the accident initially takes place in a local context, the risk gets distributed transnationally (it cannot be confined to one place or even to a single nation-state). Radioactivity does not respect geographical boundaries, being blown across large parts of Europe. Since the radioactive fallout is not immediately visible, Beck recognises that technologically mediated communication becomes significant in breaking the news of risk and in the dissemination of advice to the public. Nevertheless, as he makes clear, the expert scientific advice on offer through media is marked by contradictions. There is deep uncertainty, at both an institutional and a personal level, about what to do in the short term. Furthermore, an element of uncertainty continues into the future because, as Giddens (1999: 29) says of Chernobyl: 'No one knows what its long-term consequences will be.'

If we look at the case of mad cow disease, 'the BSE episode', or at the cultivation of genetically modified crops, then much the same uncertainty is evident. The future health risks are unknown. They are, to be precise, what Giddens (1999) labels 'known unknowns'. For ordinary consumers of food, there are potential health hazards and dilemmas to be confronted in the course of daily living. John Tulloch and Deborah Lupton (2003) present us with findings from research into everyday experiences of risk, and 'lay risk knowledges', in Britain and Australia, reporting amongst other things on some interesting responses to the issue of 'GM foods'. One of their interviewees draws a parallel that is pertinent to my current discussion: 'I don't think the companies who play around with genetics have ever done enough to be sure of the implications ... take any major advance in science ... like nuclear energy – people haven't researched that well enough' (in Tulloch and Lupton 2003: 76). This person is well aware that there are serious unknowns associated with modern science, leading to a lack of trust in the reliability of particular scientific 'advances'. Of course, whilst it is possible to act cautiously in order to minimise any harm from genetically modified food products, it would be impossible to gain physical protection from another nuclear incident on the scale of Chernobyl.

It would also be impossible to adopt and maintain a general attitude of distrust with regard to all 'expert systems' in the modern world. Again, that 'would paralyse ordinary day-to-day life' (Giddens 1990: 132). In his notes on disembedding mechanisms, certain elements of which I have already summarised in my discussion of extensionality, Giddens (1990; 1991) points out that in order to get on with everyday existence today it is necessary for lay individuals to put trust or faith in many abstract systems of technical knowledge they cannot fully comprehend. This is because expert systems are mechanisms that 'penetrate virtually all aspects of social life in conditions of modernity' (Giddens 1991: 18).

An initial example of routinely relying on technical know-how or expertise is that of inhabiting a modern house. 'Simply by sitting in my house', Giddens (1990: 27) remarks, 'I am involved in an expert system, or a series of such systems, in which I place my reliance.' He explains that his understanding of the knowledge employed by the architect and builder is very limited, yet if he is going to climb the stairs (without fear of the building collapsing) then faith is required in their professional competence, and in the knowledge they have used in designing and constructing the house. We might add that contemporary residential settings depend on specialist systems for the provision of running water, electric lighting and so on.

Giddens' tale of sitting in his house is followed up when he offers us other examples that have to do with technologies of transportation:

> When I go out of the house and get into a car, I enter settings which are thoroughly permeated by expert knowledge – involving the design

and construction of automobiles, highways, intersections, traffic lights and many other items. Everyone knows that driving a car is a dangerous activity, entailing the risk of accident. In choosing to go out in the car, I accept that risk, but rely upon the aforesaid expertise to guarantee that it is minimised as far as possible. ... When I park the car at the airport and board a plane, I enter other expert systems, of which my own technical knowledge is at best rudimentary.

(Giddens 1990: 28)

In this narrative of travelling by road and air, his emphasis is on the relationship or the tension between trust and risk factors. He recognises that there is a degree of danger involved in driving (statistically, it is riskier than flying), but still makes his 'faceless commitment' to the systems of car construction, road building and traffic control.

Alongside the faceless commitments made by lay actors to abstract systems of expertise, Giddens also identifies the operation of what he chooses to call 'face-work commitments' (a rather looser use of the term than that originally found in Goffman 1967). Those latter commitments are made in specific social contexts, 'access points' at which the human representatives of expert systems encounter ordinary members of the public in physically co-present, face-to-face interaction. Here, there is a process of 'reembedding ... the ... recasting of disembedded social relations so as to pin them down (however partially or transitorily) to local conditions of time and place' (Giddens 1990: 79–80). For instance, returning to his travel story, he comments on how 'the studied casualness and calm cheer of air crew personnel are probably as important in reassuring passengers as any number of announcements demonstrating statistically how safe air travel is' (Giddens 1990: 86). The 'demeanour' of the representatives in this type of situation is designed to display a 'manifest trustworthiness' and an 'attitude of "business-as-usual"'.

So far, in our consideration of the academic literature on risk in relation to trust and trustworthiness, little has been said about media. Beck did acknowledge that technologically mediated communication was a key source of (confusing) information in the case of Chernobyl and, to be fair, his social theory does not altogether neglect the significance of print and electronic media in defining risks (see Beck 2000). At this juncture, though, I want us to think in greater depth about what we could usefully label 'the mediation of security and anxiety' in modern society.

My starting point for exploring that phenomenon is Giddens' discussion of the demeanour of institutional representatives in their dealings with lay individuals. He thinks of this purely in terms of face-to-face communications conducted in 'local conditions of time and place' (Giddens 1990: 80), but I would argue that we might expand on his model so as to incorporate the performances of, for example, particular kinds of television presenter for distant audience members. Silverstone (1993), in his analysis of television as a transi-

150

tional object bound up with the maintenance of ontological security, briefly compares the demeanour of 'air hostesses' with that of weather announcers. In both jobs, he suggests, there is an attempt to 'provide reassurance' and 'project confidence'. Through their casual and cheerful screen personae, the presenters of weather reports 'even in times of bad weather … encourage or reassure the viewer that tomorrow will be (basically) all right' (Silverstone 1993: 588).

For Silverstone (1993: 588–9), however, it is the genre of news that has 'pride of place' in this regard because there 'it is possible to see most clearly the dialectical articulation of anxiety and security – and the creation of trust':

> Reassurance is provided … levels of anxiety … are ameliorated both in terms of the structure of the news as a programme (the tidying of papers, mutual smiles and silent chat following a 'human interest' story complete news bulletins, except under exceptional circumstances of crisis or catastrophe, all over the world), and in terms of its reliability and frequency. … And it is this, as well as (or as much as) … its role as a provider of information … which needs to be understood if we are to recognize the basis for television's persistent importance in everyday life.

So his understanding of news is that it constitutes a site of 'anxiety creation and resolution'. Watching it, he implies, gives viewers a repeated impression of the riskiness and unpredictability of the world, yet this genre is nonetheless characterised by what Silverstone (1999: 119) later describes as its 'iterative familiarities', such as the 'news readers whose voices and faces we recognise, structures … that we understand, can predict and … take for granted'. Whilst his theoretical assumptions are not based on an empirical study of people watching news programmes, research carried out some years ago in the USA by Mark Levy (1982) seems to support parts of Silverstone's analysis (it also connects with the work of Horton and Wohl 1986, since Levy is interested in para-interactions with television news presenters). He confirms that many viewers see 'newscasters' as familiar and reassuring figures, with a 'history of "shared" experiences' being accumulated over time.

Of course, the human representatives of scientific expert systems (spokespeople for the nuclear power industry, for instance) will occasionally make appearances on screen themselves, using media as a point of public access in order to try to manage a crisis of confidence or promote a particular institutional position. John Corner *et al.* (1990: 16) look at the example of a promotional video produced by the Central Electricity Generating Board in Britain, which aims 'to address the increased public anxiety about nuclear energy following the Chernobyl disaster and to put the case for the economic necessity of nuclear power'. Its 'communicative design' borrows heavily from television's 'established "current affairs" discourses', including the use of an established television presenter and interviewer, Brian Walden, known for his seemingly 'impartial' journalistic style. In the course of the video, he questions the chair of the electricity board about risks posed by nuclear power generation. Their interview is 'an exercise in persuasive theatricality ... designed to show the strengths of the interviewee's position' (Corner *et al.* 1990: 18), but this does not mean that viewers will necessarily accept the promotional message on offer or remain unaware of the discursive strategies being employed.

Relations between media texts and audiences, as we saw in the last chapter, are interdiscursive. Interpretative responses will be varied and uneven, depending on the knowledge and commitment brought to bear on output by different groups of readers. Corner *et al.* (1990: 75–7) present evidence of a highly critical interpretation made by certain members of an environmental pressure group, invited by the researchers to watch the promotional video, who say of Walden: 'He was very much pro-nuclear, wasn't he, as if he was presenting ... the industry's case ... to use him in a partial setting I don't think really works.' These viewers are far from convinced or reassured by the attempt to ease public fears.

A mediation, and 'dialectical articulation' (Silverstone 1993), of security and anxiety is not only evident in instances of broadcasting or video communication. It is also possible to identify a tension between experiences of trust and risk in interactions around, as well as via, the internet. In the previous chapter, I referred to a study of children's uses of computer-mediated communication (Holloway and Valentine 2003), in which it is reported that parents often perceive the internet as a 'risky space' because of its potential to connect the family home with 'dangerous strangers' and pornographic images (fears associated with the social construction of the child as a figure especially vulnerable to risks, see Macdonald 2003). Sarah Holloway and Gill Valentine (2003) explain that there is now 'net nanny' software available for the purpose of electronically 'policing children's activities' online, which promises to reduce parental risk-anxiety. They proceed to reflect on how all of this is tied up with intergenerational relations of trust, and perhaps a lack of trust, in domestic cultures.

Joost van Loon (2000) is a social theorist who seeks to extend Beck's thesis on the risk society to the domain of online communications. The main concept in his argument is 'cyberrisks', and the examples he gives of such virtual environmental risks include the danger of credit card 'cyberfraud' and that 'hallmark of cyberrisks, the computer virus' (van Loon 2000: 238). This metaphor of the virus, in his view, comes into common use at roughly the same time as 'the arrival of AIDS on the global mediascape': 'Hence, being infected with a computer virus became associated with unsafe computing, or worse with deviant forms of computing' (van Loon 2000: 239; and see Tulloch and Lupton 1997 on television representations of risk in relation to HIV/AIDS).

Regarding anxieties over cyberfraud that are associated with the giving of personal information in an online setting, Silverstone (1999: 116) presents us with the following reflection on one of his own internet shopping experiences:

> I click onto Amazon.com, the Internet bookstore. 'Safe and easy ordering – guaranteed!' A page of reassurance. I will never need to

worry about credit-card safety, since every transaction will be 100 per cent safe. ... I am assured that there is safety in numbers: over 3 million customers have safely shopped with Amazon without credit-card fraud. And I am assured that the technology is safe. Secure Server Software ... the industry standard, encrypts all my personal information so that it cannot be read as 'the information travels over the Internet'. If I am still worried all I have to do is enter the last five numbers of my credit card and I will be given instructions on ordering by phone. Am I reassured? What is going on here?

Much the same articulation of security and anxiety that Silverstone saw in television news is what 'is going on here'. As he goes on to reply, echoing Giddens, 'I am being asked to trust an abstract system' (Silverstone 1999: 116–7), and in these particular circumstances the risk-anxiety anticipated in advance by the creators of this site has to do with the internet's relative novelty as a medium for the purchase of goods (compared with, say, the telephone or even 'the securities of the face-to-face ... the dust of my local bookshop').

Whereas transactions in a physically local bookshop that gets visited on a regular basis may still involve contact with someone whose face looks familiar, and who perhaps has a trustworthy demeanour, online shopping is more impersonal (which, we need to remember, could be experienced by some people as preferable). In the media setting Silverstone describes, there is no other person for him to interact with, as there would most likely be over the telephone. Rather, there is an electronic page. Nevertheless, it is clear from what he says that the typed text on the page employs what, in another context, critical discourse analyst Norman Fairclough (1994) has called synthetic personalisation. Its authors attempt to construct the feeling of a one-to-one, interpersonal encounter with the reader and potential customer.

Labour

Returning to earlier comments about the demeanour of aircraft cabin crew, I refer next to some of the arguments advanced by a feminist sociologist, Arlie Hochschild (1983), in an account of the training and employment experiences of that group of workers known to Americans as 'flight attendants'. Her starting point, familiar from the Marxist tradition, is the exploitation of various sorts of labour by capitalist organisations for the purpose of generating profits. She is concerned to define an increasingly important type of labour in the modern economy, though, and to distinguish it from more traditional ways of categorising the work people do, taking the job of the flight attendant (usually a woman's job) as her main case study:

The flight attendant does physical labor when she pushes heavy metal carts through the aisles, and she does mental work when she prepares for … emergency landings and evacuations. But in the course of doing this physical and mental labor, she is also doing something more, something I define as emotional labor.

(Hochschild 1983: 6–7)

For many employees today, she contends (particularly for those working in the rapidly expanding service sector, see Noon and Blyton 1997), 'human feeling' is the key capacity being exploited. 'Pink collar' workers in the service industries are often required to display and to manage emotions, their own and others', in the course of doing jobs that involve them in routine encounters with customers. Crucially, for Hochschild (1983: 5), 'the emotional style of offering the service is part of the service itself'.

My intention below is to show how Hochschild's concept of emotional labour is applicable not only to cabin crew or other employees who have to deal face-to-face with members of the public in physical, workplace settings. In addition, it might be helpful in the field of media studies for thinking about jobs entailing interactions at a distance by means of an electronic medium such as the telephone. Indeed, her lengthy description and analysis of the work of flight attendants is supplemented by a shorter discussion of 'the bill collector' who pursues debtors 'voice-to-voice' by calling them up. If the flight attendant does 'emotion work' partly in order 'to enhance the status of the customer and entice further sales by … friendliness', then bill collectors can 'sometimes deliberately deflate the status of the customer with distrust and anger' (Hochschild 1983: 16).

Central to the construction of a 'workplace identity' for flight attendants is the act of smiling, which is believed by their employers to 'project a warm personality'. On a training course, new recruits to an American airline are told: 'Your smile is your biggest asset – use it' (in Hochschild 1983: 105). They are also encouraged to imagine the passengers as 'personal guests' in their living rooms. The largely impersonal social relations with customers are supposed to be seen, then, 'as if they were personal'. A 'safe homey atmosphere' should be maintained in the aircraft at all times, they are instructed, even when there is extreme danger to the passengers. One flight attendant who spoke with Hochschild (1983: 107) proudly declares that if 'we were going to make a ditching in water … I think I would probably – and I think I can say this for most of my fellow flight attendants – be able to keep them from being too worried about it'.

Clearly, a fair amount of job commitment and performative skill is needed if passengers are to be made to feel always welcome and reassured (and from the perspective of the customer, emotional labour is 'potentially good' for the experience of flying), but Hochschild insists that this comes at a 'human cost' for the worker. There is a physical price to pay for smiling consistently on a long-haul trip, which many flight attendants find to be exhausting, yet she suggests it is the emotional cost that is most important for us to recognise. From her theoretical and political perspective, emotional labour involves an institutional

154

appropriation of sincerity and sociability for financial gain. The company 'stakes a claim' on 'private territories' that were once predominantly associated with leisure worlds. More specifically, Hochschild (1983: 97) notes that it is 'a certain type of outgoing middle-class sociability' which frequently gets appropriated in the promotion of an airline's corporate image. I have serious doubts about her division between a 'false self', which is acted or presented at work, and a 'true self' that is damaged as a result (see also Lupton 1998). Still, she raises vital questions to do with the suppression and commercialisation of feelings in the public world of employment.

Two further, significant features of the study are her concern with the standardisation of self-presentation and emotional labour in the airline industry, and the consideration she gives to the supervision or monitoring of that work. Flight attendants in the company where Hochschild did the majority of her field research complied with an 'appearance code' that required them to be weighed periodically. She reports that they could be reprimanded, suspended and ultimately fired for being over the stipulated 'maximum allowable weight'. In addition, 'they were constantly reminded that their own job security ... rode on a smiling face' (Hochschild 1983: 104).

Airline officials see a 'professional' flight attendant as somebody who has fully 'accepted the rules' of standardisation and that acceptance tends to lead to a self-regulation of personal appearance, behaviour and feeling in accordance with corporate policy. While Hochschild does not cite Michel Foucault's writings on discipline, surveillance and power (see especially Foucault 1979; 1980), preferring Goffman's on the presentation of self and the 'arts of impression management' in daily living (most notably Goffman 1959), the ideas of the former theorist would provide another possible way of conceptualising the social conditions and practices of flight attendants. Although it proves difficult, in Foucault's theory of power, to see how there might be any agency that is not completely determined in advance by institutional structures, his thoughts on the disciplinary shaping of bodies and subjectivities do strike a chord with the ethnographic account Hochschild gives.

Issues of emotion, standardisation and surveillance are significant in a later analysis of working practices in telephone call centres ('communication factories') too (Cameron 2000). Perhaps the most evident parallel between the findings of Hochschild (1983) and Deborah Cameron (2000) is the emphasis in each workplace setting on smiling. This may be surprising given the fact that there are no visual cues available to the interlocutor in telephone talk, yet Cameron (2000: 105) observes: 'It is extremely common to find the instruction to "smile" being given to telephone workers (and other "invisible" workers, such as those who make public announcements at airports and railway stations).' Obviously, whether or not smiling is considered appropriate will depend very much on the nature of the call or announcement (it would be inappropriate for the bill collectors interviewed by Hochschild), but Cameron discovers the smile to be a feature of emotional labour that the trainers and supervisors of 'telephone workers' broadly recommend.

Attending to the verbal cues given by workers in a call centre, Cameron notes that the employers seek to 'standardise' output or, in other words, to 'technologise' (Fairclough 1992) the talk by styling and scripting it. 'The goal', she explains, 'is to give customers a completely uniform and consistent experience of dealing with the organization, regardless of which employee they find themselves talking to' (Cameron 2000: 100). It is the company's identity and 'brand image' that takes priority:

> When the notion of 'branding' is extended to the verbal and other behaviour of employees ... language is regulated to ensure operators function ... as embodiments of a single corporate persona. ... By standardizing speech performance, and particularly by requiring the expression of 'standard' personality traits ('outgoingness') and emotional states ('excitement'), the call centre regime imposes on workers the demand to present themselves in a way the company determines, down to the last detail. ... The call centre regime is not alone here, of course. But the extent of scripting and the intensity of surveillance in call centres make them a particularly extreme case of institutional control over individuals' self-presentation.
>
> (Cameron 2000: 101)

Supervisors assess the performances of operators (who are encouraged, in turn, to engage in self-assessment) by taping and replaying a selection of the mediated interactions they have with customers.

Like Hochschild's flight attendants, the telephone workers who spoke to Cameron found their emotional labour to be 'hard work' and 'interpersonally demanding'. Having to construct and maintain a 'helpful and cheery service persona' throughout a shift lasting several hours, whilst under constant pressure to meet 'call handling targets', is a stressful experience. The pressures of reproducing that service day after day mean many such workers do not see themselves as having made a permanent career choice. Rather, they are in it 'for a few years', ready and willing to move within that industry in the meantime to secure better pay or working hours.

As Cameron (2000: 120–1) reminds us, telephone services are not only provided by workers in call centres: 'Another type of telephone service ... is the "sex line" ... which customers call (and for which they pay ... by the minute) to be aroused by erotic talk, produced by someone who enacts, over the phone, a fantasy sexual persona.' The workplaces in this instance are usually the private households of 'sex line workers', who are contacted by a central switchboard and asked to take a call. Despite the obvious substantive differences between the kinds of talk they produce, Cameron argues that the call centre employee and the sex line worker are both involved in ongoing emotional labour, in displaying and managing feelings on an everyday basis, and must each adopt a 'stylised' working identity (perhaps a series of identities, in the example of 'phone sex').

Gary Gumpert (1990), in media and communications, and Kira Hall (1995), from cultural anthropology, offer commentaries on phone sex that are relevant to our wider interests in this chapter. To begin with, they each recognise that the absence of visual cues in telephone communication allows for a greater degree of flexibility in the presentation of self than would typically be found in face-to-face, co-present interaction. As I will discuss later, similar points are made by other academics in relation to computer-mediated communication. In addition, both Gumpert and Hall reveal that new recruits to sex line work are trained in the adoption of certain fantasy personae or scenarios, which are drawn from what Hall (1995) terms the 'limited field of discourse' associated with the genre of pornography. Having said that, she reports that there are female 'fantasy makers' in San Francisco who perceive themselves as powerful manipulators of this discourse, particularly when they work for 'women-owned' commercial services. Gumpert (1990: 148) discovers, too, that some calls are monitored 'for the expressed purpose of controlling the quality of performance rendered by the employees'. The male manager of a phone sex company tells him the women have to be able to 'give good phone'. Again, we are brought back to those issues of standardisation and surveillance raised by Hochschild and Cameron.

Finally in this section, I want us to link Gumpert's work on phone sex with far more general matters that have to do with the distinctive feelings, and also the spatial arrangements, of familiarity and 'strangeness' in modern life (see Giddens 1990, who touches on these experiences in his notes towards a 'phenomenology of modernity'). Clearly, part of the appeal of phone sex services for their (chiefly male) users is the promise of 'arousal' in a 'remote relationship' with a stranger, which is 'free of obligation and responsibility between the consenting parties, except for satisfaction and service being provided' (Gumpert 1990: 149). On the face of it, the customer is purchasing a private, fleeting and anonymous telephonic intimacy with 'no ties' beyond the frame of the fantasy episode, and few of the risks attached to a physically co-present sexual encounter with an unknown other. However, Gumpert qualifies this perception in two ways. Based on his investigation of a phone sex company in the USA, he states that there is actually encouragement of 'an ongoing relationship between client and sexual partner' (Gumpert 1990: 148), with financial incentives for the sex line worker who can narrate regular, coherent and knowable personae for her 'call-back' clients. He goes on to note that the 'privacy of this sexual dyad is a façade where anonymity is only provided for the distant "hooker"' (Gumpert 1990: 149). Even if the mediated interaction is not recorded for supervisory purposes, callers still run an 'implicit risk' of publicity in conducting the transaction, because they effectively reveal their identities when supplying credit card data to the switchboard receptionist.

Drawing together several of the arguments covered in this book, then, my conclusion to the present section of the chapter is an observation that senses of the familiar and the strange, or the personal and the impersonal, are mapped on to the changing situational geography of social life in an increasingly complicated fashion. In modern times, the division between knowing and not knowing others is no longer such a clear split 'between people who are "here" and people who are "somewhere else"' (Meyrowitz 1985: 122). Many now have the opportunity to experience forms of familiarity (and strangeness) at a distance via media, in addition to the kinds of intimacy (and practices of civil inattention) that are found in circumstances of physical proximity.

Performativity

Up to this point, there have already been quite a few references to the notion of 'performances' (as in the acting or performing of particular roles and scripts in jobs requiring emotional labour, for instance). Performance is an important concept in Goffman's 'dramaturgical model' of self-presentation within different social settings (Goffman 1959), a model that continues to be of relevance for the analysis of modern communication, including interactions or quasi-interactions conducted via the internet and broadcasting. Specific applications of his approach, focusing on the presentation of self on 'personal homepages' (Cheung 2000), and on the construction and long-term maintenance of self-identity in radio DJ talk (Brand and Scannell 1991; Scannell 1996), serve to demonstrate that continuing relevance. However, Goffman is by no means the only thinker on matters of identity to make use of the general idea of performance.

Philosopher Judith Butler (1999) elaborates a theory of 'performativity' as she seeks to reconceptualise gender, proposing that gendered identities are always performatively produced. To put her argument as straightforwardly as possible, she is asserting that there are no femininities or masculinities outside of their 'iterative' performances in day-to-day life. 'There is no gender identity behind the expressions of gender', insists Butler (1999: 33), because 'identity is performatively constituted by the very "expressions" that are said to be its results.'

Hall (2001) points out that the significance of the term 'performative' in this context can be connected to the ordinary language philosophy and 'speech act theory' of John Austin (1962). There, utterances are understood as performative in the sense that they act on the world rather than, or sometimes as well as, describing it. To borrow Austin's phrase, verbal expressions 'do things'. As Cameron (1997: 49) explains:

> Just as ... Austin ... maintained that illocutions like 'I promise' do not describe a pre-existing state of affairs but actually bring one into being, so Butler claims that 'feminine' and 'masculine' are not what we are, nor traits we have, but effects we produce by way of particular things we do. ... Gender has constantly to be reaffirmed and publicly displayed by repeatedly performing particular acts in accordance with the cultural norms (themselves historically and socially constructed, and consequently variable) which define 'masculinity' and 'femininity'.

According to Butler, gender is 'always a doing' (we are reminded here of the language of ethnomethodology). If her emphasis is on bodily expression, on a repeated stylisation of the body that 'congeals' in time 'to produce the appearance ... of a natural sort of being' (Butler 1999: 43–4), then it may also be possible for us to relate the case she puts back to the phenomenon of speech acts, since 'people are who they are because of (among other things) the way they talk' (Cameron 1997: 49; and see Malone 1997 for a similar theoretical position derived from the writings of Goffman).

Objections to Butler's theory of performativity have come from rather different directions. On the one hand, in a retrospective commentary on her own work, written some years after its original publication, she wonders whether there is a danger that her account will lead gender to be read as 'simply a self-invention' (Butler 1999: xxv). Hall (2001: 182), on the other hand, makes the following criticism: 'For Butler ... actors are little more than ventriloquists, iterating the gendered acts that have come before them ... only ... resignification ... (and Butler points to ... drag performance) can turn this iterability on its ugly head.' So while Butler is worried about being seen to invest too much importance in personal creativity, Hall actually suggests that too much emphasis is placed there on the reproduction of 'cultural norms', save for the occasional transgressive act of cross-dressing.

Despite the objections and apparent contradictions, I believe there is a way of hanging on to these ideas about the performative dimension of social life. Indeed, in my view, notions of performance and performativity can be useful to us in our thinking on various forms of cultural identity (that is, if we understand creativity and reproduction not as opposing elements but as interdependent). Performances in a range of contexts are best made sense of in terms of what Giddens (1993) names the structuration of social practices. There is a ' "structure/ agency" tension that circulates around the concept of performance' (Tulloch 1999: 3–4).

While Butler's focus is on gender (and related issues of sexuality, see also Bell and Valentine 1995), the relevance of notions of performance and performativity need not be restricted to that area alone. For example, it might even be possible for us to recognise that there is a performative dimension to social class. If we reflect back on ideas about cultural distinction and dispositions that are found in the work of Bourdieu (1984), it is clear that he understands the reproduction of class cultures and identities as, at least on one level, the consequence of 'a doing' (involving distinctive styles of speech as well as bodily dispositions, see Bourdieu 1991). Similarly, when Paul Willis (1977) examines the social reproduction of working-class masculinities, his interest is partly in creative, situated performances of class and gender. Beverley Skeggs (1997), too, explores the acts and process of 'becoming respectable', in her study of social class and femininity, referring in passing to Butler on performativity. Of course, it is important to guard against any interpretation of class positions as simply 'self-inventions', since the creative enterprise of constructing identity through narrative or performance always gets done within certain 'conditions of existence', particular economic and discursive limits, of which a theorist like Bourdieu keeps us keenly aware. At the same time, though, we must avoid thinking of class identities and differences as just being mechanically reproduced on a structural level, with no meaningful social action and no potential for change or cultural resistance.

National identity is also 'staged' and performed, according to Tim Edensor (2002), in eventful state ceremonies and popular cultural celebrations, as well as in 'habitual performances of everyday life'. In a later section of the chapter, our attention will shift to the performance of national, and transnational or diasporic, identities. John Urry (2003: 6) goes so far as to suggest that the global is enacted: 'to perform the global implies that many individuals and organizations mobilize around and orchestrate phenomena that possess and demonstrate a global character'. He argues that images of the globe and expressions of globalisation may themselves be contributing to the constitution of a 'global space'. This is a valid point, particularly when we consider, say, the cultural significance of photographs of the 'whole earth' taken from outside its atmosphere, so long as Urry's argument does not lead us to the problematic assumption that globalisation is nothing more than a discursive construct. As I stated in the first part of this volume, the origins of global social change precede the recent popularity of 'globalisation talk'.

MUDding

When Thompson (1995: 233) wrote of mediated symbolic materials providing 'new arenas for self-experimentation', new ways of 'exploring possibilities, imagining alternatives, experimenting with the project of the self', internet interactions did not feature in his thinking, and yet some theorists of computer-mediated communication claim that the online environments known as MUDs are prime sites for 'identity play' (I will be concerned here, in particular, with Turkle 1996a; 1996b; and Bassett 1997). These theorists tend to stress the performative construction of identities, and the narrative and theatrical elements of 'MUDding': 'MUDs are a new ... genre ... of collaborative writing, with things in common with performance art ... improvisational theater ... and script writing' (Turkle 1996a: 157). Through their computer keyboards, participants are jointly authoring fantasy stories and settings for role-playing games, in which it is usual for them to create characters or enact selves that are apparently quite different to those they perform in offline social contexts. A fair degree of presentational flexibility is available there because the participants are visible to each other only through typed text on the computer screen.

Caroline Bassett (1997: 545), in her study of 'performing in cyberspace' and 'doing gender' online, notes that: 'Gender-switching is part of the subcultural furniture in ... MUDs.' She reports that there is a generalised uncertainty about the offline gender identities of other 'players'. Sherry Turkle (1996b), too, comes across several instances of 'virtual cross-dressing' (like Bassett, she acknowledges a debt to the work of Butler). However, both Bassett and Turkle recognise that there are limitations to this playing with the (gendered) presentation of self. For Bassett (1997: 538), then, there is an identifiable tension 'between gender play on the one hand, and a fairly rigid adherence to gender norms on the other', with players often 'conforming to rigid stereotypes of "their" chosen gender'. The MUD featured in her study is therefore, in many ways, 'a highly conventional place'. In Turkle's analysis of MUDding, there is the interesting observation that virtual cross-dressing can pose difficulties, especially when participants are faced with the challenge of 'maintaining this fiction' over time. It may require hard work in order 'to pass' convincingly and consistently as a woman or a man in computer-mediated interaction, if the necessary roles are not already familiar from other situations (see Turkle 1996b: 212–13).

The limitations outlined by Bassett and Turkle are significant. Although their writings certainly do foreground play, creativity and flexibility, they confirm once again that identity is not merely a self-invention. Narratives and performances of gendered self, even those that might seem highly playful and transgressive, will always have to draw on existing symbolic resources and cultural conventions. In addition, these limitations remind us that we must not fall into the trap of treating MUDs as places 'apart from the rest of social life' (Miller and Slater 2000: 4). As Lori Kendall (2002: 8) puts it, online communications are not part of 'a separate sovereign world': 'Nobody inhabits only cyberspace.' Identities presented while MUDding 'cannot be separated from the off-line physical person who constructs them' (Valentine 2001: 56). On a similar tack, Christine Hine (2000: 39) proposes that 'online and offline worlds are connected in complex ways'. Indeed, she feels that Turkle manages to go some way towards investigating the complex connections, since 'Turkle chose not to report on online interactions unless she had also met face-to-face the person involved' (Hine 2000: 22).

Turkle's research is 'multi-sited' and incorporates a mixture of methods. In her investigation of MUDding, she carries out one-to-one and group interviews whilst 'hanging out' with players away from the computer screen, in addition to her participant observation in virtual places (playing in the MUD herself). She tries to understand precisely how participants' presentations of self in various sites, physical and virtual, are articulated. To give a flavour of this approach and to open up a critique of her theoretical position, I will briefly summarise two of the individual case studies that she offers us. These examples feature the emotions, experiences and performances of American college students who are enthusiastic MUDders. We will see that the young men here have a good deal in common, since both speak about coming to the internet with long-standing troubles in life. However, Turkle suggests the social-psychological consequences of their virtual play are markedly different.

Stewart, the first case, is a graduate student who 'has had heart trouble since he was a child' and who, as a result of his health problem, has been forced to live 'within a small compass' (Turkle 1996a: 162). Corporeal existence, for him, is mainly divided between a science laboratory and a dormitory room at college. MUDding, in which he participates for 'at least 40 hours' per week, broadens his horizons in some ways through virtual travel. He explains to Turkle (1996a: 163) 'with delight that his favorite MUD is ... on a computer in Germany and has many European players':

> On the German MUD, Stewart shaped a character named Achilles, but he asks his MUD friends to call him Stewart as much as possible. ... The room he has built for Achilles on the MUD is elegant, romantic, heavily influenced by Ralph Lauren advertising. ... There are books, a roaring fire, cognac, a cherry mantel 'covered with pictures of Achilles' friends from around the world'. ... MUDs have brought Stewart the only romance ... he has ever known. At a social event held in virtual space, a 'wedding' of two regular players on the German-based MUD ... Achilles met Winterlight ... Stewart, who has known little success with women, was able to charm this desirable player.

Turkle proceeds to relate the story of Achilles' 'virtual dating' of Winterlight, leading to 'a formal engagement ceremony' in the MUD.

Online, the character that Stewart plays has the charm and confidence to 'win the girl', yet those performative skills are not translated into his offline life. According to Turkle (1996a: 167), MUDding does 'nothing to alter Stewart's sense of himself as withdrawn, unappealing and flawed'. In contrast, she takes the second case of Robert, who is apparently able to 'learn from' his MUDding experiences. These experiences help to facilitate what she calls a 'working through' of his difficulties, which have to do with prior 'severe disruptions' in Robert's family circumstances (he describes his father as an 'abusive alcoholic' who 'lost his good job' because of heavy drinking and then left to work in another part of the USA).

Initially, when Robert began MUDding at college, it was as a way of 'not thinking about anything else', of escaping his emotional troubles. After a frantic period in which he spent most of his waking hours on the internet, though, he developed a strong sense of confidence in his personal abilities:

> Much of Robert's play on MUDs was serious work because he took on responsibilities in cyberspace equivalent to those of someone with a full-time job. Robert became a highly placed administrator of a new MUD. It needed to be built and maintained. Players needed to be recruited and trained. Robert told me that he had never before 'been in charge of anything'. Now his MUD responsibilities were enormous. Building and maintaining a MUD is a large and complicated task. There is technical programming work. New objects made by individual players need to be carefully reviewed to make sure that they do not

interfere with the basic technical infrastructure of the MUD. There is management work. People need to be assigned jobs, taught the rules of the MUD and put into a chain of command. And there is political work. The MUD is a community of people whose quarrels need to be adjudicated and whose feelings need to be respected. On his MUD, Robert did all of this, and by all accounts, he did it with elegance, diplomacy and aplomb.

(Turkle 1996a: 169–70)

The comparative assessment that Turkle makes of the students' experiences seems a reasonable one. If Stewart is frustrated by an inability to be more like the 'ego ideal' character he creates for himself, then Robert feels reassured of his social worth because of MUDding, finding that 'he excels at negotiation and practical administration' (Turkle 1996a: 170). Turkle has an admirable ethnographic desire to see 'through the eyes' of the people she studies. Having said that, an emphasis on the 'therapeutic' potential of MUDs and a borrowing from the language of psychotherapy brings her to occasionally dubious, pathologising judgements. So, for instance, she ends up arguing that players must have 'a self that is healthy enough to be able to grow' (Turkle 1996a: 173) if they are to benefit from MUDding. Another example would be her assertion that an advantage held by Robert over Stewart is the relationship he has with a 'competent mother', whereas Stewart's mother 'has always been terribly distressed by his illness' (Turkle 1996a: 165). Still, this is not the only shortcoming in Turkle's conceptual framework.

More importantly, I believe there are limitations to Turkle's analysis that flow directly from her enthusiastic adoption of a poststructuralist theoretical perspective on fragmented, 'distributed' subjectivities (she chooses to refer to it as a postmodernist view of 'identity-as-multiplicity'). Apart from the fact that this perspective sits rather awkwardly beside the type of psychotherapeutic judgements about 'healthy selves' and 'good parenting' mentioned above, I very much doubt whether it provides the most appropriate conceptualisation of her empirical data on Stewart and Robert. Instead, my interpretation would be that they are each striving to 'secure some subjective continuity ... some integrity' (Johnson 1986: 301) in their reflexive biographies or symbolic projects of the self. In the account Turkle (1996a: 163) gives of Stewart, she remarks on his insistence that he 'wants to feel' his 'MUD life' can be incorporated into daily social life outside the MUD, 'that MUDs simply allow him to be a better version of himself'.

Community

Most of this final chapter has focused on aspects of the self and self-identity in modern society. I turn next, via the concept of community, to the constitution of collective identities (while recognising that there is no neat dividing line

163

between the individual and the collective, as senses of 'belonging' are often a significant element of selfhood and personal feeling). Communities of different sorts are touched on in my discussion here, from those that form in physically 'local social relations' (Crow and Allan 1994) to the construction of 'virtual community' (Rheingold 1995) or communities in cyberspace (Jones 1995; Smith and Kollock 1999), but it is necessary to start with some general observations on the idea of community.

Anthropologist Anthony Cohen (1989: 12) offers us an initial summary, in the passage reproduced below, of what he understands to be the principal use of the concept of community:

> A reasonable interpretation of the word's use would seem to imply two related suggestions: that the members of a group of people (a) have something in common with each other, which (b) distinguishes them in a significant way from the members of other putative groups. 'Community' thus seems to imply simultaneously both similarity and difference. The word ... expresses a relational idea: the opposition of one community to others or to other social entities.

Pursuing this basic point about 'similarity and difference', his interest is in how people 'think with' the cultural symbols available to them, in order to construct commonalities and mark boundaries (see also Cohen 1986). A similar point is made by Edward Said (1978: 54), when he refers to the practices of 'imaginative geography': 'A group of people living on a few acres of land will set up boundaries between ... its immediate surroundings and the territory beyond ... designating ... a familiar space which is "ours" and an unfamiliar space beyond ... which is "theirs" .'

Given our earlier concerns with the separation of time and space or the disembedding of social systems, we need to take care not to assume that community and its boundary are always tied to physical 'territory'. Indeed, Said is suggesting that even when the social relations of a group are highly localised, concentrated within 'a few acres of land', their collective identity still has to be 'imagined' (and the boundary of community symbolised) in opposition to other people and places. As Cohen (1989: 18) puts it, 'it is appropriate to consider "the idea of villageness" as symbolic'. It is also appropriate for us to consider the potentially varied meanings of 'villageness' for the inhabitants of a local settlement. If we recall the research on rural villages in Cambridgeshire reported by Doreen Massey (1995), especially her differentiation between the locals and the incomers, she clearly demonstrates that there is no single, homogeneous community mapped on to a physical place (for a review of further empirical studies, which identify localised divisions between established groups of 'insiders' and incoming 'outsiders', see Crow and Allan 1994). Of course, Massey's work is a reminder, too, that local place boundaries may be constantly, if unevenly, crossed or permeated by way of corporeal and electronic mobilities.

Consequently, the scope of terms like community and 'milieu' are currently being reassessed, with particular regard to trans-local and transnational connections (for example, see several of the contributions to Eade 1997).

Probably the most widely cited argument that communities are imagined appears in the writing of an historian, Benedict Anderson (1991), who seeks to explain the rise of 'national consciousness'. His specific historical analysis of nationhood resonates with the broader working definition of community summarised by Cohen (1989), since he is interested in the symbolic construction of similarities and differences. 'The nation is imagined as limited', notes Anderson (1991: 7), 'because even the largest of them, encompassing perhaps a billion living human beings, has finite, if elastic, boundaries, beyond which lie other nations.'

Anderson's theory of nations as imagined communities deserves our close attention, partly because he sees print media and their uses as important in processes of community formation. The 'extraordinary mass ceremony' of reading a newspaper, then, provides symbolic resources with which readers supposedly think the nation into existence each day, creating a 'confidence of community in anonymity':

> The significance of this mass ceremony ... is paradoxical. It is performed in silent privacy, in the lair of the skull. Yet each communicant is well aware that the ceremony he [*sic*] performs is being replicated simultaneously by thousands (or millions) of others of whose existence he [*sic*] is confident ... this ceremony is incessantly repeated at daily or half-daily intervals throughout the calendar. What more vivid figure for the secular, historically clocked, imagined community can be envisioned?
>
> (Anderson 1991: 35)

Paddy Scannell and David Cardiff (1991; and see Cardiff and Scannell 1987) might well respond to his rhetorical question by arguing that, in fact, the simultaneous reception of radio or television programmes provided by British public service broadcasting (the repeated ritual of watching a BBC evening news bulletin would be a classic instance of this simultaneity) is a 'more vivid figure for' the imagined national community. However, as was suggested in the opening chapter, a recent 'proliferation of broadcast channels, through cable and satellite television ... may ... play a significant part in deconstructing national cultures' (Morley and Robins 1995: 68). In any case, imagining the nation is a necessarily problematic act to begin with, because it requires numerous social inequalities and cultural differences within any 'national community' to be negotiated. For that reason, Stuart Hall (1992b: 296) insists on approaching national culture, of which the press and broadcasting can only be elements, as not 'simply a point of allegiance, bonding and symbolic identification' but also a 'structure of cultural power'.

Some criticisms of Anderson's theory are made by Edensor (2002). He repeats a common complaint 'that Anderson's focus on the imagined seems to ignore the socio-political realities of power and the organisational structures of the state', before going on to propose that Anderson puts an 'excessive' emphasis on print media and presents an analysis of nationalism which 'remains rooted in a historical perspective' (Edensor 2002: 7). Nevertheless, his commentary invites us to credit the historian for recognising a link between national sentiment and the habitual performances of 'the quotidian'. Although Anderson describes the simultaneous reading of national daily newspapers as an extraordinary ceremony, in truth it is experienced as a profoundly ordinary, uneventful practice, rather like watching the nightly television news.

Another theorist to connect senses of national community with practices of everyday life is social psychologist Michael Billig (1995), who coins the phrase 'banal nationalism' (later, we meet the related term 'banal transnationalism', Aksoy and Robins 2003). Refusing to accept the view that nationalism is confined to isolated moments of ' "hot" nationalist passion', he looks to ground the reproduction of national identities in the banal (though far from benign) 'flagging' of nationhood. In the following extract from his book, Billig (1995: 45–6) advances this argument:

> Certainly, each nation has its national days, which disrupt the normal routines. ... These are conventional carnivals of surplus emotion, for the participants expect to have special feelings, whether of joy, sorrow or inebriation. ... The great days of national celebration are patterned so that the national flag can be consciously waved both metaphorically and literally. However, these are by no means the only social forms which sustain what is loosely called national identity. In between times ... privately waved flags may be wrapped up and put back in the attic, ready for next year ... but that is not the end of flagging. All over the world, nations display their flags, day after day. Unlike the flags on the great days, these flags are largely unwaved, unsaluted, unnoticed.

To borrow Scannell's terms, we could say that Billig is more interested in dailiness than eventfulness, and like Anderson he attends to national daily newspapers as a way of flagging imagined community. However, whereas Anderson focuses on the simultaneous, repeated ritual of their consumption, Billig emphasises the habitual use of certain 'little words' by journalists in the production of national daily newspapers. These words go 'mostly unnoticed' by readers, yet they constitute 'a routine "deixis", which is continually pointing to the national homeland as the home of the readers' (Billig 1995: 11).

Earlier in this book, I explained how deictic expressions are a routine feature of face-to-face interaction in physical settings (Levinson 1983), where they 'index' a shared visual reference, and sometimes a jointly known and evaluated context (Volosinov 1976). In the case of the 'homeland deixis' of which Billig

(1995: 107) writes, where references are made, for example, to 'this country' or even just to ' "the" nation', there is 'no object to indicate ... what is there to point to?' Still, what readers are being encouraged to imagine here is a 'national place of "us", conceived as a community' (Billig 1995: 107).

In addition to the use of particular deictic expressions, distinctive styles of discourse may be significant in the performance or imagination of community. A helpful illustration for our purposes, since it is concerned with 'mundane enactments of belonging' (also, since it brings together the study of national identity with ideas about the internet and 'diasporas', on to which we will move next), can be found in an investigation of doing being 'Trini' carried out by Daniel Miller and Don Slater (2000). One of the instances of performing 'Trini-ness', both online and offline, that they describe for us is a form of talk known in Trinidad as 'the lime'.

'Liming' is the communicative style employed by participants in an internet chat room called *de Rumshop Lime*. It is an attempt to simulate a specific type of physically co-present interaction:

> The 'lime' especially evokes the street corner, where males traditionally exchanged innuendo and banter with passing females and aimed to hear about whatever was happening. The rumshop is a local, down-market drinking place ... another favourite place to lime. ... The term 'lime' is regarded as quintessentially Trini ... 'liming' was the word generally used to describe chatting online and other non-serious uses of the internet, as it would describe any similar hanging out. The Internet comes to be seen simply as liming extended to ... another social space.
>
> (Miller and Slater 2000: 88–9)

My initial discussion of the research done by Miller and Slater, at the end of the first part of this book, established their reluctance to use the concept of virtuality. The chat room interactions that they analyse, then, are understood as an extension of offline life to 'another social space', rather than as a feature of some discrete, virtual existence. They note how 'Trini youth could pursue their lime' (Miller and Slater 2000: 89) with a degree of continuity across different sites, moving from school to street to internet communication.

Miller and Slater are conscious of the pitfalls of homogenising groups of people around a category such as 'Trinidadians' (just as Harindranath 2000 was suspicious of reifying 'Indians' in a study of 'documentary meanings', cited in the last chapter). Trinidad has to be imagined as a community 'across a complex ethnic mix and a geographical dispersion across the globe' (Miller and Slater 2000: 6). There are notable differences between 'home-based Trinis', who try 'to present an ideal Trinidad to the rest of the world' (Miller and Slater 2000: 93) when they are online, and 'diasporic Trinis', who have a nostalgic tendency to regard the internet as somewhere 'to recover through re-enactment' what they miss by living away.

Nevertheless, Miller and Slater do identify Trini-ness as an ongoing cultural 'project', through which a sense of collective 'integrity' is sought.

For Howard Rheingold (1995), a theorist of computer-mediated communication who does employ the notion of the virtual, the work of Anderson on the imagination of community is attractive as a way of conceptualising the ties that bind together social groups in cyberspace. After all, Anderson is talking about a process in which shared access to textual information provides the possibility of imagining a 'togetherness' that stretches well beyond face-to-face human contacts. On this basis, maybe nations themselves could be thought of as virtual communities of a kind, although the application of Anderson's ideas to online identities and relationships is not always helpful, according to Matthew Hills (2001).

Instead of applying the concept of imagined community, Hills prefers to label a group of 'cult media' fans on the internet as a 'community of imagination' (he is especially concerned with those fans at *alt.tv.X-Files*, who debate issues arising from their viewing of an American television show). His justification for this distinction, which appears at first sight to be merely an exercise in theoretical hair-splitting, is that the participants in *alt.tv.X-Files* form 'a community which, rather than ... imagining itself in clocked time, constitutes itself precisely through a common affective engagement' (Hills 2001: 154), or through a 'common respect' for and imaginative relationship with a specific popular fiction. The internet affords many live, synchronous electronic encounters, such as those evident in MUDs and chat rooms of various sorts, but the fan site that Hills explores is a 'bulletin board service' displaying the asynchronous postings of *X-Files* fans. Writers and readers of these postings are logging on at different times. Therefore, there is not quite the same 'coincidence in the temporality of information ... the "mass ceremony"' (Hills 2001: 154) that Anderson highlights when he writes about the importance of simultaneity for imagining a nation. Neither is there the same reliance on 'routines and repetitions' for community building.

Whilst Hills (2001: 151) adds greater complexity to our understanding of the constitution of modern community, opposing the way in which, in his opinion, 'Anderson's work has been more or less simplistically transferred to cyberspace', Manuel Castells (2001) adopts another position. He believes that, rather than conceiving of social groupings (including those developed or sustained through electronic media use) primarily as communities, it is better to begin by thinking of them as being formed within networks. That is, he wants to displace the now widely accepted notion of virtual community with his theory of the network society (Castells 1996) and, more particularly, with a set of reflections on 'networked individualism' (Castells 2001).

An emphasis on personalised networking in Castells (2001) is prefigured in the work of sociologist Barry Wellman (1988). In re-evaluating the 'community question', well before his own subsequent engagement with the internet (for instance, Wellman 1997), Wellman considered the importance of what he chooses to call 'non-local social networks' (actually trans-local), which people establish by means of physical transport and telephone connections. Continuing along this line of thought, and drawing on Wellman's empirical research, Castells (2001: 130–2) contends that today:

> Increasingly ... the development of the Internet provides an appro-
> priate material support for the diffusion of networked individualism ...
> individuals build their networks, on-line and off-line, on the basis of
> their interests, values, affinities and projects. ... New technological
> developments seem to enhance the chances for networked individu-
> alism to become the dominant form of sociability ... cell-telephony fits
> a social pattern organized around ... individualized interaction, based
> on the selection of time, place and partners of the interaction.

Whatever we make of such a bold assessment of the pace and direction of change in the early 2000s, it is worth us noticing how the emerging, 'cellular' and personalised 'structures of sociability' identified by Castells seem to differ from the sociable mood that Scannell (1996) associates with broadcasting from the mid-1930s onwards (and see Bauman 2000, for a comparable thesis on 'individualisation' in the coming age 'augured by cellular telephones').

Diasporas

At the start of the preceding section, we saw how Cohen (1989) approaches community as 'a relational idea' implying both similarity and difference. His emphasis there on the opposition between bounded, though symbolic and imagined, group identities does have a good deal of explanatory value, but I now want us to interrogate this binary relation of one culture or community 'which is "ours"' to another 'which is "theirs"' (Said 1978) by exploring what have been termed 'diaspora communities' (Gillespie 2000). In the words of Paul Gilroy (1997: 303–4), a key thinker on diasporas (see especially Gilroy 1993), 'there are trends at work which make this bounded belonging poten-tially less relevant to the process of identity-formation':

> The movement of ... people across national boundaries, technologies
> that deliver modern instantaneous communication ... and globaliza-
> tion in all its forms are some of the forces determining the
> contemporary context of identity. ... I use the concept of diaspora to
> illuminate the trans-national workings of identity-formation. ...
> Diasporas are the result of the 'scattering' of peoples, whether as the
> result of war, oppression, poverty, enslavement or the search for better
> economic and social opportunities, with the inevitable opening of their
> culture to new influences and pressures. Diaspora as a concept, there-
> fore, offers new possibilities for understanding identity.

Of course, as Hall (1992b) puts it, the arrival of the Rest in the West may in certain circumstances lead to an intensified polarisation of groups. There is sometimes a 'strong defensive reaction' from members of 'dominant ethnic groups who feel threatened' by the presence of others and, in response to racism and exclusion, 'a strategic retreat to more defensive identities amongst the minority communities themselves' (Hall 1992b: 308). Each of these groupings, in its own way, entails a search for the safety and security of closed community in what is deemed to be an unsafe, 'insecure world' (Bauman 2001). However, there are also alternative routes or 'detours of identity', which require our attention to 'in-between' cultures (Gilroy 1997).

Hall (1992b) writes of the formation of 'cultures of hybridity'. Living in such cultures, he asserts, means learning 'to speak two cultural languages, to translate and negotiate between them' (Hall 1992b: 310). Marie Gillespie (2002) employs a similar vocabulary in reflecting back on her study of young Punjabi Londoners, referring to their 'cross-cultural navigations' and 'cosmopolitan consciousness' (see also Qureshi 2003 on the reflexive negotiation and performance of identities among young 'Edinburgh Pakistanis', especially her important conclusion that in future it will be necessary to address struggles for 'personal coherence' or integrity in a state of plural belongings).

Certain qualifications might be made at this point. Following John Tomlinson (1999), we have to recognise that the concept of 'the hybrid' (whilst it points helpfully towards instances of intensified cultural mixing associated with globalisation) has some 'tricky connotations'. In part, this is because of its derivation 'from notions of breeding in plants and animals' (Tomlinson 1999: 143). Above all, though, there is the danger of assuming that such a thing as 'cultural purity' existed prior to, or still exists alongside, the emergence of these ' "mongrel" forms'. Putting it another way, there is an implicit, if unintended, essentialism in the arguments about hybridity that circulate in social and cultural theory. For that reason, Tomlinson (1999: 147) wonders whether it would be preferable for us to find 'a different term that does not trail behind it all the residual biologism of "the hybrid" metaphor'.

A further note of caution is sounded by Ien Ang (1994; 2001). She warns that the 'imagined community of ... diaspora ... cannot be envisioned in any ... homogeneous way' (Ang 2001: 36). One of her own particular interests is in how, within different segments of the global 'Chinese diaspora', in Australia, America, Malaysia and elsewhere, 'Chineseness ... acquires its peculiar form and content in dialectical junction with ... diverse local conditions' (Ang 2001: 35). Diasporas, then, are just as much about 'where you're at', specifically, as they are about 'where you're from' (or else where earlier generations were from) originally.

As part of a wider investigation into the significance of media and their uses across the 'Turkish diaspora' in Western Europe, Asu Aksoy and Kevin Robins (2003) listen to what Turkish-speaking people in London have to say about the Turkish-language television that is now available to them via satellite broadcasting. The researchers point out that Turkish migrant populations in Western Europe are not predominantly tuning in to services 'specifically targeted at "Turks abroad"'. Instead, viewers are able to watch exactly what is being broadcast simultaneously in 'the country of origin'. Aksoy and Robins (2003: 92–3) believe that this is 'the key innovation in the lives of Turkish migrants ... the ability to routinely watch television from Turkey'. However, they are keen to add that 'London Turks' are not only viewing 'television from Turkey', as many will also be 'very familiar with British television', and so 'Turkish programmes are ... watched and thought about with an awareness of British television in mind ... migrant viewers ... operate in and across two cultural spaces (at least) – Turkish and British' (Aksoy and Robins 2003: 103). Although Aksoy and Robins are highly critical of existing 'diasporic media and cultural studies', wishing to distance themselves from much of the previous academic literature in that area (and see Aksoy and Robins 2000), their work on television audiences is, to my mind, precisely an examination of people's cross-cultural navigations between where they are at and where they are from.

Considering their focus on the transnational movement of images and sounds (alongside the transnational migration and resettlement of people), it is a surprise to discover that Aksoy and Robins choose to draw centrally on Scannell (1996; 2000). As they remark, 'Scannell's overall project ... is very national in orientation ... essentially a ... national phenomenology of broad-casting' (Aksoy and Robins 2003: 99–100). Despite this, his concern with the pleasures of ordinariness and, in particular, with what he names the 'for-anyone-as-someone structure' of (national) broadcasting's address to its listeners and viewers (Scannell 2000), is still of interest to them. Let me try to unpack their arguments about television and banal transnationalism in greater detail.

'The key to understanding transnational Turkish television', assert Aksoy and Robins (2003: 95), 'is its relation to banality.' They suggest that, like television viewers in other contexts, London Turks are predominantly looking to televi-sion from Turkey for a feeling of ordinariness. This enjoyable, reassuring confirmation of the 'ordinary, banal reality' of day-to-day Turkish life comes with a sense that Turkey is, experientially, being brought closer. There is, in relation to some of the output, a production of 'warm and nostalgic feelings'. At the same time, though, 'migrants can also find Turkish channels disturbing, unsettling, frustrating' (Aksoy and Robins 2003: 97). The passage below is taken from the transcription of an interview with a woman they call Hüyla, who reports a strong emotional response to watching Turkish news programmes:

> I'm irritated by the news. ... You might find it funny but, really, you sit in front of the television, you are going to watch the news, you are relaxed, everybody is curious about what's happening in Turkey; and then it says, 'Good evening viewers, today four cars crashed into each other'. ... They show these things, people covered in blood. People who know nothing about rescuing, trying to drag these people out,

> they pull them, and in front of your eyes people die. … Somebody dies
> in front of you and they show this … this is like torture … for me it is.
>
> (in Aksoy and Robins 2003: 96)

Her reaction is not an isolated instance, either, for it seems that an 'often intense discomfort' with watching the news from Turkey was an issue raised by several of the interviewees.

Aksoy and Robins (2003: 102) account for the irritation or discomfort of migrants as follows:

> Transnational viewers are often disconcerted because, on … occasions, they cannot relate to Turkish programmes as a natural, ordinary, unremarkable, everyday entitlement. … In the transnational context, there is a problem with the mode of address. Broadcasting works on the basis of what Scannell calls a 'for-anyone-as-someone' structure of address: it is addressing a mass audience, and yet appears to be addressing the members of that audience personally, as individuals. … In the Turkish case, it seems that viewers may often be made to feel like no one in particular. The conditions no longer exist for feeling at home in … Turkish broadcasting culture.

When they observe how, in many instances, the 'conditions no longer exist' for a London Turk to experience television from Turkey (especially news programmes) as addressed to her or him in person, 'as someone', their point is that migrant viewers are no longer able to watch it 'from the inside'. Rather such viewers are 'compelled to think about Turkish culture in the light of other cultural experiences' (Aksoy and Robins 2003: 103). As I mentioned earlier, one of those other experiences is that of British broadcasting with its occasionally different conventions of visual representation and constructions of ordinariness or banality.

Remarkably similar findings are presented by Roza Tsagarousianou (2001), whose analysis of media and diasporas includes reflections on the consumption practices of Greek-Cypriot migrants living in London. She tells us that, on the one hand, diasporic radio and television services help to create an environment in which certain audience members experience a sense of reconnection with their perceived 'homeland'. So some people express an appreciation of this recently available media output. For example, a woman declares: 'I can really feel at home … listen to people talk in my language, music that I understand' (in Tsagarousianou 2001: 163). On the other hand, though, there are expressions of resentment at being positioned as 'appendages of a "home audience"' in Greece. There are also criticisms of the 'standards' of Greek television, such as: 'The quality of the image is not at all good … these movies are so old – we have seen them again and again … one expects more' (in Tsagarousianou 2001: 165). We could reasonably assume that the judgement above is based on a cross-cultural comparison with other forms of broadcasting that are available in the UK.

Dwellings

Bringing this final chapter of the book to a close, I want us to think about self and collective identity in relation to 'a variety of ways of dwelling' (Urry 2000: 157). So having just considered experiences of diasporic communication, and having already encountered broader debates about trans-local and transnational flows or mobilities, we need to look a little more closely at ideas of 'home' and to 'ask how, in a world of flux, forms of … dwelling are sustained and reinvented' (Morley 2000: 13). As James Clifford (1992; 1997) acknowledges, travelling of different sorts has to be conceptualised in conjunction with practices of dwelling. There is a clear parallel here with the way in which, in my much earlier discussion of globalisation and time–space transformations, our thoughts turned ultimately to questions of place. For Urry (2000: 133), then, 'dwellings' are socially constituted when people feel themselves to belong somewhere, 'to be … at home in a place' (and see Heidegger 1993).

Houses or apartments are perhaps the most obvious examples of dwelling places, being invested by their inhabitants with meanings of home and 'at-homeness' (Seamon 1979), frequently through acts of 'consumption as appropriation' (for instance, see Miller 1990; Gullestad 1993). A home, in this sense of the word, is far more than simply a physical place in which to take shelter. It also has an emotional resonance that is captured in popular phrases such as 'home is where the heart is', 'there's no place like home' and 'home sweet home' (Jagose *et al.* 2003), which convey feelings of belonging and attachment. Of course, it should be remembered, too, that the precise manner in which home gets constituted will vary across divisions of social class (Bennett *et al.* 1999), and the making of 'home life' is traditionally a highly gendered activity (see especially Hunt 1989). Homes are domestic sites of difference and power as well as places 'to dwell'.

Media are significant in constructions of home, and so it is now important for me to expand on comments made previously in this book concerning information and communication technologies in daily social contexts. Silverstone (1999: 88) tells an intriguing story below, presumably based on personal observation, of television as an integral part of the home life of a youngster:

> A little girl … comes home from school on a summer's afternoon. She runs into the sitting room of her suburban house, throws her empty lunch box on the sofa and switches on the television. She plonks herself in front of it, kneeling on the rug. After a few minutes the garden beckons and out she goes. Down to the bottom and the swing. The television set is still on, and mother, from her panoptic view in the kitchen, noticing that her daughter is no longer watching, comes in and switches it off. The girl reacts immediately and as soon as her mother has left the sitting room runs back in, switches it on and returns to the swing, barely in earshot. What can be made of this fragment of everyday life? What might it tell us about the media's role? …

> This is the childhood world of house and home. A garden. A kitchen.
> A mother. ... And within it, now, media. The television. ... On and off.

Allowing for the problematic assumption of universal experience that seems to lie behind his reference to 'the childhood world' (what he describes above is surely a very particular experience of suburban family living), Silverstone correctly identifies the potential contribution of television, even as a provider of background sounds, to contemporary feelings of being at home. Yet television is not the only electronic medium to be appropriated in the project of turning a house into a home. In addition to radio, which began years before to play that domestic role, Elaine Lally (2002) has shown us how the computer can get incorporated into household dwelling practices.

Lally's main interest (we came across her work in my commentary on technologies-as-texts) is in the domestication of technology. This is an interest shared by David Morley (2003), although he goes on to examine 'a quite different story', namely the way in which electronic media are also implicated in a transformation or reinvention of dwelling that he calls the 'dislocation of domesticity', which involves a technological mobilisation of home. His account of the transformation revolves around the case of the mobile phone:

> Evidently, one of the things that the mobile phone does is to dislocate the idea of home, enabling its user, in the words of the Orange advertising campaign in the UK, to 'take your network with you, wherever you go'. ... As we know, the mobile phone call ... radically disrupts the physical space of the public sphere in a variety of ways, annoying others with its insistent demand for attention or imposing 'private' conversation on those near its user ... what the mobile phone does is to fill the space of the public sphere with the chatter of the hearth, allowing us to take our homes with us, just as a tortoise stays in its shell wherever it travels.
>
> (Morley 2003: 451–3)

Stretching a concept employed by Clifford (1992; 1997), it is possible to understand such privatised mobility as a kind of (often fairly localised) 'dwelling-in-travel' (there are additional links with the argument put forward by Castells 2001, regarding the emergence of networked individualism).

When Morley observes a dislocation of domesticity in mobile phone use and, incidentally, in the 'ambient television' (McCarthy 2001) found in public places like waiting rooms and airport lounges, he is not implying that objects such as the static telephone and the television set have ceased to be common household fixtures. A continued interest of his is in the connections that media forge between the domestic home and other ' "spaces of belonging" (and identity) at different geographical scales ... in which people think of themselves as being "at home" ' (Morley 2001: 425). These connections permit, for some people, imaginative dwelling in a 'national place of "us"' (Billig 1995: 107) and what Urry (2000) terms a 'virtual dwellingness', by which he means a sense of belonging in an online 'somewhere', a virtual place. On the subject of transnational diasporas, Hall (1992b: 310) notes that members of migrant groups may feel an attachment to different collective homes 'at one and the same time', as when the television viewers interviewed by Aksoy and Robins (2003) 'operate in and across' Turkish and British 'cultural spaces' (see also Olwig 1999, for discussion of a complex instance of plural belongings in which corporeal travel is not regarded as being in opposition to, but rather the prerequisite for, constructing 'proper homes'). This type of diasporic experience must be compared, of course, with that of far more (physically) 'sedentary' populations in modern societies (Morley 2000). However, we would do well to recall that, even for members of those relatively more settled and rooted groups, identity is often still formed in circumstances of imaginative or virtual travel (Urry 2000; 2002) along particular routes, and in locales which are usually 'thoroughly penetrated by … social influences quite distant from them' (Giddens 1990: 18–19).

Chapter 5 has once again revisited some of those ideas about cyclicity and extensionality that were examined in the first part of the book, although the emphasis in this concluding chapter was put firmly on the social formations of self and community in a global context. At the outset, Giddens' thoughts on self-identity and reflexivity, and also on the distinctive tension or dynamic between feelings of security and anxiety in contemporary social existence, were considered at length. There, I discussed several instances of that dynamic, in urban practices of civil inattention, for example, or else in experiences of watching the news and shopping on the internet. My commentary then shifted to matters of emotional labour, a concept initially employed by Hochschild in her analysis of work in the service sector that entails certain kinds of face-to-face and voice-to-voice (electronically mediated) encounter with customers. Such jobs, it was noted, involve the standardised performance of an appropriate persona and demeanour, and this point raises wider issues to do with identity and performativity, which were pursued partly in relation to Turkle's research on the playful type of computer-mediated communication that is known as MUDding. In the later sections of the chapter, my main concern was with constructions of collective identity. For instance, I considered the case of diasporas and cross-cultural navigations in modern societies, before arriving in the end at crucial questions of home and belonging. Answering these requires attention to how dwellings are being constituted today on different geographical scales, from the level of the private household to that of transnational communities. Furthermore, Morley proposes that the public users of mobile phones are now engaged in a novel dislocation of domesticity and mobilisation of home.

AFTERWORD

Since I have already provided summaries at the end of each chapter, and as connections between the materials in different chapters have been made at various points throughout, this afterword does not try to offer a full-blown conclusion to the book as a whole. Rather, my intention here is briefly to fore-ground a further distinctive feature of the book, beyond those features outlined to begin with in the introduction (its specific thematic structure, its attempt to bridge an established divide between the study of mass and interpersonal communications, its insistence on understanding media in their broad social and cultural contexts, and so on). An important part of the book's claim to origi-nality, as a work of review and synthesis, is its bringing together of ways of thinking about media and communications, and about social life more generally, that are conventionally regarded as being separate from one another, or even as mutually exclusive theoretical tendencies in the humanities and social sciences.

On the one hand, then, we have encountered a number of approaches in which the focus is on the cooperative achievement of intelligibility and social order, and on the practical accomplishment or performance of rituals, selves and worlds. Our journey through this book has involved us in considering, for example, particular phenomenological and ethnomethodological perspectives, as well as the sociology of Erving Goffman and some of the literature associated with discourse pragmatics or politeness theory. It would be fair to say that none of these approaches has been central to the academic field of media studies to date. Indeed, there will be many media courses in higher education that are currently taught without any mention of such work. In my view, this is a great pity because the ideas emerging out of that wide tradition of social analysis are crucial if we want to appreciate the detail of how everyday and institutional life gets done. That is why I chose to discuss at length Paddy Scannell's writings on the development of methodical and reproducible techniques for doing broad-casting (especially Scannell 1995; 1996), including his reflections on the constitution of modern forms of sociability.

Scannell is able to make use of the insights of phenomenology, ethnomethodology and conversation analysis, in addition to the theory of struc-turation advanced by Anthony Giddens (1984), but in order to do so he feels the need to set aside the vocabulary of a (now arguably mainstream) critical paradigm in media and cultural studies. Although I am clearly sympathetic to the kind of project he has embarked on, and have started to suggest how it might be pursued in the study of electronically mediated communication via telephone and the internet (see also Hutchby 2001), I do not agree with him that it is necessary for us to wipe the slate clean of all previous concepts in critical media analysis (ideology, hegemony, texts, readings, cultural politics and so forth). So, on the other hand, we have encountered ideas in this book, of inequality, difference and power relations, which will probably be more familiar to most media students and lecturers. My feeling is that those concerns with conflicting social interests and locations, which are broadly shared by proponents of cultural studies and the political-economy perspective, despite continuing disputes over precisely where meaning and power lie, cannot simply be jettisoned.

Apart from anything else, the concerns of critical researchers in several academic areas allow us to recognise the profound unevenness of what Giddens (1990) identifies as the phenomenological aspects of late modernity. Doreen Massey's comments on theories that tend to assume a singular experience of globalising processes (Massey 1992; 1994), and David Morley's critique of Scannell on constructions of fun or sociability in radio and television programmes (Morley 2000), are valuable instances of a critical approach in action. These authors choose to highlight moments of social exclusion, as opposed to those of inclusion and commonality on which a writer like Scannell is primarily focused. What we must strive to do, of course, is to combine the merits of consensus and critical views of society, acknowledging the fact that cooperation and social division are both contributing, simultaneously, to the character of contemporary life.

BIBLIOGRAPHY

Adam, B. (1995) *Timewatch: the social analysis of time*, Cambridge: Polity Press.

Aksoy, A. and Robins, K. (2000) 'Thinking across spaces: transnational television from Turkey', *European Journal of Cultural Studies* 3: 345–67.

——(2003) 'Banal transnationalism: the difference that television makes', in K. Karim (ed.) *The Media of Diaspora*, London: Routledge.

Allan, G. (1979) *A Sociology of Friendship and Kinship*, London: Allen and Unwin.

——(1989) *Friendship: developing a sociological perspective*, Hemel Hempstead: Harvester Wheatsheaf.

Althusser, L. (1984) 'Ideology and ideological state apparatuses (notes towards an investigation)', in *Essays on Ideology*, London: Verso.

Anderson, B. (1991) *Imagined Communities: reflections on the origin and spread of nationalism*, revised edn, London: Verso.

Ang, I. (1985) *Watching* Dallas: *soap opera and the melodramatic imagination*, London: Methuen.

——(1990) 'Melodramatic identifications: television fiction and women's fantasy', in M. Brown (ed.) *Television and Women's Culture: the politics of the popular*, London: Sage.

——(1991) *Desperately Seeking the Audience*, London: Routledge.

——(1992) 'Living-room wars: new technologies, audience measurement and the tactics of television consumption', in R. Silverstone and E. Hirsch (eds) *Consuming Technologies: media and information in domestic spaces*, London: Routledge.

——(1994) 'On not speaking Chinese', *New Formations* 24: 1–18.

——(2001) *On Not Speaking Chinese: living between Asia and the West*, London: Routledge.

Anthias, F. (1999) 'Theorising identity, difference and social divisions', in M. O'Brien, S. Penna and C. Hay (eds) *Theorising Modernity: reflexivity, environment and identity in Giddens' social theory*, Harlow: Longman.

Appadurai, A. (1996) *Modernity at Large: cultural dimensions of globalization*, Minneapolis MN: University of Minnesota Press.

Atkinson, K. and Moores, S. (2003) ' "We all have bad bad days": attending to face in broadcast troubles-talk', *The Radio Journal: international studies in broadcast and audio media* 1: 129–46.

Augé, M. (1995) *Non-Places: introduction to the anthropology of supermodernity*, London: Verso.

Austin, J. (1962) *How to Do Things with Words*, Cambridge MA: Harvard University Press.

Bakhtin, M. (1986) *Speech Genres and Other Late Essays*, eds C. Emerson and M. Holquist, Austin TX: University of Texas Press.

179

Baran, S. and Wallis, R. (1990) *The Known World of Broadcast News*, London: Routledge.

Barnard, S. (2000) *Studying Radio*, London: Arnold.

Barthes, R. (1968) *Elements of Semiology*, New York: Hill and Wang.

——(1973) *Mythologies*, London: Paladin.

——(1975) *The Pleasure of the Text*, New York: Hill and Wang.

——(1977) 'Rhetoric of the image', in *Image – Music – Text*, New York: Hill and Wang.

——(1979) *The Eiffel Tower and Other Mythologies*, New York: Hill and Wang.

——(1984) *Camera Lucida: reflections on photography*, London: Fontana.

——(1985) 'On photography', in *The Grain of the Voice: interviews 1962–1980*, New York: Hill and Wang.

Bassett, C. (1997) 'Virtually gendered: life in an on-line world', in K. Gelder and S. Thornton (eds) *The Subcultures Reader*, London: Routledge.

Baudrillard, J. (1988) *Selected Writings*, ed. M. Poster, Cambridge: Polity Press.

Bauman, Z. (1990) *Thinking Sociologically*, Oxford: Blackwell.

——(1998) *Globalization: the human consequences*, Cambridge: Polity Press.

——(2000) *Liquid Modernity*, Cambridge: Polity Press.

——(2001) *Community: seeking safety in an insecure world*, Cambridge: Polity Press.

Bausinger, H. (1984) 'Media, technology and daily life', *Media, Culture and Society* 6: 343–51.

Baym, N. (2000) *Tune In, Log On: soaps, fandom and online community*, Thousand Oaks CA: Sage.

Beck, U. (1992a) 'From industrial society to risk society: questions of survival, structure and ecological enlightenment', *Theory, Culture and Society* 9: 97–123.

——(1992b) *Risk Society: towards a new modernity*, London: Sage.

——(1999) *World Risk Society*, Cambridge: Polity Press.

——(2000) 'Foreword', in S. Allan, B. Adam and C. Carter (eds) *Environmental Risks and the Media*, London: Routledge.

Beck, U., Giddens, A. and Lash, S. (1994) *Reflexive Modernization: politics, tradition and aesthetics in the modern social order*, Cambridge: Polity Press.

Beck, U. and Willms, J. (2004) *Conversations with Ulrich Beck*, Cambridge: Polity Press.

Bell, D. and Valentine, G. (1995) 'The sexed self: strategies of performance, sites of resistance', in S. Pile and N. Thrift (eds) *Mapping the Subject: geographies of cultural transformation*, London: Routledge.

Bennett, T. (1986) 'Introduction: popular culture and "the turn to Gramsci"', in T. Bennett, C. Mercer and J. Woollacott (eds) *Popular Culture and Social Relations*, Milton Keynes: Open University Press.

Bennett, T., Emmison, M. and Frow, J. (1999) *Accounting for Tastes: Australian everyday cultures*, Cambridge: Cambridge University Press.

Bettelheim, B. (1960) *The Informed Heart*, New York: Free Press.

Bhabha, H. (ed.) (1990) *Nation and Narration*, London: Routledge.

Billig, M. (1995) *Banal Nationalism*, London: Sage.

Blum-Kulka, S. (1997) 'Discourse pragmatics', in T. van Dijk (ed.) *Discourse as Social Interaction*, London: Sage.

Blumler, J. and Katz, E. (eds) (1974) *The Uses of Mass Communications: current perspectives on gratifications research*, Beverly Hills CA: Sage.

Boden, D. and Molotch, H. (1994) 'The compulsion of proximity', in R. Friedland and D. Boden (eds) *NowHere: space, time and modernity*, Berkeley and Los Angeles CA: University of California Press.

Boltanski, L. (1999) *Distant Suffering: morality, media and politics*, Cambridge: Cambridge University Press.

Bonner, F. (2003) *Ordinary Television: analyzing popular TV*, London: Sage.

Bourdieu, P. (1984) *Distinction: a social critique of the judgement of taste*, London: Routledge and Kegan Paul.

——(1991) *Language and Symbolic Power*, ed. J. Thompson, Cambridge: Polity Press.

——(1993a) 'Outline of a sociological theory of art perception', in *The Field of Cultural Production: essays on art and literature*, Cambridge: Polity Press.

——(1993b) 'The art of standing up to words', in *Sociology in Question*, London: Sage.

Brand, G. and Scannell, P. (1991) 'Talk, identity and performance: *The Tony Blackburn Show*', in P. Scannell (ed.) *Broadcast Talk*, London: Sage.

Braudel, F. (1973) *The Mediterranean and the Mediterranean World in the Age of Philip II*, London: Fontana.

Brown, M. (1994) *Soap Opera and Women's Talk*, Thousand Oaks CA: Sage.

Brown, P. and Levinson, S. (1987) *Politeness: some universals in language usage*, Cambridge: Cambridge University Press.

Brunsdon, C. (1981) '*Crossroads*: notes on soap opera', *Screen* 22(4): 32–7.

——(1984) 'Writing about soap opera', in L. Masterman (ed.) *Television Mythologies: stars, shows and signs*, London: Comedia.

——(1995) 'Satellite dishes and the landscapes of taste', in E. Carter, J. Donald and J. Squires (eds) *Cultural Remix: theories of politics and the popular*, London: Lawrence and Wishart/New Formations.

——(1997) *Screen Tastes: soap opera to satellite dishes*, London: Routledge.

——(2000) *The Feminist, the Housewife and the Soap Opera*, Oxford: Oxford University Press.

Brunsdon, C. and Morley, D. (1978) *Everyday Television:* Nationwide, BFI television monograph no.10, London: British Film Institute.

Bryant, C. and Jary, D. (2001) 'Anthony Giddens: a global social theorist', in C. Bryant and D. Jary (eds) *The Contemporary Giddens: social theory in a globalizing age*, Basingstoke: Palgrave.

Bucholtz, M. (2000) ' "Thanks for stopping by": gender and virtual intimacy in American shop-by-television discourse', in M. Andrews and M. Talbot (eds) *All the World and Her Husband: women in twentieth-century consumer culture*, London: Cassell.

Buckingham, D. (1997) 'Electronic child abuse? Rethinking the media's effects on children', in M. Barker and J. Petley (eds) *Ill Effects: the media/violence debate*, London: Routledge.

Bull, M. (2000) *Sounding Out the City: personal stereos and the management of everyday life*, Oxford: Berg.

——(2004) ' "To each their own bubble": mobile spaces of sound in the city', in N. Couldry and A. McCarthy (eds) *MediaSpace: place, scale and culture in a media age*, London: Routledge.

Butler, J. (1999) *Gender Trouble: feminism and the subversion of identity*, 2nd edn, New York: Routledge.

Cairncross, F. (1997) *The Death of Distance: how the communications revolution will change our lives*, London: Orion Books.

Cameron, D. (1997) 'Performing gender identity: young men's talk and the construction of heterosexual masculinity', in S. Johnson and U. Meinhof (eds) *Language and Masculinity*, Oxford: Blackwell.

——(2000) *Good to Talk? Living and working in a communication culture*, London: Sage.

Cardiff, D. and Scannell, P. (1987) 'Broadcasting and national unity', in J. Curran, A. Smith and P. Wingate (eds) *Impacts and Influences: essays on media power in the twentieth century*, London: Methuen.

Casey, E. (1993) *Getting Back into Place: toward a renewed understanding of the place-world*, Bloomington and Indianapolis IN: Indiana University Press.

Castells, M. (1996) *The Information Age: economy, society and culture – Vol. 1, The Rise of the Network Society*, Malden MA: Blackwell.

——(2001) *The Internet Galaxy: reflections on the Internet, business and society*, Oxford: Oxford University Press.

——(2002) 'The Internet and the network society', in B. Wellman and C. Haythornthwaite (eds) (2002) *The Internet in Everyday Life*, Malden MA: Blackwell.

Chambers, I. (1994) *Migrancy, Culture, Identity*, London: Routledge.

Chaney, D. (2002) *Cultural Change and Everyday Life*, Basingstoke: Palgrave.

Charlesworth, S. (1999) *A Phenomenology of Working Class Experience*, Cambridge: Cambridge University Press.

Cheung, C. (2000) 'A home on the Web: presentations of self on personal homepages', in D. Gauntlett (ed.) *Web.Studies: rewiring media studies for the digital age*, London: Arnold.

Chodorow, N. (1978) *The Reproduction of Mothering: psychoanalysis and the sociology of gender*, Berkeley and Los Angeles CA: University of California Press.

Clifford, J. (1992) 'Traveling cultures', in L. Grossberg, C. Nelson and P. Treichler (eds) *Cultural Studies*, New York: Routledge.

——(1997) *Routes: travel and translation in the late twentieth century*, Cambridge MA: Harvard University Press.

Cohen, A. (ed.) (1986) *Symbolising Boundaries: identity and diversity in British cultures*, Manchester: Manchester University Press.

——(1989) *The Symbolic Construction of Community*, London: Routledge.

Collins, R. (1990) 'The language of advantage: satellite television in Western Europe', in *Television: policy and culture*, London: Unwin Hyman.

——(1992) *Satellite Television in Western Europe*, revised edn, Acamedia research monograph no.1, London: John Libbey.

Corner, J., Harvey, S. and Lury, K. (1994) 'Culture, quality and choice: the re-regulation of TV 1989–91', in S. Hood (ed.) *Behind the Screens: the structure of British television in the nineties*, London: Lawrence and Wishart.

Corner, J., Richardson, K. and Fenton, N. (1990) *Nuclear Reactions: form and response in 'public issue' television*, Acamedia research monograph no.4, London: John Libbey.

Corrigan, P. (1983) 'Film entertainment as ideology and pleasure: towards a history of audiences', in J. Curran and V. Porter (eds) *British Cinema History*, London: Weidenfeld and Nicolson.

Cottle, S. (1998) 'Ulrich Beck, "risk society" and the media: a catastrophic view?', *European Journal of Communication* 13: 5–32.

Couldry, N. (1999) 'Remembering Diana: the geography of celebrity and the politics of lack', *New Formations* 36: 77–91.

——(2000a) *The Place of Media Power: pilgrims and witnesses of the media age*, London: Routledge.

——(2000b) *Inside Culture: re-imagining the method of cultural studies*, London: Sage.

——(2001) 'Everyday royal celebrity', in D. Morley and K. Robins (eds) *British Cultural Studies: geography, nationality and identity*, Oxford: Oxford University Press.

Coward, R. (1984) *Female Desire: women's sexuality today*, London: Paladin.

Crisell, A. (1994) *Understanding Radio*, 2nd edn, London: Routledge.

Crow, G. and Allan, G. (1994) *Community Life: an introduction to local social relations*, Hemel Hempstead: Harvester Wheatsheaf.

Cuff, E., Sharrock, W. and Francis, D. (1998) *Perspectives in Sociology*, 4th edn, London: Routledge.

Cunningham, S. and Jacka, E. (1996) 'Australian television in world markets', in J. Sinclair, E. Jacka and S. Cunningham (eds) *New Patterns in Global Television: peripheral vision*, Oxford: Oxford University Press.

Dant, T. (1999) *Material Culture in the Social World: values, activities, lifestyles*, Buckingham: Open University Press.

Dayan, D. (1998) 'Particularistic media and diasporic communications', in T. Liebes and J. Curran (eds) *Media, Ritual and Identity*, London: Routledge.

——(1999) 'Media and diasporas', in J. Gripsrud (ed.) *Television and Common Knowledge*, London: Routledge.

Dayan, D. and Katz, E. (1992) *Media Events: the live broadcasting of history*, Cambridge MA: Harvard University Press.

de Certeau, M. (1984) *The Practice of Everyday Life*, Berkeley and Los Angeles CA: University of California Press.

Derrida, J. (1976) *Of Grammatology*, Baltimore MD: Johns Hopkins University Press.

DiMaggio, P. (1987) 'Classification in art', *American Sociological Review* 52: 440–55.

Dittmar, H. (1992) *The Social Psychology of Material Possessions: to have is to be*, Hemel Hempstead: Harvester Wheatsheaf.

Douglas, M. (1966) *Purity and Danger: an analysis of concepts of pollution and taboo*, London: Routledge and Kegan Paul.

Drew, P. and Chilton, K. (2000) 'Calling just to keep in touch: regular and habitualised telephone calls as an environment for small talk', in J. Coupland (ed.) *Small Talk*, Harlow: Longman.

Drew, P. and Wootton, A. (1988) *Erving Goffman: exploring the interaction order*, Cambridge: Polity Press.

Duck, S. (1999) *Relating to Others*, 2nd edn, Buckingham: Open University Press.

du Gay, P., Hall, S., Janes, L., Mackay, H. and Negus, K. (1997) *Doing Cultural Studies: the story of the Sony Walkman*, London: Sage/Open University Press.

Durkheim, E. (1964) *Rules of Sociological Method*, New York: Free Press.

Duruz, J. and Johnson, C. (1999) 'Mourning at a distance: Australians and the death of a British Princess', in A. Kear and D. Steinberg (eds) *Mourning Diana: nation, culture and the performance of grief*, London: Routledge.

Eade, J. (ed.) (1997) *Living the Global City: globalization as local process*, London: Routledge.

Easthope, A. (1986) *What a Man's Gotta Do: the masculine myth in popular culture*, London: Paladin.

Edensor, T. (2002) *National Identity, Popular Culture and Everyday Life*, Oxford: Berg.

Ellis, J. (1982) *Visible Fictions: cinema, television, video*, London: Routledge and Kegan Paul.

Erikson, E. (1950) *Childhood and Society*, New York: Norton.

Fairclough, N. (1989) *Language and Power*, Harlow: Longman.

——(1992) *Discourse and Social Change*, Cambridge: Polity Press.

——(1994) 'Conversationalization of public discourse and the authority of the consumer', in R. Keat, N. Whiteley and N. Abercrombie (eds) *The Authority of the Consumer*, London: Routledge.

——(1995) *Media Discourse*, London: Edward Arnold.

——(2000) *New Labour, New Language?* London: Routledge.

Felski, R. (2000) 'The invention of everyday life', *New Formations* 39: 15–31.

Finnegan, R. (1997) ' "Storying the self": personal narratives and identity', in H. Mackay (ed.) *Consumption and Everyday Life*, London: Sage/Open University Press.

Fischer, C. (1991) ' "Touch someone": the telephone industry discovers sociability', in M. Lafolette and J. Stine (eds) *Technology and Choice: readings from* Technology and Culture, Chicago IL: University of Chicago Press.

Fiske, J. (1987) *Television Culture*, London: Methuen.

——(1991) 'Popular discrimination', in J. Naremore and P. Brantlinger (eds) *Modernity and Mass Culture*, Bloomington and Indianapolis IN: Indiana University Press.

Fiske, J., Hodge, R. and Turner, G. (1987) *Myths of Oz: readings in Australian popular culture*, Boston MA: Unwin Hyman.

Flew, T. (2005) *New Media: an introduction*, 2nd edn, Melbourne: Oxford University Press.

Foucault, M. (1979) *Discipline and Punish: the birth of the prison*, Harmondsworth: Penguin Books.

——(1980) *Power/Knowledge: selected interviews and other writings 1972–1977*, ed. C. Gordon, Brighton: Harvester Press.

Fowler, R. (1991) *Language in the News: discourse and ideology in the press*, London: Routledge.

Frissen, V. (1995) 'Gender is calling: some reflections on past, present and future uses of the telephone', in K. Grint and R. Gill (eds) *The Gender-Technology Relation*, London: Taylor & Francis.

Frow, J. (1987) 'Accounting for tastes: some problems in Bourdieu's sociology of culture', *Cultural Studies* 1: 59–73.

——(1995) *Cultural Studies and Cultural Value*, Oxford: Oxford University Press.

Garfinkel, H. (1984) *Studies in Ethnomethodology*, Cambridge: Polity Press.

Gauntlett, D. and Hill, A. (1999) *TV Living: television, culture and everyday life*, London: Routledge/British Film Institute.

Gell, A. (1986) 'Newcomers to the world of goods: consumption among the Muria Gonds', in A. Appadurai (ed.) *The Social Life of Things: commodities in cultural perspective*, Cambridge: Cambridge University Press.

Geraghty, C. (1981) 'The continuous serial: a definition', in R. Dyer, C. Geraghty, M. Jordan, T. Lovell, R. Paterson and J. Stewart, *Coronation Street*, BFI television monograph no.13, London: British Film Institute.

——(1991) *Women and Soap Opera: a study of prime time soaps*, Cambridge: Polity Press.

Giddens, A. (1979) *Central Problems in Social Theory: action, structure and contradiction in social analysis*, Berkeley and Los Angeles CA: University of California Press.

——(1981) *A Contemporary Critique of Historical Materialism – Vol. 1, Power, Property and the State*, Basingstoke: Macmillan.

——(1984) *The Constitution of Society: outline of the theory of structuration*, Cambridge: Polity Press.

——(1987a) 'Time and social organization', in *Social Theory and Modern Sociology*, Cambridge: Polity Press.

——(1987b) 'Structuralism, post-structuralism and the production of culture', in *Social Theory and Modern Sociology*, Cambridge: Polity Press.

——(1990) *The Consequences of Modernity*, Cambridge: Polity Press.

——(1991) *Modernity and Self-Identity: self and society in the late modern age*, Cambridge: Polity Press.

——(1992) *The Transformation of Intimacy: sexuality, love and eroticism in modern societies*, Cambridge: Polity Press.

——(1993) *New Rules of Sociological Method: a positive critique of interpretative sociologies*, 2nd edn, Cambridge: Polity Press.

——(1994) 'Living in a post-traditional society', in U. Beck, A. Giddens and S. Lash, *Reflexive Modernization: politics, tradition and aesthetics in the modern social order*, Cambridge: Polity Press.

——(1999) *Runaway World: how globalisation is reshaping our lives*, London: Profile Books.

——(2001) *Sociology*, 4th edn, Cambridge: Polity Press.

Giddens, A. and Pierson, C. (1998) *Conversations with Anthony Giddens: making sense of modernity*, Cambridge: Polity Press.

Gillespie, M. (1993) 'Soap viewing, gossip and rumour amongst Punjabi youth in Southall', in P. Drummond, R. Paterson and J. Willis (eds) *National Identity and Europe: the television revolution*, London: British Film Institute.

——(1995) *Television, Ethnicity and Cultural Change*, London: Routledge.

——(1997) 'Local uses of the media: negotiating culture and identity', in A. Sreberny-Mohammadi, D. Winseck, J. McKenna and O. Boyd-Barrett (eds) *Media in Global Context: a reader*, London: Arnold.

——(2000) 'Transnational communications and diaspora communities', in S. Cottle (ed.) *Ethnic Minorities and the Media: changing cultural boundaries*, Buckingham: Open University Press.

——(2002) 'Dynamics of diasporas: South Asian media and transnational cultural politics', in G. Stald and T. Tufte (eds) *Global Encounters: media and cultural transformation*, Luton: University of Luton Press.

Gilroy, P. (1993) *The Black Atlantic: modernity and double consciousness*, London: Verso.

——(1997) 'Diaspora and the detours of identity', in K. Woodward (ed.) *Identity and Difference*, London: Sage/Open University Press.

Gledhill, C. (1997) 'Genre and gender: the case of soap opera', in S. Hall (ed.) *Representation: cultural representations and signifying practices*, London: Sage/Open University Press.

Goffman, E. (1959) *The Presentation of Self in Everyday Life*, New York: Anchor Books.

——(1963) *Behavior in Public Places: notes on the social organization of gatherings*, New York: Free Press.

——(1967) *Interaction Ritual: essays on face-to-face behavior*, New York: Pantheon Books.

——(1981) 'Radio talk: a study of the ways of our errors', in *Forms of Talk*, Philadelphia PA: University of Pennsylvania Press.

——(1983) 'The interaction order', *American Sociological Review* 48: 1–17.

Graham, S. (2000) 'The end of geography or the explosion of place? Conceptualizing space, place and information technology', in M. Wilson and K. Corey (eds) *Information Tectonics: space, place and technology in an electronic age*, Chichester: Wiley.

Gramsci, A. (1971) *Selections from the Prison Notebooks of Antonio Gramsci*, eds Q. Hoare and G. Nowell-Smith, London: Lawrence and Wishart.

Gray, A. (1987) 'Behind closed doors: video recorders in the home', in H. Baehr and G. Dyer (eds) *Boxed In: women and television*, London: Pandora Press.

——(1992) *Video Playtime: the gendering of a leisure technology*, London: Routledge.

——(1999) 'Audience and reception research in retrospect: the trouble with audiences', in P. Alasuutari (ed.) *Rethinking the Media Audience: the new agenda*, London: Sage.

Gregory, D. and Urry, J. (eds) (1985) *Social Relations and Spatial Structures*, Basingstoke: Macmillan.

Griffin, C. (1985) *Typical Girls? Young women from school to the job market*, London: Routledge and Kegan Paul.

Gripsrud, J. (2002) *Understanding Media Culture*, London: Arnold.

Grodin, D. and Lindlof, T. (1996) 'The self and mediated communication', in D. Grodin and T. Lindlof (eds) *Constructing the Self in a Mediated World*, Thousand Oaks CA: Sage.

Gullestad, M. (1993) 'Home decoration as popular culture: constructing homes, genders and classes in Norway', in T. del Valle (ed.) *Gendered Anthropology*, London: Routledge.

Gumpert, G. (1990) 'Remote sex in the information age', in G. Gumpert and S. Fish (eds) *Talking to Strangers: mediated therapeutic communication*, Norwood NJ: Ablex.

Gumpert, G. and Cathcart, R. (eds) (1986) *Inter/Media: interpersonal communication in a media world*, 3rd edn, New York: Oxford University Press.

Habermas, J. (1989) *The Structural Transformation of the Public Sphere: an inquiry into a category of bourgeois society*, Cambridge: Polity Press.

Hägerstrand, T. (1975) 'Space, time and human conditions', in A. Karlqvist, L. Lundqvist and F. Snickars (eds) *Dynamic Allocation of Urban Space*, Farnborough: Saxon House.

Hall, K. (1995) 'Lip service on the fantasy lines', in K. Hall and M. Bucholtz (eds) *Gender Articulated: language and the socially constructed self*, New York: Routledge.

——(2001) 'Performativity', in A. Duranti (ed.) *Key Terms in Language and Culture*, Malden MA: Blackwell.

Hall, S. (1980a) 'Encoding/decoding', in S. Hall, D. Hobson, A. Lowe and P. Willis (eds) *Culture, Media, Language: working papers in cultural studies, 1972–79*, London: Hutchinson.

——(1980b) 'Recent developments in theories of language and ideology: a critical note', in S. Hall, D. Hobson, A. Lowe and P. Willis (eds) *Culture, Media, Language: working papers in cultural studies, 1972–79*, London: Hutchinson.

——(1982) 'The rediscovery of "ideology": return of the repressed in media studies', in M. Gurevitch, T. Bennett, J. Curran and J. Woollacott (eds) *Culture, Society and the Media*, London: Methuen.

——(1991) 'The local and the global: globalization and ethnicity', in A. King (ed.) *Culture, Globalization and the World-System: contemporary conditions for the representation of identity*, Basingstoke: Macmillan.

——(1992a) 'The West and the Rest: discourse and power', in S. Hall and B. Gieben (eds) *Formations of Modernity*, Cambridge: Polity Press/Open University.

——(1992b) 'The question of cultural identity', in S. Hall, D. Held and A. McGrew (eds) *Modernity and Its Futures*, Cambridge: Polity Press/Open University.

Hall, S., Angus, I., Cruz, J., Derian, J., Jhally, S., Lewis, J. and Schwichtenberg, C. (1994) 'Reflections upon the encoding/decoding model: an interview with Stuart

Hall', in J. Cruz and J. Lewis (eds) *Viewing, Reading, Listening: audiences and cultural reception*, Boulder CO: Westview Press.

Hannerz, U. (1996) *Transnational Connections: culture, people, places*, London: Routledge.

——(2001) 'Thinking about culture in a global ecumene', in J. Lull (ed.) *Culture in the Communication Age*, London: Routledge.

Harindranath, R. (2000) 'Ethnicity, national culture(s) and the interpretation of television', in S. Cottle (ed.) *Ethnic Minorities and the Media: changing cultural boundaries*, Buckingham: Open University Press.

Harries, D. (ed.) (2002) *The New Media Book*, London: British Film Institute.

Harvey, D. (1989a) *The Condition of Postmodernity: an enquiry into the origins of cultural change*, Oxford: Blackwell.

——(1989b) *The Urban Experience*, Oxford: Blackwell.

Heidegger, M. (1962) *Being and Time*, Oxford: Blackwell.

——(1993) 'Building, dwelling, thinking', in *Basic Writings*, ed. D. Krell, London: Routledge.

Held, D., McGrew, A., Goldblatt, D. and Perraton, J. (1999) *Global Transformations: politics, economics and culture*, Cambridge: Polity Press.

Hemmings, S., Silva, E. and Thompson, K. (2002) 'Accounting for the everyday', in T. Bennett and D. Watson (eds) *Understanding Everyday Life*, Oxford: Blackwell/Open University Press.

Hendy, D. (2000) *Radio in the Global Age*, Cambridge: Polity Press.

Henriques, J., Hollway, W., Urwin, C., Venn, C. and Walkerdine, V. (1984) *Changing the Subject: psychology, social regulation and subjectivity*, London: Methuen.

Heritage, J. (1984) *Garfinkel and Ethnomethodology*, Cambridge: Polity Press.

Herman, E. and McChesney, R. (1997) *The Global Media: the new missionaries of corporate capitalism*, London: Cassell.

Hermes, J. (1993) 'Media, meaning and everyday life', *Cultural Studies* 7: 493–506.

——(1995) *Reading Women's Magazines: an analysis of everyday media use*, Cambridge: Polity Press.

Hills, M. (2001) 'Virtually out there: strategies, tactics and affective spaces in on-line fandom', in S. Munt (ed.) *Technospaces: inside the new media*, London: Continuum.

Hine, C. (2000) *Virtual Ethnography*, London: Sage.

Hirsch, E. (1992) 'The long term and the short term of domestic consumption: an ethnographic case study', in R. Silverstone and E. Hirsch (eds) *Consuming Technologies: media and information in domestic spaces*, London: Routledge.

——(1998) 'New technologies and domestic consumption', in C. Geraghty and D. Lusted (eds) *The Television Studies Book*, London: Arnold.

Hobsbawm, E. and Ranger, T. (eds) (1983) *The Invention of Tradition*, Cambridge: Cambridge University Press.

Hobson, D. (1980) 'Housewives and the mass media', in S. Hall, D. Hobson, A. Lowe and P. Willis (eds) *Culture, Media, Language: working papers in cultural studies, 1972–79*, London: Hutchinson.

——(1989) 'Soap operas at work', in E. Seiter, H. Borchers, G. Kreutzner and E-M. Warth (eds) *Remote Control: television, audiences and cultural power*, London: Routledge.

Hochschild, A. (1983) *The Managed Heart: commercialization of human feeling*, Berkeley and Los Angeles CA: University of California Press.

Hodge, R. and Kress, G. (1988) *Social Semiotics*, Cambridge: Polity Press.

Holloway, S. and Valentine, G. (2003) *Cyberkids: children in the information age*, London: RoutledgeFalmer.

Holmes, J. (1995) *Women, Men and Politeness*, Harlow: Longman.

Hopper, R. (1992) *Telephone Conversation*, Bloomington and Indianapolis IN: Indiana University Press.

Horton, D. and Wohl, R. (1986) 'Mass communication and para-social interaction: observations on intimacy at a distance', in G. Gumpert and R. Cathcart (eds) *Inter/Media: interpersonal communication in a media world*, 3rd edn, New York: Oxford University Press.

Hubbard, P., Kitchin, R. and Valentine, G. (eds) (2004) *Key Thinkers on Space and Place*, London: Sage.

Hunt, P. (1989) 'Gender and the construction of home life', in G. Allan and G. Crow (eds) *Home and Family: creating the domestic sphere*, Basingstoke: Macmillan.

Hutchby, I. (2001) *Conversation and Technology: from the telephone to the Internet*, Cambridge: Polity Press.

Innis, H. (1950) *Empire and Communications*, Oxford: Oxford University Press.

——(1951) *The Bias of Communication*, Toronto: University of Toronto Press.

Jackson, S. and Moores, S. (eds) (1995) *The Politics of Domestic Consumption: critical readings*, Hemel Hempstead: Prentice Hall/Harvester Wheatsheaf.

Jagose, A., Martin, F. and Healy, C. (2003) 'At home in the suburb', in F. Martin (ed.) *Interpreting Everyday Culture*, London: Arnold.

Jameson, F. (1991) *Postmodernism, or the Cultural Logic of Late Capitalism*, London: Verso.

Jamieson, L. (1998) *Intimacy: personal relationships in modern societies*, Cambridge: Polity Press.

Jancovich, M., Faire, L. and Stubbings, S. (2003) *The Place of the Audience: cultural geographies of film consumption*, London: British Film Institute.

Janelle, D. (1991) 'Global interdependence and its consequences', in S. Brunn and T. Leinbach (eds) *Collapsing Space and Time: geographic aspects of communication and information*, London: HarperCollins.

Jarvis, H., Pratt, A. and Cheng-Chong Wu, P. (2001) *The Secret Life of Cities: the social reproduction of everyday life*, Harlow: Prentice Hall.

Jaworski, A. and Coupland, N. (1999) 'Editors' introduction to Part Four: negotiating social relationships', in A. Jaworski and N. Coupland (eds) *The Discourse Reader*, London: Routledge.

Jefferson, G. (1984) 'The organisation of laughter in talk about troubles', in M. Atkinson and J. Heritage (eds) *Structures of Social Action: studies in conversation analysis*, Cambridge: Cambridge University Press.

Jefferson, G. and Lee, J. (1992) 'The rejection of advice: managing the problematic convergence of a "troubles-telling" and a "service encounter"', in P. Drew and J. Heritage (eds) *Talk at Work: interaction in institutional settings*, Cambridge: Cambridge University Press.

Jensen, J. (1992) 'Fandom as pathology: the consequences of characterization', in L. Lewis (ed.) *The Adoring Audience: fan culture and popular media*, London: Routledge.

Johnson, L. (1981) 'Radio and everyday life: the early years of broadcasting in Australia, 1922–1945', *Media, Culture and Society* 3: 167–78.

——(1988) *The Unseen Voice: a cultural history of early Australian radio*, London: Routledge.

Johnson, R. (1986) 'The story so far: and further transformations?', in D. Punter (ed.) *Introduction to Contemporary Cultural Studies*, Harlow: Longman.

Jones, S. (ed.) (1995) *CyberSociety: computer-mediated communication and community*, Thousand Oaks CA: Sage.

Katz, E. and Liebes, T. (1985) 'Mutual aid in the decoding of *Dallas*: preliminary notes from a cross-cultural study', in P. Drummond and R. Paterson (eds) *Television in Transition: papers from the first International Television Studies Conference*, London: British Film Institute.

Kear, A. and Steinberg, D. (eds) (1999) *Mourning Diana: nation, culture and the performance of grief*, London: Routledge.

Kendall, L. (2002) *Hanging Out in the Virtual Pub: masculinities and relationships online*, Berkeley and Los Angeles CA: University of California Press.

King, A. (1980) 'A time for space and a space for time: the social production of the vacation house', in A. King (ed.) *Buildings and Society: essays on the social development of the built environment*, London: Routledge and Kegan Paul.

Kitchin, R. (1998) *Cyberspace: the world in the wires*, Chichester: Wiley.

Lacan, J. (1977) *Écrits: a selection*, London: Tavistock Publications.

Lally, E. (2002) *At Home with Computers*, Oxford: Berg.

Langer, J. (1981) 'Television's "personality system"', *Media, Culture and Society* 3: 351–65.

Larsen, P. (1999) 'Imaginary spaces: television, technology and everyday consciousness', in J. Gripsrud (ed.) *Television and Common Knowledge*, London: Routledge.

Lash, S. and Urry, J. (1994) *Economies of Signs and Space*, London: Sage.

Leal, O. (1990) 'Popular taste and erudite repertoire: the place and space of television in Brazil', *Cultural Studies* 4: 19–29.

Levinson, P. (1999) *Digital McLuhan: a guide to the information millennium*, London: Routledge.

Levinson, S. (1983) *Pragmatics*, Cambridge: Cambridge University Press.

Lévi-Strauss, C. (1977) *Structural Anthropology – Vol. 1*, Harmondsworth: Penguin Books.

Levy, M. (1982) 'Watching TV news as para-social interaction', in G. Gumpert and R. Cathcart (eds) *Inter/Media: interpersonal communication in a media world*, 2nd edn, New York: Oxford University Press.

Leyshon, A. (1995) 'Annihilating space? The speed-up of communications', in J. Allen and C. Hamnett (eds) *A Shrinking World? Global unevenness and inequality*, Oxford: Oxford University Press/Open University Press.

Liebes, T. (1998) 'Cultural differences in the retelling of television fiction', in R. Dickinson, R. Harindranath and O. Linné (eds) *Approaches to Audiences: a reader*, London: Arnold.

Liebes, T. and Katz, E. (1990) *The Export of Meaning: cross-cultural readings of* Dallas, New York: Oxford University Press.

Ling, R. and Yttri, B. (2002) 'Hyper-coordination via mobile phones in Norway', in J. Katz and M. Aakhus (eds) *Perpetual Contact: mobile communication, private talk, public performance*, Cambridge: Cambridge University Press.

Livingstone, S. (2002) *Young People and New Media: childhood and the changing media environment*, London: Sage.

Livingstone, S. and Lunt, S. (1994) *Talk on Television: audience participation and public debate*, London: Routledge.

Lull, J. (1980) 'The social uses of television', *Human Communication Research* 6: 197–209.

——(1990) *Inside Family Viewing: ethnographic research on television's audiences*, London: Routledge.

Lull, J. and Hinerman, S. (eds) (1997) *Media Scandals: morality and desire in the popular culture marketplace*, Cambridge: Polity Press.

Lupton, D. (1998) *The Emotional Self: a sociocultural exploration*, London: Sage.

Lury, K. (1996) 'Television performance: being, acting and "corpsing"', *New Formations* 27: 114–27.

McCarthy, A. (2001) *Ambient Television: visual culture and public space*, Durham NC: Duke University Press.

McChesney, R. (1998) 'Media convergence and globalisation', in D. Thussu (ed.) *Electronic Empires: global media and local resistance*, London: Arnold.

Macdonald, M. (2003) *Exploring Media Discourse*, London: Arnold.

McGuigan, J. (1996) *Culture and the Public Sphere*, London: Routledge.

Mackay, H. (1995) 'Technological reality: cultured technology and technologized culture', in B. Adam and S. Allan (eds) *Theorizing Culture: an interdisciplinary critique after postmodernism*, London: UCL Press.

——(2000) 'The globalization of culture?', in D. Held (ed.) *A Globalizing World? Culture, economics, politics*, London: Routledge/Open University Press.

MacKenzie, D. and Wajcman, J. (eds) (1985) *The Social Shaping of Technology: how the refrigerator got its hum*, Milton Keynes: Open University Press.

McLuhan, E. and Zingrone, F. (1997a) 'Introduction', in E. McLuhan and F. Zingrone (eds) *Essential McLuhan*, London: Routledge.

——(eds) (1997b) *Essential McLuhan*, London: Routledge.

McLuhan, M. (1964) *Understanding Media: the extensions of man*, London: Routledge and Kegan Paul.

McLuhan, M. and Fiore, Q. (1967) *The Medium is the Massage: an inventory of effects*, Harmondsworth: Penguin Books.

McRobbie, A. (1991) 'Settling accounts with subcultures: a feminist critique', in *Feminism and Youth Culture: from* Jackie *to* Just Seventeen, Basingstoke: Macmillan.

Malone, M. (1997) *Worlds of Talk: the presentation of self in everyday conversation*, Cambridge: Polity Press.

Manning, P. (1992) *Erving Goffman and Modern Sociology*, Cambridge: Polity Press.

Marriott, S. (1995) 'Intersubjectivity and temporal reference in television commentary', *Time and Society* 4: 345–64.

Massey, D. (1992) 'A place called home?', *New Formations* 17: 3–15.

——(1993) 'Power-geometry and a progressive sense of place', in J. Bird, B. Curtis, T. Putnam, G. Robertson and L. Tickner (eds) *Mapping the Futures: local cultures, global change*, London: Routledge.

——(1994) *Space, Place and Gender*, Cambridge: Polity Press.

——(1995) 'The conceptualization of place', in D. Massey and P. Jess (eds) *A Place in the World? Places, cultures and globalization*, Oxford: Oxford University Press/Open University Press.

——(1998) 'The spatial construction of youth cultures', in T. Skelton and G. Valentine (eds) *Cool Places: geographies of youth cultures*, London: Routledge.

Masterman, L. (ed.) (1984) *Television Mythologies: stars, shows and signs*, London: Comedia.

Matrix Collective (1984) *Making Space: women and the man-made environment*, London: Pluto Press.

Mattelart, A. (2000) *Networking the World, 1794–2000*, Minneapolis MN: University of Minnesota Press.

Mattelart, M. (1986) 'Women and the cultural industries', in R. Collins, J. Curran, N. Garnham, P. Scannell, P. Schlesinger and C. Sparks (eds) *Media, Culture and Society: a critical reader*, London: Sage.

Meyrowitz, J. (1985) *No Sense of Place: the impact of electronic media on social behavior*, New York: Oxford University Press.

——(1994) 'Medium theory', in D. Crowley and D. Mitchell (eds) *Communication Theory Today*, Cambridge: Polity Press.

——(2003) 'Canonic anti-text: Marshall McLuhan's *Understanding Media*', in E. Katz, J. Peters, T. Liebes and A. Orloff (eds) *Canonic Texts in Media Research: Are there any? Should there be? How about these?*, Cambridge: Polity Press.

Miller, D. (1987) *Material Culture and Mass Consumption*, Oxford: Blackwell.

——(1990) 'Appropriating the state on the council estate', in T. Putnam and C. Newton (eds) *Household Choices*, London: Futures Publications.

——(1992) '*The Young and the Restless* in Trinidad: a case of the local and the global in mass consumption', in R. Silverstone and E. Hirsch (eds) *Consuming Technologies: media and information in domestic spaces*, London: Routledge.

——(1997) 'Consumption and its consequences', in H. Mackay (ed.) *Consumption and Everyday Life*, London: Sage/Open University Press.

Miller, D. and Slater, D. (2000) *The Internet: an ethnographic approach*, Oxford: Berg.

Miller, T. and McHoul, A. (1998) *Popular Culture and Everyday Life*, London: Sage.

Misztal, B. (1996) *Trust in Modern Societies: the search for the bases of social order*, Cambridge: Polity Press.

——(2000) *Informality: social theory and contemporary practice*, London: Routledge.

Mitchell, W. (1995) *City of Bits: space, place and the Infobahn*, Cambridge MA: MIT Press.

Moores, S. (1993) *Interpreting Audiences: the ethnography of media consumption*, London: Sage.

——(1996) *Satellite Television and Everyday Life: articulating technology*, Acamedia research monograph no.18, Luton: John Libbey Media/University of Luton Press.

——(1997) 'Broadcasting and its audiences', in H. Mackay (ed.) *Consumption and Everyday Life*, London: Sage/Open University Press.

——(2000) *Media and Everyday Life in Modern Society*, Edinburgh: Edinburgh University Press.

——(2003a) 'Thinking metaphorically about media and globalization', in D. Demers (ed.) *Globalization and Mass Communication: papers presented at the 2002 Center for Global Media Studies Conference*, Spokane WA: Marquette Books.

——(2003b) 'Media, flows and places', Media@lse electronic working paper no.6, London School of Economics and Political Science.

——(2003c) 'Oltre il senso di Meyrowitz: il luogo è istantaneamente pluralizzato (non marginalizzato) nelle pratiche d'uso dei media elettronici', *C:Cube (Cultura, Comunicazione, Consumo)* 3: 113–22.

——(2004) 'The doubling of place: electronic media, time-space arrangements and social relationships', in N. Couldry and A. McCarthy (eds) *MediaSpace: place, scale and culture in a media age*, London: Routledge.

Morley, D. (1980) *The Nationwide Audience: structure and decoding*, BFI television monograph no.11, London: British Film Institute.

——(1981) 'The *Nationwide* audience: a critical postscript', *Screen Education* 39: 3–14.

191

——(1986) *Family Television: cultural power and domestic leisure*, London: Comedia.

——(1992) *Television, Audiences and Cultural Studies*, London: Routledge.

——(1996) 'The geography of television: ethnography, communications and community', in J. Hay, L. Grossberg and E. Wartella (eds) *The Audience and Its Landscape*, Boulder CO: Westview Press.

——(2000) *Home Territories: media, mobility and identity*, London: Routledge.

——(2001) 'Belongings: place, space and identity in a mediated world', *European Journal of Cultural Studies* 4: 425–48.

——(2003) 'What's "home" got to do with it? Contradictory dynamics in the domestication of technology and the dislocation of domesticity', *European Journal of Cultural Studies* 6: 435–58.

Morley, D. and Brunsdon, C. (1999) *The* Nationwide *Television Studies*, London: Routledge.

Morley, D. and Robins, K. (1995) *Spaces of Identity: global media, electronic landscapes and cultural boundaries*, London: Routledge.

Mosco, V. (1996) *The Political Economy of Communication: rethinking and renewal*, London: Sage.

Moyal, A. (1989) 'The feminine culture of the telephone: people, patterns and policy', *Prometheus* 7: 5–31.

——(1992) 'The gendered use of the telephone: an Australian case study', *Media, Culture and Society* 14: 51–72.

Mumford, L. (1973) *Interpretations and Forecasts*, London: Secker and Warburg.

Murdock, G. (1989) 'Class stratification and cultural consumption: some motifs in the work of Pierre Bourdieu', in F. Coalter (ed.) *Freedom and Constraint: the paradoxes of leisure*, London: Routledge.

——(1993) 'Communications and the constitution of modernity', *Media, Culture and Society* 15: 521–39.

Murdock, G., Hartmann, P. and Gray, P. (1992) 'Contextualizing home computing: resources and practices', in R. Silverstone and E. Hirsch (eds) *Consuming Technologies: media and information in domestic spaces*, London: Routledge.

Murray, R. (1989) 'Fordism and post-Fordism', in S. Hall and M. Jacques (eds) *New Times: the changing face of politics in the 1990s*, London: Lawrence and Wishart/Marxism Today.

Noon, M. and Blyton, P. (1997) *The Realities of Work*, Basingstoke: Macmillan.

Ochberg, R. (1994) 'Life stories and storied lives', in A. Lieblich and R. Josselson (eds) *The Narrative Study of Lives: exploring identity and gender*, Thousand Oaks CA: Sage.

Olwig, K. (1999) 'Travelling makes a home: mobility and identity among West Indians', in T. Chapman and J. Hockey (eds) *Ideal Homes? Social change and domestic life*, London: Routledge.

Olwig, K. and Hastrup, K. (eds) (1997) *Siting Culture: the shifting anthropological object*, London: Routledge.

O'Sullivan, T. (1991) 'Television memories and cultures of viewing, 1950–65', in J. Corner (ed.) *Popular Television in Britain: studies in cultural history*, London: British Film Institute.

Papastergiadis, N. (2000) *The Turbulence of Migration: globalization, deterritorialization and hybridity*, Cambridge: Polity Press.

Paterson, R. (1993) 'Planning the family: the art of the television schedule', in M. Alvarado, E. Buscombe and R. Collins (eds) *The* Screen Education *Reader: cinema, television, culture*, Basingstoke: Macmillan.

Penacchioni, I. (1984) 'The reception of popular television in Northeast Brazil', *Media, Culture and Society* 6: 337–41.

Petrie, D. and Willis, J. (eds) (1995) *Television and the Household: reports from the BFI's audience tracking study*, London: British Film Institute.

Pickering, M. (1997) *History, Experience and Cultural Studies*, Basingstoke: Macmillan.

Plummer, K. (1995) *Telling Sexual Stories: power, change and social worlds*, London: Routledge.

Potter, J. and Wetherell, M. (1987) *Discourse and Social Psychology: beyond attitudes and behaviour*, London: Sage.

Pred, A. (1996) 'The choreography of existence: comments on Hägerstrand's time-geography and its usefulness', in J. Agnew, D. Livingstone and A. Rogers (eds) *Human Geography: an essential anthology*, Oxford: Blackwell.

Qureshi, K. (2003) 'Performing selves and belongings: the reflexive negotiation of identities among "Edinburgh Pakistanis"', unpublished Ph.D. thesis, Open University.

Radway, J. (1987) *Reading the Romance: women, patriarchy and popular literature*, London: Verso.

——(1988) 'Reception study: ethnography and the problems of dispersed audiences and nomadic subjects', *Cultural Studies* 2: 359–76.

Rakow, L. (1992) *Gender on the Line: women, the telephone and community life*, Urbana and Chicago IL: University of Illinois Press.

Rath, C-D. (1985) 'The invisible network: television as an institution in everyday life', in P. Drummond and R. Paterson (eds) *Television in Transition: papers from the first International Television Studies Conference*, London: British Film Institute.

Rheingold, H. (1995) *The Virtual Community: finding connection in a computerized world*, London: Minerva.

Richardson, K. and Meinhof, U. (1999) *Worlds in Common? Television discourse in a changing Europe*, London: Routledge.

Ricoeur, P. (1974) *The Conflict of Interpretations: essays in hermeneutics*, Evanston IL: Northwestern University Press.

Robins, K. (1995) 'The new spaces of global media', in R. Johnston, P. Taylor and M. Watts (eds) *Geographies of Global Change: remapping the world in the late twentieth century*, Oxford: Blackwell.

——(1996) 'Cyberspace and the world we live in', in J. Dovey (ed.) *Fractal Dreams: new media in social context*, London: Lawrence and Wishart.

Roche, M. (2000) *Mega-Events and Modernity: Olympics and Expos in the growth of global culture*, London: Routledge.

Rosengren, K., Wenner, L. and Palmgreen, P. (eds) (1985) *Media Gratifications Research: current perspectives*, Beverly Hills CA: Sage.

Sacks, H. (1984) 'On doing "being ordinary"', in M. Atkinson and J. Heritage (eds) *Structures of Social Action: studies in conversation analysis*, Cambridge: Cambridge University Press.

——(1995) *Lectures on Conversation*, ed. G. Jefferson, Oxford: Blackwell.

Sacks, H., Schegloff, E. and Jefferson, G. (1974) 'A simplest systematics for the organization of turn-taking for conversation', *Language* 50: 696–735.

Said, E. (1978) *Orientalism*, London: Routledge and Kegan Paul.

Sarup, M. (1996) *Identity, Culture and the Postmodern World*, ed. T. Raja, Edinburgh: Edinburgh University Press.

Saussure, F. de (1983) *Course in General Linguistics*, eds C. Bally and A. Sechehaye, London: Duckworth.

Scannell, P. (1988) 'Radio times: the temporal arrangements of broadcasting in the modern world', in P. Drummond and R. Paterson (eds) *Television and Its Audience: international research perspectives*, London: British Film Institute.

——(1991) 'Introduction: the relevance of talk', in P. Scannell (ed.) *Broadcast Talk*, London: Sage.

——(1992) 'Public service broadcasting and modern public life', in P. Scannell, P. Schlesinger and C. Sparks (eds) *Culture and Power: a* Media, Culture and Society *reader*, London: Sage.

——(1995) 'For a phenomenology of radio and television', *Journal of Communication* 45(3): 4–19.

——(1996) *Radio, Television and Modern Life: a phenomenological approach*, Oxford: Blackwell.

——(1998) 'Media – language – world', in A. Bell and P. Garrett (eds) *Approaches to Media Discourse*, Oxford: Blackwell.

——(1999) '*Blind Date* and the phenomenology of fun', in J. Stokes and A. Reading (eds) *The Media in Britain: current debates and developments*, Basingstoke: Macmillan.

——(2000) 'For-anyone-as-someone structures', *Media, Culture and Society* 22: 5–24.

Scannell, P. and Cardiff, D. (1991) *A Social History of British Broadcasting – Vol. 1, 1922–1939: serving the nation*, Oxford: Blackwell.

Schegloff, E. (1986) 'The routine as achievement', *Human Studies* 9: 111–51.

——(2002) 'Beginnings in the telephone', in J. Katz and M. Aakhus (eds) *Perpetual Contact: mobile communication, private talk, public performance*, Cambridge: Cambridge University Press.

Schiller, H. (1979) 'Transnational media and national development', in K. Nordenstreng and H. Schiller (eds) *National Sovereignty and International Communication*, Norwood NJ: Ablex.

——(1985) 'Electronic information flows: new basis for global domination?', in P. Drummond and R. Paterson (eds) *Television in Transition: papers from the first International Television Studies Conference*, London: British Film Institute.

——(1992) *Mass Communications and American Empire*, 2nd edn, Boulder CO: Westview Press.

Schlesinger, P. (1991) 'On national identity (i): cultural politics and the mediologists', in *Media, State and Nation: political violence and collective identities*, London: Sage.

——(1993) 'Wishful thinking: cultural politics, media and collective identities in Europe', *Journal of Communication* 43(2): 6–17.

Seamon, D. (1979) *A Geography of the Lifeworld: movement, rest and encounter*, New York: St Martin's Press.

Sennett, R. (1998) *The Corrosion of Character: the personal consequences of work in the new capitalism*, New York: Norton.

Silj, A. (1988) *East of* Dallas: *the European challenge to American television*, London: British Film Institute.

Silverstone, R. (1990) 'Television and everyday life: towards an anthropology of the television audience', in M. Ferguson (ed.) *Public Communication: the new imperatives*, London: Sage.

——(1993) 'Television, ontological security and the transitional object', *Media, Culture and Society* 15: 573–98.

——(1994) *Television and Everyday Life*, London: Routledge.

——(1999) *Why Study the Media?*, London: Sage.

Silverstone, R. and Haddon, L. (1996) 'Design and the domestication of information and communication technologies: technical change and everyday life', in R. Mansell and R. Silverstone (eds) *Communication by Design: the politics of communication technologies*, Oxford: Oxford University Press.

Silverstone, R., Hirsch, E. and Morley, D. (1991) 'Listening to a long conversation: an ethnographic approach to the study of information and communication technologies in the home', *Cultural Studies* 5: 204–27.

——(1992) 'Information and communication technologies and the moral economy of the household', in R. Silverstone and E. Hirsch (eds) *Consuming Technologies: media and information in domestic spaces*, London: Routledge.

Simmel, G. (1950) *The Sociology of Georg Simmel*, ed. K. Wolff, New York: Free Press.

Skeggs, B. (1997) *Formations of Class and Gender: becoming respectable*, London: Sage.

Slevin, J. (2000) *The Internet and Society*, Cambridge: Polity Press.

Smith, M. and Kollock, P. (eds) (1999) *Communities in Cyberspace*, London: Routledge.

Spigel, L. (1992a) 'Installing the television set: popular discourses on television and domestic space, 1948–1955', in L. Spigel and D. Mann (eds) *Private Screenings: television and the female consumer*, Minneapolis MN: University of Minnesota Press.

——(1992b) *Make Room for TV: television and the family ideal in postwar America*, Chicago IL: University of Chicago Press.

Standage, T. (1998) *The Victorian Internet: the remarkable story of the telegraph and the nineteenth century's online pioneers*, London: Weidenfeld and Nicolson.

Stones, R. (ed.) (1998) *Key Sociological Thinkers*, Basingstoke: Macmillan.

Storey, J. (2001) *Cultural Theory and Popular Culture: an introduction*, 3rd edn, Harlow: Prentice Hall/Pearson Education.

Sussex Technology Group (2001) 'In the company of strangers: mobile phones and the conception of space', in S. Munt (ed.) *Technospaces: inside the new media*, London: Continuum.

Tester, K. (2001) *Compassion, Morality and the Media*, Buckingham: Open University Press.

Thomas, R. (1995) 'Access and inequality', in N. Heap, R. Thomas, G. Einon, R. Mason and H. Mackay (eds) *Information Technology and Society: a reader*, London: Sage/Open University Press.

Thompson, E. (1993) 'Time, work-discipline and industrial capitalism', in *Customs in Common*, Harmondsworth: Penguin Books.

Thompson, J. (1990) *Ideology and Modern Culture: critical social theory in the era of mass communication*, Cambridge: Polity Press.

——(1994) 'Social theory and the media', in D. Crowley and D. Mitchell (eds) *Communication Theory Today*, Cambridge: Polity Press.

——(1995) *The Media and Modernity: a social theory of the media*, Cambridge: Polity Press.

——(2000) *Political Scandal: power and visibility in the media age*, Cambridge: Polity Press.

Thornton, S. (1995) *Club Cultures: music, media and subcultural capital*, Cambridge: Polity Press.

Thussu, D. (1998) 'Introduction', in D. Thussu (ed.) *Electronic Empires: global media and local resistance*, London: Arnold.

——(2000) *International Communication: continuity and change*, London: Arnold.

Tomlinson, J. (1991) *Cultural Imperialism: a critical introduction*, London: Pinter.

——(1999) *Globalization and Culture*, Cambridge: Polity Press.

Tsagarousianou, R. (2001) ' "A space where one feels at home": media consumption practices among London's South Asian and Greek Cypriot communities', in R. King and N. Wood (eds) *Media and Migration: constructions of mobility and difference*, London: Routledge.

Tulloch, J. (1999) *Performing Culture: stories of expertise and the everyday*, London: Sage.

——(2000) ' "Landscapes of fear": public places, fear of crime and the media', in S. Allan, B. Adam and C. Carter (eds) *Environmental Risks and the Media*, London: Routledge.

Tulloch, J. and Lupton, D. (1997) *Television, AIDS and Risk: a cultural studies approach to health communication*, Sydney: Allen and Unwin.

——(2003) *Risk and Everyday Life*, London: Sage.

Tunstall, J. (1977) *The Media Are American: Anglo-American media in the world*, London: Constable.

Turkle, S. (1996a) 'Parallel lives: working on identity in virtual space', in D. Grodin and T. Lindlof (eds) *Constructing the Self in a Mediated World*, Thousand Oaks CA: Sage.

——(1996b) *Life on the Screen: identity in the age of the Internet*, London: Weidenfeld and Nicolson.

Turnock, R. (2000) *Interpreting Diana: television audiences and the death of a princess*, London: British Film Institute.

Urry, J. (1990) *The Tourist Gaze: leisure and travel in contemporary societies*, London: Sage.

——(1991) 'Time and space in Giddens' social theory', in C. Bryant and D. Jary (eds) *Giddens' Theory of Structuration: a critical appreciation*, London: Routledge.

——(1995) *Consuming Places*, London: Routledge.

——(2000) *Sociology Beyond Societies: mobilities for the twenty-first century*, London: Routledge.

——(2002) 'Mobility and proximity', *Sociology* 36: 255–74.

——(2003) *Global Complexity*, Cambridge: Polity Press.

Valentine, G. (2001) *Social Geographies: space and society*, Harlow: Prentice Hall/Pearson Education.

van Loon, J. (2000) 'Mediating the risks of virtual environments', in S. Allan, B. Adam and C. Carter (eds) *Environmental Risks and the Media*, London: Routledge.

Varis, T. (1984) 'The international flow of television programs', *Journal of Communication* 34(1): 143–52.

Volosinov, V. (1976) 'Discourse in life and discourse in art (concerning sociological poetics)', in *Freudianism: a Marxist critique*, New York: Academic Press.

——(1986) *Marxism and the Philosophy of Language*, Cambridge MA: Harvard University Press.

Wakeford, N. (1999) 'Gender and the landscapes of computing in an Internet café', in M. Crang, P. Crang and J. May (eds) *Virtual Geographies: bodies, space and relations*, London: Routledge.

Wallace, P. (1999) *The Psychology of the Internet*, Cambridge: Cambridge University Press.

Wark, M. (1994) *Virtual Geography: living with global media events*, Bloomington and Indianapolis IN: Indiana University Press.

Waters, M. (1995) *Globalization*, London: Routledge.

Wellman, B. (1988) 'The community question re-evaluated', in M. Smith (ed.) *Power, Community and the City*, New Brunswick NJ: Transaction Books.

——(1997) 'An electronic group is virtually a social network', in S. Kiesler (ed.) *The Culture of the Internet*, Hillsdale NJ: Lawrence Erlbaum.

Wellman, B. and Haythornthwaite, C. (eds) (2002) *The Internet in Everyday Life*, Malden MA: Blackwell.

Wernick, A. (1991) *Promotional Culture: advertising, ideology and symbolic expression*, London: Sage.

Williams, K. (2003) *Understanding Media Theory*, London: Arnold.

Williams, R. (1990) *Television: technology and cultural form*, 2nd edn, London: Routledge.

Willis, P. (1977) *Learning to Labour: how working-class kids get working-class jobs*, Aldershot: Saxon House.

Wilson, T. (1993) *Watching Television: hermeneutics, reception and popular culture*, Cambridge: Polity Press.

Winnicott, D. (1965) *The Maturational Processes and the Facilitating Environment*, London: Hogarth.

——(1974) *Playing and Reality*, Harmondsworth: Penguin Books.

Wood, J. (1993) 'Repeatable pleasures: notes on young people's use of video', in D. Buckingham (ed.) *Reading Audiences: young people and the media*, Manchester: Manchester University Press.

Wynne, D. (1990) 'Leisure, lifestyle and the construction of social position', *Leisure Studies* 9: 21–34.

Young, M. (1992) 'Time, habit and repetition in day-to-day life', in A. Giddens (ed.) *Human Societies: an introductory reader in sociology*, Cambridge: Polity Press.

INDEX

'accent', wider definition than typically found in sociolinguistics 107
Adam, B. 4, 13–14, 37, 39
AIDS on global mediascape 152
'air hostesses', compared with weather announcers providing reassurance 151
Aksoy, A. 166, 170–2, 175
All My Children, qualifiers and 98–9
Allan, G. 77, 164
Althusser, L. 105–7, 109, 144
American college students, enthusiastic MUDders 161
American Express 52
American teenagers, considered to be 'free' by Punjabi youth 118
analysis of work in service sector 175
Anderson, B. 31, 165–6, 168
Ang, I. 20, 25, 79, 113–14, 116, 170
Anthias, F. 143
Appadurai, A. 54–5
Arabs and Israelis, interviews about *Dallas* 114–15
Atkinson, K. 93–7
'attention to face', interaction and 93
audiences, fragmentation and dispersal of 33
Augé, M. 51
Austin, J., 'speech act theory' 158
Australia, death of Diana and 80
Australian culture, traditionally looked outwards 131, 133

BA 52
Bakhtin, M. 108
Baran, S. 48
Barnard, S. 95
Barthes, R. 5; analysis of photography and 133, 136, 138; connotative signs, 'second–order semiological system' 105, 109; myth central concept of his early work 105–6; news photography and 136; photographs of his mother 137; production of bourgeois myth 107; *punctum* in relation to *studium* 136; role of media in contemporary 'systems of signification' 104; 'semiology' and 103; 'symbolic' messages at level of 'connotation' 104–5; 'technologies-as-texts' and myth 122; 'that-has-been' effect of photography 137; work on connotation and myth 138
Bassett, C. 160–1
Baudrillard, J. 42
Bauman, Z. 53–4, 142, 169
Bausinger, H. 17, 24, 135
Baym, N. 98–9
BBC, commitment to 'principle of universal availability' 31; 'outside broadcasting activities' 29–30
BBC News 24 digital station 25
BBC Nine O'clock News, moved to *BBC Ten O'clock News* 24
BBC research unit (1930s) 21
Beck, U. 37, 49, 53; Chernobyl accident (1980s) 148, 150; manufactured uncertainties 148; 'world risk society' 146–7, 150, 152
'becoming respectable', act and process of 159
Bell, D. 159
Bennett, T. 109, 120, 131–3, 173
Berlin Wall, fall of 31
Bettelheim, B. 11
Beverly Hills 90210, Punjabi youth in Southall and 118
Bhabha, H. 143
Big Breakfast, The 18
Billig, M. 166–7, 174–5
Black, Cilla 86

Black movement, term black = beautiful 109

Blair, Tony, verbal presentation as 'normal person' 78

Blind Date 85–8

BlueSky 91

Blum-Kulka, S. 94, 107

Blumler, J. 100

Blyton, P. 154

Boden, D. 70, 81

body language, feature of daily social interaction 141–2

Boltanski, L. 145

Bonner, F. 23

Bourdieu, P. 5, 127–32, 131; characteristics of popular taste 130; concept of 'cultural capital' 128–9, 159; identity and particular economic and discursive limits 160; 'judgement of taste' and 129–30; unequal distribution of cultural capital and 138; values and practices of 'distinction' 127; ways gender relations intersect with social class 130

Brand, G. 158

'branding' 156; of channels 25

Braudel, F. 14

Brazilian city, television as 'material object' in 122, 124

'bricks', mobiles considered 'too big' and 'too old' 124

Britain, predominant 'whiteness' of public service broadcasting 33

broadcasting, 'institutional authority' 84; national calendar of public events 30; new technologies and temporal arrangements 25; part of seriality and spatiality of everyday life 23; 'pattern of output', times of paid labour and leisure 21; permits a live 'witnessing' of remote happenings 63; sociability of 83–4

Brown, M. 29

Brown, P. 93–4, 96–8

Brunsdon, C. 98, 109, 123, 127–8

Bryant, C. 36

BSE episode 149

Bucholtz, M. 27

Buckingham, D. 82

Bull, M. 63

Butler, J. 158–9, 161

Cairncross, F. 43

calendar, characterised by its repetitiveness 29, 38–9

'calendrical time' 29, 33

call centre talk standardised 156–7

Cameron, D. 61, 155–6, 159

capitalism, businesses in the global economy and 52

Cardiff, D. 18, 84, 165

Casey, E. 64, 101

Castells, M. 4; 'flows of information, technology, images, sounds and symbols' 54; 'networked individualism' 168–9, 174; 'network society' 36, 52–3, 58; 'text-based virtual reality' 65

Cathcart, R. 99

celebrities, judged on talent but also on personality 78

Central Electricity Generating Board, promotional video 151

Chambers, I. 63

Chaney, D. 92

Charlesworth, S. 88

Chernobyl accident (1980s) 148–51

Cheung, C. 158

children, singled out as 'others' vulnerable to negative effects of media 82, 125, 152

Chilton, K. 88, 90

'Chineseness', diverse local conditions and 170

Chodorow, N. 120

Christmas Day speech, tradition and 15–16, 29

cinema, tends to be consumed as 'special event' in public contexts 24

'civil inattention' 101, 142

Clifford, J. 54, 59, 173–4

Clinton, Bill, Monica Lewinsky and 78

'clock time', modern industrial societies and 13–14, 33, 38–9

CNN news channel 25

Coca-Cola 52, 117–18

Coca-Cola or 'Coke', outside USA 117

Cohen, A. 139, 164–5, 169

Coke, global commodity 118

Cold War, research to surpass technology of Soviet Union 46

collective identities, constitution of 163–4, 175

Collins, R. 25

commodification of learning, conversational style of advertising and 92

'commodification of space', separation of private household from public workplace 12–13

communication media, bound up with

those of transportation 40; detach phenomenon of publicness from common locale 31

communication technologies, potential influences apart from content 42

communities, concept of and construction of collective identities 163–4, 167; role of satellite television in deconstructing 165

'communities of high presence-availability', pre-modern cultures and 70

'community of imagination', cult media fans on the internet 168

'compassion fatigue' 146

computer, social life of in contemporary households 124–6, 174

computer virus 152

computer-mediated communication, uses of 152

computer-mediated interaction, way of thinking about face and politeness 98

consumers, 'colonising' of imagination of 56–7

consumption 2

conversation analysis 2

conversation analysts, telephonic sociability and 89

'conversationalisation', 'ideological function' 92–3; media and other public discourses 91–2; 'realised in variety of linguistic features' 92

Corner, J. 32; promotional video and 151–2

Coronation Street 27–9

'corporeal travel' 54

Corrigan, P. 121

Cottle, S. 147

Couldry, N. 33, 62–3, 80, 134

Coupland, N. 94

Coward, R. 106, 109

credit card 'cyberfraud' 152

Crisell, A. 95

'critical situations', certitudes of routine threatened 11

Crow, G. 164

Cuff, E. 33

'cultural norms', too much emphasis on reproduction of 159

Cunningham, S. 58

'cyberrisks' 152

cyberspace, communities in 164; 'flaming' in 90

cyclicity 4, 9, 26, 30, 35, 175; dailiness 16–20; eventfulness 29–34; hourliness 25–7; lifetime 27–9; ordinariness 22–5; programmes or segments recur on regular timed basis 26; routines 10–14; scheduling 20–2; seriality 19–20; structuration 9–10; traditions 14–16

dailiness 9, 16–20, 33, 135–6

Dallas 79, 113–15, 117

Dant, T. 123

'day-to-day', marked practices of repetition 11

Dayan, D. 29, 31, 55

daytime broadcasting, women who do housework and childcare 21

de Certeau, M. 25

'decoding' of television programmes, viewers and 106

deictic expressions, routine feature of face-to-face interaction 166

deixis, context of printed text or television commentary and 71

'deixis' or 'indexicality' in pragmatics and ethnomethodology 108

'deregulation', decrease in influence of national broadcasting in Western Europe 32

Derrida, J. 111

'developing world', global 'unevenness' and inequality 50

Diana, Princess of Wales 31, 79–81

'diaspora communities' 169

diasporas, as much about 'where you're at' as 'where you're from' 170, 175

'diasporic public spheres' 54–5

DiMaggio, P. 132

Disney 52, 57

Dittmar, H. 123

'docu-soap' 19

'domestication of public utterance' 84

Dorothy, 'what to like' in a picture 131–2

'doubling of interaction', way of theorising interaction mix of social life 99

doubling or pluralisation, simultaneous mixing of interactions 102

Douglas, M. 63

Drew, P. 88, 90, 93

du Gay, P. 63

Duck, S. 69–70

durée of daily life 14–15, 70

Durkheim, E. 53

Duruz, J. 80

Eade, J. 165

Easthope, A. 105

Edensor, T. 160, 166
'Edinburgh Pakistanis', identities among young 170
electric telegraph 41, 45
'electronic empires' 56
electronic flows, consequences for boundaries 60
electronic media, 'mobility of the human body' no longer necessary 41
'electronically immediate' relationships, television presenter and audience 72–3
Ellis, J. 19, 24, 60
'emergence of the weekend', 'important leisure institution' 13
emotional labour, employees who deal face-to-face with public 154; human cost of for worker 154–6; performances and 158; sex line and 156
empires, dominance of powerful organisations and business leaders 56
'empty space' 39
Erikson, E. 139
'escapism', often derogatory term in judging romance readers 119
ethnomethodology 2, 12
ethnomethods, definition 99–100
European migrants, travelling to America in nineteenth century 41–2
eventfulness 9, 29–34
extensionality 4, 35, 175; empires 56–8; flow 53–6; globalisation 35–7; medium 42–6; network 51–3; permeability 58–64; shrinking 46–50; stretching 38–46; unevenness 50–1; virtuality 64–6

face, 'public self-image' of participant in encounter 93
face-to-face communication 2, 4, 60, 70–5, 83, 150
faceless commitments by lay actors, abstract systems of expertise and 150
Fairclough, N. 78, 91–3, 153, 156
'fallacy', assumption that media texts treated as meaningful 134
'false self' and 'true self' 155
'family communication patterns', part played by television viewing 99
'fandom as pathology' 82
feelings of safety and danger, related to class, gender and 143
Felski, R. 12
'feminine time', 'structurelessness' of 21
feminist perspective 106, 127–8

film analysis 141
'financial exclusion', information-haves and information-have-nots 50
Finnegan, R. 143
Fiore, Q. 43–4
Fischer, C. 88
Fiske, J. 105, 128
Flew, T. 2
'flexible accumulation', Harvey and 47
flexitime, 'reward' of employees, does not liberate from employer's 'intimate grip' 27
'flexitime' work patterns, 'new capitalism' and 26–7
'flight attendants' 153–6
'forms of inner speech and narrative' 143–4
Foucault, M. 13, 155
Fowler, R. 92
Freud, S. 107
friendliness in social interaction, 'not a given' but 'communicative accomplishment' 98
Frissen, V. 88
Frow, J. 128, 132

Garfinkel, H. 12, 99, 140–1
Gates, Bill (Microsoft Corporation) 56
Gauntlett, D. 22, 77
'gay', multiaccentuality of term 109
Gell, A. 123
gender, 'always a doing' 159; factor in shaping telephone as 'technology for sociability' 88; 'key variable' in time-use research by BBC's research unit 21–2; no identity behind expressions of 158; pieces of domestic technology and 126
'gender-switching', 'part of subcultural furniture in MUDs' 160
genetically modified (GM) crops 149
Geraghty, C. 19, 27–8, 128
Giddens, A. 2, 153; basic trust in familiar others 140–2; broadcasting's ordinariness 23; on Chernobyl and 'known unknowns' 149; commodification of space 61; degrees of security felt by those in different social positions 142–3; 'extensional transformations' on global scale 35–6; familiarity generated by mediated experience, 'reality inversion' 42; formation of the self and 139, 141, 175; ideas on disembedding and time–space distanciation 66; institutional

representatives in dealings with lay individuals 150; irreversible passing away of lifetime 14, 27, 137; metaphors of stretching 51–3; modernity a new element of risk and a novel 'risk culture' 147–8; modernity and transformation of time and space 38, 43; money as 'symbolic token', 'standardised value' 39–40; 'new risks and uncertainties' of late modernity 37; ontological insecurity and 17; 'phenomenology of modernity' 157, 178; 'place becomes increasingly phantasmagoric' in modernity 44, 58; 'postmodern', term for movements in the arts 48; 'practical consciousness' 12; printed text and electronic signal modernity's distinct media 69–70; 'reflexivity' and 143–4, 146; 'reverse colonisation' 57; 'reversible time' 14–15; risks and uncertainties of late modernity 146; rooms categorised in usage of time and space 13; routinisation 22; 'satellite communication' 41, 48; sitting in a house or using car 149–50; social interaction 69; spatial representation associated with modern map drawing 39; television as part of ordinary life 24; theory of structuration 9–10, 34, 159, 177–8; thoughts on self-identity and reflexivity 175; time and space 3–4, 69; 'time-geography' 10–11; time–space transformations 44–6; tradition of Christmas speech 15–16, 29; transformation in process of social reproduction 19; transnational 'finance and capital flows' 40; universalisation as consequence of modernity 49

Gillespie, M. 55–6, 116–19, 169–70

Gillian, 'upwardly mobile' woman and taste 131

Gilroy, P. 169–70

Gledhill, C. 128

'global American electronic invasion', earth 'under electronic siege' 56

global capitalism, political economists of communication and 118

global context, social formations of self and community 175

'global dangers' 37

global economics, unevenness of 57, 66

'global modernity', brings things from a distance 60

global shrinkage, places move closer together in travel or communication time 49–50

global social change, precedes popularity of 'globalisation talk' 160

global warming 37

globalisation 35; Europe's expansion and 39; global space and 160; has not eliminated localised communication 113; increase in transnational 'finance and capital flows' 40; 'is far from new' 35; money and media of communication significant mechanisms in process of 52; multifaceted or differentiated social phenomenon 45; national sentiment and 133; 'reorganisation' of time–space relations and 36; speed and intensity of in recent years 60; transformation of localities and 54; unevenness of 37, 50–1, 57, 66

GMTV, presentation by Eamonn Holmes and Fiona Phillips 76

Goffman, E. 5, 177; ' unfocused interaction' between unknown others 142; 'civil inattention' 101, 142; 'dramaturgical model' of self-presentation 158; face as 'public self-image' of participant in encounter 93–4; 'face-to-face' interaction 60, 70, 98, 150; idea of performance and 158; presentation of self and 'arts of impression management' 155; sociology of 177

Graham, S. 65

Gramsci, A. 109

Gray, A. 111, 126, 135

Greek-Cypriot migrants living in London, consumption practices of 172

Greenpeace 52

Gregory, D. 10

'grief' for Jill Dando 79

Griffin, C. 131

Gripsrud, J. 2

Grodin, D. 146

Gulf War 31

Gullestad, M. 131, 173

Gumpert, G. 61, 99, 157

Habermas, J. 33

Haddon, L. 124

Hägerstrand, T. 10, 21

Hall, K. 157–9

Hall, S. 5; 'black = beautiful' 109; consequences of arrival of the Rest in the West 35, 55, 170; encoding and decoding of television messages 109, 111, 127; 'ideo-

logical propositions of the text' 112;
images never offer faithful reflection of
'the real' 135; messages being decoded
'full and straight' 118, 127; migrant
groups attachment to different collective
homes 175; migrant populations and 55;
'moments' of television
'production/circulation and consumption'
110; national culture 'structure of
cultural power' 165; 'significant clusterings' 111; signification has degree of
fluidity to it 110; 'subjectivity', critique
of model of 141; terms like 'the nation'
and 'the people' 109; thinking and ideas
of Barthes and Volosinov 138

Hannerz, U. 51

Harindranath, R. 115, 167

Harries, D. 2

Harvey, D. 4, 36; capitalist economic
transformations 52; economic aspects of
globalisation 50; economic determinism
and 47; experiential collapsing-in of the
globe 48, 66; metaphor of shrinking 51;
'postcapitalist' society and 49; postmodern architectural forms and 48;
time–space compression 43, 46–7

Hastrup, K. 55

Have a Go! 84–8

Haythornthwaite, C. 65

'hedging devices', specific instances of
phone-in talk 94, 97–8

Heidegger, M. 14, 27, 62, 85, 137, 173

Held, D. 45

Hemmings, S. 21

Hendy, D. 74

Henriques, J. 144

Heritage, J. 12

Herman, E. 57

Hermes, J. 18, 133–5

'high-consequence risk', global nuclear
annihilation 147

Hill, A. 22, 77

Hills, M. 168

Hine, C. 161

Hinerman, S. 78

Hirsch, E. 123

Hobsbawm, E. 15, 30

Hobson, D. 21, 29, 128

Hochschild, A. 5, 153–7, 175

Hodge, R. 106

Holloway, S. 125, 152

Hollywood cinema, versus television's
'personality system' 76

Holmes, J. 97

Home and Away 57

Hopper, R. 71

Horton, D. 5; audience feel have 'got to
know' person on screen 73, 75–8, 151;
'continuing relationship' with audience
members 95; intimacy at a distance 102;
'pathological' mediated relationships
81–4; role of studio audience 86

'hourliness' 26

Hubbard, P. 2

human cultures, 'reflexive monitoring of
action' 146

Hunt, S. 101, 173

Hutchby, I. 45, 61, 88–91, 178

Hüyla, response to watching Turkish news
programmes 171–2

'hyperreality', notion that media images
represent prior reality 42

identity 139; community 163–9; diasporas
169–72; dwellings 173–5; inattention
141–3; labour 153–8; MUDding 160–3;
performativity 158–60; reflexivity
143–6; risk 146–53; trust 139–41

identity formation, trends in 169–70

Indians, cultural differences and similarities among 115, 167

'individualisation', cellular telephones and
169

industrial revolution, synchronisation of
labour and 12

Innis, H. 42–4, 46, 56

interaction 69; conversationalisation 91–3;
doubling 99–102; face 93–8; friendliness
98–9; grief 78–81; intimacy 74–8; mix
73–4; pathologisation 81–3; sociability
83–91; typology 69–73

'internal pluralism', replaced by 'external
pluralism' 25

international travel 54

internet and broadcasting, interactions or
quasi-interactions 158

Internet fora, traditional images and experiences persist in 102

internet, the, chat on like face-to-face
exchanges at cocktail party 90; chat on
soap operas not 'dominated by men' 98;
'cult media' fans on a 'community of
imagination' 168; 'diasporas' and 167;
example of technology for one purpose
used for others 46; experiences of trust
and risk in interactions around and via

152; island of Trinidad and those in global Trinidadian diaspora 66; ought to be treated as 'part of everyday life' 65; parents perceive as a 'risky space' 152; radio and television programmes transmitted via 74; set of interconnected nodes 53; treating as if it had 'cyberian apartness' from everyday 74

'intimacy at a distance' 74

IRC chat channels 74

'izzat', depends on 'chastity of daughters' 117

Jacka, E. 58
Jackson, S. 121
Jagose, A. 173
Jameson, F. 49
Jamieson, L. 77
Jancovich, M. 24, 121
Janelle, D. 49–50
Jarvis, H. 11
Jary, D. 36
Jaworski, A. 94
Jefferson, G. 95–6
Jensen, J. 82
Jewish families in Israel, use of language among 94
Johnson, C. 80
Johnson, L. 21
Johnson, R. 143–4, 163
Jones, S. 164

Katz, E. 29, 31, 100, 113–15
Kear, A. 80
Kendall, L. 65, 91, 98, 100, 102, 161
Kilroy! 19
Kilroy-Silk, Robert 19
King, A. 13
Kitchin, R. 46, 65
Kollock, P. 164
Kress, G. 106

Lacan, J. 107, 141
Lally, E. 124–6, 174
'landscapes of computing', not restricted to the realms of the virtual 102
Langer, J. 75–6, 80
language 32, 92, 94, 107–8, 141–2; meaning of words not wholly stable 12
Larsen, P. 60
Lash, S. 53–4
laughter, positive politeness and 94
'lay readers', Barthes and Coward and 106

Leal, O. 122–4
Lee, J. 95
letter writer, no option of using talk or facial expressions 71–2
Lévi-Strauss, C. 103
Levinson, S. 44, 71, 93–4, 96–8, 166
Levy, M. 151
Leyshon, A. 41–2, 47, 50–1, 62
Liebes, T. 113–15
'life-cycle', socially constructed stages in human lifetime 14
'liming', communicative style used by participants in internet chat room 167
'limited field of discourse', associated with pornography 157
Lindlof, T. 146
Ling, R. 124
linguistics 103–4
Live and Direct, hosted by Anna Raeburn 95
Liverpool, distinctive character through trade and migration 60
Livingstone, S. 101, 125
'London Turks' 171–2
longue durée 29, 34; institutional time that exceeds individual lifetimes 14–15
Lull, J. 78, 99–100, 121
Lupton, D. 149, 152, 155
Lury, K. 76, 86

McCarthy, A. 24, 174
McChesney, R., analysis of Murdoch empire and 56–7
Macdonald, M. 147
McDonalds 52, 117–19
McGuigan, J. 50
McHoul, A. 100
Mackay, H. 45, 57
MacKenzie, D. 45
McLuhan, E. 44
McLuhan, M. 4, 36, 46–7, 60; experiential collapsing-in of the globe 66; revival of his ideas since 1990s 44; 'the medium is the message' 42, 122; 'We now live in a global village' 43
McRobbie, A. 131
Malone, M. 159
'Mangel', term remained in widespread usage in Southall 117
Manilow, Barry, 'one-sided love affair' of married woman 82–3
Manning, P. 93
manufactured risks and uncertainties 148

maps 39

'marketisation' of media, public affairs media conversationalised 92

Marriott, S. 71

Marx, K. 47

'mass communications' 2, 75; monological 72

mass media, new and distinctive kind of publicness 30

Massey, D. 4, 178; 'openness of places' 58–9; research on rural villages in Cambridgeshire 164; speed and intensity of globalisation 60; unevenness and inequalities of aspects of global social change 50–1, 66

Masterman, L. 105

Matrix Collective 13

Mattelart, A. 52

Mattelart, M. 21

media, broad social and cultural context 3

media discourses, helping to structure perceptions of where risk lies 147

media and information flows, 'not simply one-way' 57

'media scandals' 78

mediated sociability, cultural and linguistic dimensions of 102

mediated symbolic forms, 'ethnic groups' beyond 'national territory' 55

medium of communication, influence over space and time 42, 44

'medium theory' 42, 44–5

'mega events', 'global' in scope 31

Meinhof, U. 4, 19, 25–7, 34

metaphor of the virus, arrival of AIDS on global mediascape 152

Meyrowitz, J. 4; book on electronic media 64; boundaries of the local more permeable today 66; 'content concerns' and 46; encounters with 'media settings' 60–2; media performance of public figures 78; 'medium' and 42–3; no longer clear split between people 'here' and 'somewhere else' 158; personal sound systems make public space private 63; relations with 'media friends' 77–9, 81; relationship with 'media friends' and 'real friends' 82–3; revival of Marshall McLuhan's ideas 44; social uses of television 99; transformation of place as 'social position' 62

Miller, D., 'cyberian apartness' of the internet 74; home life and 173; identifi-

cation of Trini-ness 168; 'Liming' in internet chat room *de Rumshop Lime* 167; meanings and identities in Trinidad 66, 133; MUDs and 161; perception of Coca-Cola in Trinidad 117–18; popularity of *The Young and the Restless* in Trinidad 115–16; suspicions of ideas about cyberspace and 'virtuality' 65–6

Miller, T. 100

Misztal, B. 90–1, 142

Mitchell, W. 64–5, 74

mobile phone, appropriate way to carry and include in one's dress 124; dislocates idea of home 174; more visible than static domestic telephone 124; talking while travelling on public transport 64

mobile phone users, 'in two places at the same time' 64

modern society, mediation of security and anxiety 150; self and self-identity in 163; traditions now translocalised 31

modernity, capitalism and industrialism, two of main dimensions of 45; interaction mix of social life has changed 73; separation of time and space pulled away from physical place 38

Molotch, H. 70, 81

money, medium of exchange 39

'mood', phenomenological analysis of culture and 87

Moores, S. 2–3, 36, 58, 62, 93–7, 121

Morley, D., broadcasting and 32–3; disagreement with Scannell over sociability in broadcasting 87, 91, 178; electronic media and transformation of dwelling 173–5; encoding and decoding television messages 109, 127; patterns of preference in media use 111–12; practices of television viewing within families 120–3, 125; proliferation of broadcasting channels 165; public users of mobile phones, dislocation of domesticity and mobilisation of home 175; transformation of localities and 54–5, 58, 60

Mornings with Kerri-Anne (Australia) 76

Morse, Samuel 41, 45

Mosco, V. 42

Moyal, A. 89–90

MUDding 160, 175

MUDs, prime sites for 'identity play' 65, 160, 168

multiaccentuality, technology-as-text 123
'multiuser domain' (virtual place) *see* MUDs
Mumford, L. 12
Murdoch, Rupert (News Corporation)
    56–7
Murdock, G. 39, 125, 132
Murray, R. 47

'narrative of the self', coherent biography
    may be constructed through 143
national community, simultaneity of radio
    and television and 165
National Health Service, fight to save from
    privatisation 31–2
national identity, 'staged' and performed in
    state ceremonies and 160
Neighbours 57–8, 116–17
'net nanny' software, electronically
    'policing children's activities' 152
Netherlands, research on readers of
    women's magazines 133; viewers' expe-
    riences of watching *Dallas* 113
'netiquette' guard against flaming 90
network and flow 52, 58
'network' and 'flow', global spread of
    institutions and relationships 36
'networked individualism' 168–9
networks, new social morphology 52
New York Times (US) 56
newspapers, 'collage effect' 48
'non-local social networks' (actually trans-
    local) 168–9
non-reciprocal intimacy, 'attractions' and
    potential 'costs' 81–2
non-terrestrial broadcasters, subscription
    channels and pay-per-view 31
Noon, M. 154
'nothing on telly', means 'nothing out of
    the ordinary' 22–3
nuclear energy, not enough research on 149

Ochberg, R. 143
Olwig, K. 55, 175
Olympic Games 31
Oprah Winfrey Show, The 19
'ordinary people', internet café as transla-
    tion landscape 102
O'Sullivan, T. 23, 123

Panorama television interview, Diana and
    'sincerity' performance 80
Panzani advertisement 104
Papastergiadis, N. 54

para-interactions with television news
    presenters 151
para-sociability, relations of intimacy with
    distant others and 83
'para-social' interaction, new type of social
    relationship 75
Paterson, R. 20
'pathological' mediated relationships,
    caution about 82
Penacchioni, I. 29
people, 'heedful' of the 'face wants' of
    others in social interaction 93; reaction
    of to young woman in train on cell
    phone to boyfriend 101
Perfect Match (Australia) 85
performances, in terms of structuration of
    social practices 159
'performative' speech act theory, signifi-
    cance of 158–9
'permeability' of boundaries in contempo-
    rary period 36
'personal homepages', presentation of self
    on 158
'personality politics' 78
Petrie, D. 22
phenomenology 2; of fun 86
'phenomenology of "going to the
    pictures"', domestic television use and
    121
phone sex 156–7
photograph, possesses an evidential force
    135
physical setting, utterances like 'here',
    'there', 'this' or 'that' and 71
Pickering, M. 144
Pickles, Wilfred 85–6
Pierson, C. 10, 15, 40, 43, 45
'pink collar' workers, service industries
    and 154
'place', pluralised rather than marginalised
    by electronically mediated communica-
    tion 66, 99; spatial locale or physical
    setting situated geographically 38
'plastic money' of credit cards, purchases
    by telephone or via Internet 40
'pleasure-producing activities', relation to
    cultures of the everyday 13
Plummer, K. 143
'politeness' 93
politeness strategies 102
'politeness theory purports to be universal'
    94
'positive politeness' 97; paying compli-

ments and use of 'in-group' identity markers 94
'post-Fordism' 47
'postmodernity', label for contemporary era 36
Potter, J. 135
'practical consciousness' 12
Pred, A. 10
predictability, ongoing skilled accomplishment 12
predictability of terrestrial programming, twentieth-century life and 26
privatised mobility, kind of 'dwelling-in-travel' 174
programme production, typically studio-based 19
public response, death of well-known figure and 78–9
public service of higher education, constructs students as consumers 92
Punjabi families, 'home videos' and 'video letters' 55
Punjabi Londoners in Southall and *Neighbours* 116–17, 170
Punjabi youth, escape from adults by going to McDonalds 119
putdownable qualities of media materials 134

qualifications or hedges, designed to mitigate offence to other group members 99
'qualifiers' to frame disagreements 98
quasi-interaction, non-reciprocal intimacy at a distance of Diana 80; practical contexts of daily life over-shadowed by 83; subdivision of mediated interaction 72–3, 75
Qureshi, K. 170
QVC shopping channel, verbal; and visual; discourses 27

radio and television, informal language may 'represent cultural democratisation' 92
Radway, J. 118–21, 134–5
Raeburn, Anna 95–8; interaction with caller Paula 96–7
Rakow, L. 89–90
Ranger, T. 15, 30
Rath, C-D. 32
'ratings', price of advertising slots in commercial broadcasting and 20
Ray (student), asking for clarification of accepted routine enquiries 140–1

reassurance 151
'recency principle', reportage close as possible to moment of occurrence 26
recursiveness, day-to-day routines and 10
reflexive or performative self 5
reflexivity, self reflexively understood in terms of biography 143
relational use of television, 'communication facilitation' 100
remote control device, symbol of condensed power relations 122
repetition, defining principle of broadcasting 19
representation 2
'reproduction', possibility of social 'change' and innovation 12
Rheingold, H. 46, 164, 168
Richard and Judy 76
Richardson, K. 4, 19, 25–7, 34
Ricoeur, P. 110, 145
risk 37, 146–53
Robert (college MUDder) 162–3
Robins, K. 31–2, 65, 165–6, 170–2, 175
Roche, M. 31
'rolling' news channels 25
romantic fiction and women's magazines 134–5
Rosengren, K. 100
routine, strongest when sanctioned by tradition 15
routinisation of day-to-day life, source of ontological security 11

Sacks, H. 23, 71, 96
Said, E., community, 'which is "ours" ' and 'which is "theirs" ' 169; *Orientalism* 35; practices of 'imaginative geography' 164
Sarup, M. 143
satellite communication, unit cost and time invariant with respect to distance 48
satellite dishes in UK (1980s and 1990s), interpretation of 123
Saussure, F. de 103–4, 107–8, 133
Saussurean linguistics, 'abstract objectivism' of 107; wider study of cultures and 104
Scannell, P. 2; broadcasting contributes to 'de-severance of the world' 61–4; broadcasting and nation calendar of public events 30; broadcasting organised by clock and calendrical time 34; 'consensus view of society' 33; dailiness and 16–18; discussion of broadcasting 9,

136, 138; doubling of place and 99; essay on temporal arrangements of broadcasting 32–3; funeral of Princess Diana and 79–80; interest in history of British broadcasting 31; national community and simultaneity of radio and television 165–6; 'national phenomenology of broadcasting' 171; phenomenology of fun in broadcasting 102–3; place as instantaneously pluralised 62; 'predictable enjoyment' by recording programmes 25; radio and television 'double reality' 63; reality 'doubled' in 'offline' room 65; role of broadcast talk and imagery to create event's aura 110; scheduling of programmes 20–34; self-identity in radio DJ talk 158; sociable dimension of radio and television 81, 83–8, 90–1, 100, 169, 177–8; studio 'institutional discursive space of radio and television' 19–20; television presenters become 'familiar companions' 77; ways broadcasting 'articulates time-structures to lifetime' 27; what is included in 'Program formats' 19

scheduling, principle of providing 'mixed programming' 20

Schegloff, E. 12, 64, 71, 89–91, 101

Schiller, H. 56–7, 115

Schlesinger, P. 32

screen performance, television viewer has multiple symbolic cues 75

Seamon, D. 173

self and collective identity 5

self-help books, 'how to live' 146

self-identity, creative enterprise 145

Sennett, R. 26

'separate sovereign world', online communications not part of 161

September 11 (2001), attack on World Trade Centre 31

serial production, creation of standardised programme formats 19

'seriality' and scheduling 18

sex line, emotional labour and 157

signification 4–5, 46, 103; acts 118–20; authentication 135–8; connotation 103–6; context 120–2; decoding 109–12; export 112–18; fallacy 133–5; meaning of 'acts' of media consumption in their own right 118; multiaccentuality 106–9; tastes 126–33; technologies 122–6

signification or meaning construction 103

signs, general science of 133

Silverstone, R. 1, 4; asked to trust an abstract system 153; on Barthes 136; dailiness and 16; 'dialectical articulation' of security and anxiety in broadcasting 152; identification with people in soap operas 28; internet shopping experiences and 152–3; plural 'mutually interdependent textualities' 122–4; reach of audience extended 'beyond physical space of house' 60; 'space for potential', trust and faith in 139–40; television as integral part of home, story about 173–4; television stitched into day-to-day routines 23–4; television as transitional object bound with ontological security 37, 150–1, 153; textuality of information and communication technologies 138

Simmel, G. 83–4, 90

siting of computers and 125

Skeggs, B. 131, 159

Sky News 25

Slater, D. 65–6, 74, 161, 167–8

Slevin, J. 46, 73–4

smiling and 155

Smith, M. 164

sociability, 'democratic structure' of 90; no objective purpose but success of sociable moment 83

sociability on the Net, often sociability with strangers 90

social actors, both 'negative face' and 'positive face' 93

social relations, 'stretched' across vast distances 36

social relationships, can be pluralised 99

'social uses typology', 'relational uses' of television in household 100

'social-semiotic theory' 103

sociological experiments with trust 140–1

sociological method, setting new rules for 53

Sony 52, 58, 59

Sony 'Walkman', public spaces made private 63

'space of flows' 53–4

'space for potential', separation of 'me' from 'not me' 139

Spigel, L. 23

Standage, T. 52

standardisation 19, 38–40, 157

standardisation and surveillance of service 157
standardisation of time measurement 13–14
Steinberg, D. 80
Stewart (MUDder with heart trouble) 161–3
Stones, R. 2
Storey, J. 1
story of Achilles' virtual dating of Winterlight 162
'strict barriers and firm counter-forces', serving to restrict human movement 54
'structure/agency' tension, around concept of performance 159
studio audiences, and 'a kind of participation' to those watching elsewhere 77; role of in *Blind Date* 86–7
Sun newspaper 18
Sussex Technology Group 64, 124

'talk on television', styles of lay expression 100–1
technological determinism, problems associated with 89; separation of technology from society 45; weaknesses of first-generation medium theory 44–5
technology, access to not always equally available to men and women 125
telephone, gendered technology 89
telephone call centres ('communication factories') 155
telephone conversation, accentuates oral cues 71-2
telephone industry, 'discovery' of sociability 88
telephone visiting, regarded as frivolous and unnecessary and discouraged 88
'telephonic convergence' 49
television, part of the 'fabric' of ordinary daily life 24
television personalities, self-presentation of 76–7
'television talk', strangers in the home and 100
Tester, K. 146
theoretical tools, talk-in-interaction and 9
theory of 'informality' in contemporary culture 90
theory of network society 168–9
theory of 'performativity' 158
theory of structuration 9, 13, 16, 33–4, 36
This Morning, presentation by Richard Madeley and Judy Finnigan 76

Thomas, R. 50
Thompson, E. 12
Thompson, J. 1, 5, 112–13; commentary on Radway's book 120; computer technology and 74; doubling of interaction and 99, 102; 'extended availability' of media messages in time and space 35; face-to-face interaction and 70–1; 'instantaneity' of modern telecommunications 40–1; 'intimacy at a distance' 74; mediated quasi-interaction 72; 'mediated symbolic materials' key feature of self-formation 145, 160; mediated visibility a double-edged sword 78; 'new arenas for self-experimentation' 160; new kinds of social relationships between individuals 73; new media of communication, new at point of introduction 70; non-reciprocal intimacy at a distance 81–3; qualitative audience researchers and 112–13; reflexive project of self-identity 146; 'reinvention of publicness' 30–1; self and experience in 'mediated world' 144; temporal and spatial dimensions of culture 44; territorial units 'realigning' as result of economics 32; 'three forms or types of interaction' 69; typology of interactions 74–5, 102; virtuality and 64
Thornton, S. 128
Thussu, D. 56–7
time and space 3–4
Time Warner 57
'time zones', international system 39
'time-geography' 10
time-measurement, standardisation and globalisation of 38
time–space compression, 'condition of postmodernity' 46
Times, The (UK) 56
Today radio programme 17–18
Tomlinson, J., concept of 'the hybrid' has 'tricky connotations' 170; cultural imperialism and work of Liebes and Katz 115; 'discourse of media imperialism' 57; 'global modernity' brings things from a distance 60; globalisation is 'uneven' 51; 'mediated proximity' and 70; people experience what globalisation 'brings to them' 54
traditions in modern society, translocalised 31
transnational migration and resettlement 3
Trini-ness, identification of 168; the Internet and 66, 167

Tsagarousianou, R. 172
Tulloch, J. 143, 149, 152, 159
'tuning in' to personal stereo, 'tunes out' sounds of the city 63
Tunstall, J. 56
'Turkish diaspora' in Western Europe 170–2
Turkish-speaking people in London 170–1
Turkle, S. 5, 65, 160–3, 175
'turn-taking', talk-in interaction 71
Turnock, R. 79–80
two 'theres' there, moments of mobile phone use 101

UK, children frequently have access to their own computer screens 125; 'pilgrimage and witnessing' following death of Diana 80–1; television presenters may come to be seen as 'familiar companions' 77
undelivered newspaper, disruption caused by 17, 24
Urry, J. 4; criticism of theory of structuration 13; 'global space' and 160; imaginative and 'virtual' travel 59–60; 'interaction mix' of corporeal and technologically mediated communication 70; 'Internet' invented for one purpose evolved into other uses 46; notions of 'network' and 'flow' 36, 52; places understood as multiplex 59; relations between corporeal, imaginative and virtual mobilities 66; self and identity in relation to variety of ways of dwelling 173; 'sociology of fluids' 53–4; 'time-geography' 10; 'time–space desynchronisation' 26; 'virtual dwelling-ness'175
USA, broadcasting organised along commercial lines 31; export of films produced in 56; phone sex company, ongoing relationship between client and partner 157; programmes during 1950s and way to draw in viewers 77; research on pluralised relationships on 'social uses of television' 99

vagabonds, on the move because pushed from behind 54
Valentine, G. 125, 152, 159, 161
van Loon, J. 152
various kinds of speech act, could 'threaten' face 93
Varis, T. 56
verbal expressions 'do things' 158

video technology, possible for viewers to disrupt schedules 24–5
'virtual community' 164, 168
'virtual cross-dressing' 161
virtual places, 'rooms' used to describe 65
virtual 'places in the cyberspace of the Net' 64
Volosinov, V. 5, 166; emphasis on 'multi-accentuality' of signs 107–9, 138; how social environments of media consumption contribute to signification 122; 'inner speech' dependent on 'semiotic material' 144; plurality of readings in intersection of differently oriented social interests 110–11; social semiotics 106, 138; utterance in essay on language as discourse 107–8

Wajcman, J. 45
Wakeford, N.(internet researcher) 102
Walden, Brian, questions about risks of nuclear power generation 151–2
Wallace, P. 90
Wallis, R. 48
Wark, M. 31
Waters, M. 36, 49
'webcasting' 74
Wellman, B. 65, 168–9
Wernick, A. 92
West, global 'terrorist networks' 52–3; Japanese communication industries and the 58
Wetherell, M. 135
Williams, K. 2
Williams, R. 22, 44–5
Willis, J. 22
Willis, P. 130–1, 159
Willms, J. 49, 53, 148
Wilson, T. 76
Winfrey, Oprah 19
Winnicott, D. 139
Wohl, R. 5; audience feel have 'got to know' person on screen 73, 75, 77–8, 151; 'continuing relationship' with audience members 95; intimacy at a distance 102; 'pathological' mediated relationships 81–4; role of studio audience 86
woman in early twenties, relationship with television 22
women, appropriation of telephone for sociable interaction 89; romantic fiction readers 118–21, 134–5
Wood, J. 125

Wootton, A. 93
'work-discipline', temporal regulation of labour 12
working class, search for social recognition of TV ownership in 123; 'set of attitudes' found in life of 130–1, 159
'working time', opposed to 'one's own' or 'free time' 12
World Cup Finals 31
World Wide Web 53; people speak of 'visiting sites' 65
Wynne, D. 130

X-Files fans 168

Young, M. 11–12
Young and the Restless, The, connect with strong sense of 'bacchanal' in Trinidad 115–16
young woman, talking to boyfriend on cell phone on train carriage 101
Yttri, B. 124

Zingrone, F. 44, 46
'zoning', repeated day after day 18